Adobe®
Dreamweaver® CS4

ILLUSTRATED

Sherry Bishop

COURSE TECHNOLOGY
CENGAGE Learning™

Australia • Brazil • Japan • Korea • Mexico • Singapore • Spain • United Kingdom • United States

COURSE TECHNOLOGY
CENGAGE Learning™

Adobe® Dreamweaver® CS4—Illustrated
Sherry Bishop

Executive Editor: Marjorie Hunt

Senior Product Manager: Karen Stevens

Associate Acquisitions Editor: Brandi Shailer

Associate Product Manager: Michelle Camisa

Editorial Assistant: Kim Klasner

Director of Marketing: Cheryl Costantini

Marketing Manager: Ryan DeGrote

Marketing Coordinator: Kristen Panciocco

Developmental Editor: Barbara Clemens

Content Project Manager: Jennifer Feltri

Art Director: Jill Ort

Print Buyer: Fola Orekoya

Text Designer: Joseph Lee, Black Fish Design

Proofreader: Camille Kiolbasa

Indexer: Sharon Hilgenberg

QA Reviewers: John Freitas, Danielle Shaw,
    Ashlee Welz Smith, Susan Whalen

Cover Artist: Mark Hunt

Compositor: GEX Publishing Services

For product information and technology assistance, contact us at
Cengage Learning Customer & Sales Support, 1-800-354-9706
For permission to use material from this text or product, submit all requests online at **www.cengage.com/permissions**
Further permissions questions can be emailed to
permissionrequest@cengage.com

ISBN-13: 978-1-4390-3579-5

ISBN-10: 1-4390-3579-2

Course Technology
20 Channel Center Street
Boston, MA 02210
USA

Cengage Learning is a leading provider of customized learning solutions with office locations around the globe, including Singapore, the United Kingdom, Australia, Mexico, Brazil, and Japan. Locate your local office at:
international.cengage.com/region

Cengage Learning products are represented in Canada by Nelson Education, Ltd.

For your course and learning solutions, visit **course.cengage.com**

Purchase any of our products at your local college store or at our preferred online store **www.ichapters.com**

Adobe product screen shot(s) reprinted with permission from Adobe Systems Incorporated

Printed in Canada
2 3 4 5 6 7 13 12 11 10 09

About This Book

Welcome to *Adobe® Dreamweaver® CS4—Illustrated*! Since the first book in the Illustrated Series was published in 1994, millions of students have used various Illustrated texts to master software skills and learn computer concepts. We are proud to bring you this new Illustrated book on the latest version of Adobe Dreamweaver CS4, the best-selling Web design software.

This new version of Dreamweaver includes some exciting new features, including enhanced support for Cascading Style Sheets and increased integration with other Adobe products such as Adobe Photoshop, Adobe Flash, and Adobe Bridge. The interface has been redesigned for a more common look with the other Adobe products. The Insert bar is now called the Insert panel and is docked on the right side of the workspace along with the other panels. The Property inspector has been divided into a CSS and HTML Property inspector when text is selected on a page. This book has incorporated many of the new program features. There is more emphasis on Cascading Style Sheets and less emphasis on the use of tables for page layout. The redesigned Help system incorporates more resources, including online content from sources outside of the Adobe Web site. Every effort has been made to enlarge the figures when possible to help you navigate the detailed panels in the Dreamweaver interface. We hope you enjoy exploring the new features as you work through the book.

The unique design of this book, which presents each skill on two facing pages, makes it easy for novices to absorb and understand new skills, and also makes it easy for more experienced computer users to progress through the lessons quickly, with minimal reading required. We hope you enjoy exploring the features of Dreamweaver CS4 as you work through this book!

Author Acknowledgments

This is the most difficult part of the entire process—properly thanking the many people who have dedicated their time and talents to create this text for you. Nicole Pinard, Vice President and Editorial Director of CTIS, and Marjorie Hunt, Executive Editor, are always at the top of my list for giving me the opportunity to work with Course Technology. Karen Stevens, the Senior Product Manager, is a talented and inspired leader. It is always a joy to work with her. She also patiently contacted the Web sites we used as examples to obtain permission for their inclusion. They add much to the flavor of the book, and I am grateful both for each of the sites and for Karen making it possible to use them.

Barbara Clemens, the Developmental Editor, is gifted and tireless in her efforts. I can always count on her to bring fresh ideas to the table. She is one of those individuals who truly brings out the best in the rest of us who are fortunate enough to work with her. Jennifer Feltri and Lorri Zdunko were our production editors, and they skillfully kept us all on schedule from start to finish. We thank them for keeping up with the many details and deadlines. The work is beautiful. I am always indebted to Jeff Schwartz and his talented team of reviewers. Ashlee Welz Smith, Danielle Shaw, Susan Whalen, and John Freitas carefully tested each step to make sure that the end product was error-free. They have a challenging job and are so appreciated. This part of the publishing process is what truly sets Course Technology apart from other publishers. Camille Kiolbasa quietly worked behind the scene to ensure that all copy errors were corrected. Thank you, Camille. Many thanks to Paula Melton, who authored the test banks.

Thank you, Adobe, for giving us this outstanding Web development tool. And I hope that as you, the learner, read and work though this book, you will begin a long and productive relationship with this marvelous program. It is an exciting tool that works easily with both the professional Web developer and the beginning design student. And, as always, thanks to my husband, Don, for his patience, understanding, and encouragement.

Sherry Bishop

Preface

Welcome to *Adobe® Dreamweaver® CS4—Illustrated.* The unique page design of the book makes it a great learning tool for both new and experienced users. Each skill is presented on two facing pages so that you don't have to turn the page to find a screen shot or finish a paragraph. See the illustration on the right to learn more about the pedagogical and design elements of a typical lesson.

This book is an ideal learning tool for a wide range of learners—the "rookies" will find the clean design easy to follow and focused with only essential information presented, and the "hot shots" will appreciate being able to move quickly through the lessons to find the information they need without reading a lot of text. The design also makes this a great reference after the course is over!

What's New in This Edition

We've made many changes and enhancements to this edition to make it the best ever. Here are some highlights of what's new:

- **CSS best practices**—The redesigned CSS and HTML Property inspectors make the integration of CSS Styles intuitive and easy to implement. All text is automatically assigned a CSS style.

- **Related Files toolbar**—The new Related Files toolbar provides easy access to the files associated with an open page file. When a page is opened in Dreamweaver, the related file names appear under the page tab. Clicking on a file name will open the file.

- **Code Navigator**—The addition of the new Code Navigator provides quick access to CSS rules. When you place the mouse pointer over a page element, the assigned CSS Style sheet file name and rule name will appear in a pop-up window. Positioning the mouse pointer over the rule name will display the rule properties.

Each two-page spread focuses on a single skill.

Concise text introduces the basic principles in the lesson and integrates a real-world case study.

UNIT
E

Dreamweaver CS4

Enhancing an Image

After you select, place, and align an image on a Web page, you can enhance it to improve its appearance. You'll need to use an image editor, such as Adobe Illustrator or Adobe Photoshop to change the image itself, for example, to remove scratches from it or significantly resize it. However, you can enhance an image in Dreamweaver using borders, cropping or resizing, adjusting its brightness, and adjusting the horizontal and vertical space around an image. **Borders** are like frames that surround an image to make it stand out on the page. **Cropping** an image removes part of the image, both visually (on the page) and physically (the file size). A cropped image is smaller and takes less time to download. **Horizontal** and **vertical space** refers to blank space above, below, or on the sides of an image that separates the image from other elements on the page. You decide to enhance the images on the about_us page by adding borders around the images, and adjusting the horizontal and vertical space around each image.

STEPS

TROUBLE
After you apply the border, your images might move to different positions than those shown in the figure, depending on the size of your Dreamweaver window. This is not a problem; you can continue with the steps.

1. Click the club house image to select it
2. Type 1 in the Border text box, then press [Tab] to apply the border size, as shown in Figure E-8
   A black border with a thickness of 1 pixel will appear around the image in the browser, replacing the default size of zero.
3. Repeat Steps 1 and 2 for the other four images
   All images will now have black borders. The borders are not visible in Dreamweaver, but you will be able to see them when you preview the document in your browser later. You notice that the surrounding text wraps closer to the sides of the images than to the bottoms of the images.

QUICK TIP
You can also use the Brightness and Contrast and Sharpen buttons to slightly adjust images. It is wise to perform major edits in an image editing program such as Adobe Photoshop. Clicking the Edit button will open the image in Photoshop if it is installed on your computer.

4. Click the club house image to select it, type 10 in the V Space text box in the Property inspector, press [Tab], type 10 in the H Space text box, press [Tab], then deselect the image
   V Space refers to vertical space above and below the image. H Space refers to horizontal space on the sides of the image. You like the way the text is more evenly wrapped around the image, so you decide to apply the same option to the other images.
5. Repeat Step 4 for the rest of the images
   The five images reflect the horizontal and vertical space settings.
6. Click the sago palm image to select it, note the W and H settings in the Property inspector, click the Crop button in the Property inspector, then click OK to close the warning message that says you are about to permanently alter the image
7. Position the pointer over the bottom-center resizing handle, as shown in Figure E-9, slowly move the handle up toward the center of the image to remove part of the lower leaves, then double-click the image to crop it
   The image appears smaller, and the Property inspector shows that the file dimensions have changed.
8. Click Edit on the Application bar (Win) or Menu bar (Mac), click Undo Crop (Win) or click Undo (Mac) to restore the image to the original size, then save the file
   The image returns its original size.

Resizing an image using the Property inspector

When you crop an image, you remove part of it. If you want to resize the whole image rather than crop it, you can select the image, then drag a selection handle toward the center of the image. Dragging a selection handle can distort the image; to resize an image while retaining its original proportions, press and hold [Shift], then drag a corner selection handle. (You can also enlarge an image using these methods.) After you drag an image handle to resize it, the image dimensions in the Property inspector appear in bold and a black Refresh icon appears to the right of the dimensions. If you click the Refresh icon, the image reverts to its original size.

Dreamweaver 106   Using and Managing Images

Hints as well as troubleshooting advice appear right where you need them—next to the step itself.

Clues to Use boxes provide concise information that either expands on the major lesson skill or describes an independent task that in some way relates to the major lesson skill.

- **Live View**—Live View is a view choice that will display an open page as though it were being viewed in a browser. This makes it easy to preview dynamic content without leaving the Dreamweaver interface.

Assignments

The lessons use The Striped Umbrella, a fictional beach resort in Florida, as the case study. The assignments on the light purple pages at the end of each unit increase in difficulty. Additional case studies provide a variety of interesting and relevant exercises for students to practice skills.

Assignments include:

- **Concepts Reviews** consist of multiple choice, matching, and screen identification questions.

- **Skills Reviews** provide additional hands-on, step-by-step reinforcement.

- **Independent Challenges** are case projects requiring critical thinking and application of the unit skills.

- **Design Quest Independent Challenges** direct students to the Internet to critique selected Web sites with regard to the features and design principles learned in each unit.

- **Real Life Independent Challenges** are practical exercises to help students with their everyday lives by creating a personal Web site of their own design. Students maintain and update this site using the skills they learn in each unit.

- **Visual Workshops** are practical, self-graded capstone projects that require independent problem solving.

Every lesson features large, full-color representations of what the screen should look like as students complete the numbered steps.

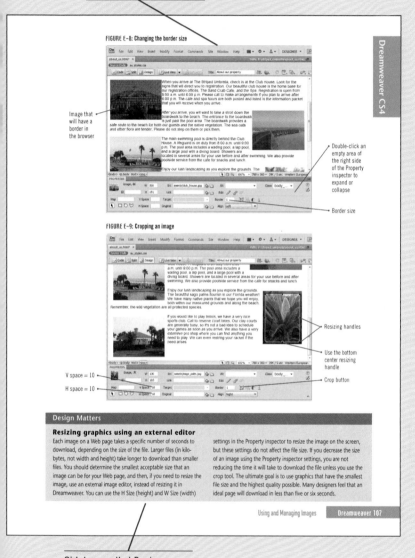

Sidebars called Design Matters introduce design theory or design tips to help students integrate basic design principles with Web site development skills.

Other Illustrated Series Titles

ADOBE® PHOTOSHOP® CS4—ILLUSTRATED CHRIS BOTELLO (1423999401)

Eight units provide essential training on using Adobe Photoshop CS4 to work with digital images, including selecting and manipulating images, working with color, adjusting color, working with layers and filters and working with shapes and type.

ADOBE® INDESIGN® CS4—ILLUSTRATED ANN FISHER (1423999398)

Eight units provide essential training on using InDesign CS4 to lay out and prepare documents for print and the Web. Coverage includes working with text, graphics, InDesign objects and master pages, linking images, and using advanced features and interactivity.

ADOBE® FLASH® CS4—ILLUSTRATED BARBARA WAXER (1439039658)

Eight units provide essential training on using Adobe Flash CS4 including creating graphics and text, using the Timeline, creating animation, creating buttons and using media, adding interactivity, and integrating with other programs.

ADOBE® PHOTOSHOP® ELEMENTS 7—ILLUSTRATED BARBARA WAXER/LISA TANNENBAUM (142399941X)

Eight units cover the basics of using Photoshop Elements to work with digital photos including managing and editing photos, adjusting contrast and color, using brushes and retouching tools, creating special effects, and sharing photos.

For more information on the Illustrated Series, please click on:
www.cengage.com/ct/illustrated

Instructor Resources

The Instructor Resources CD is Course Technology's way of putting the resources and information needed to teach and learn effectively into your hands. With an integrated array of teaching and learning tools that offer you and your students a broad range of technology-based instructional options, we believe this CD represents the highest quality and most cutting edge resources available to instructors today. Many of these resources are available at *www.cengage.com/coursetechnology*. The resources available with this book are:

- **Instructor's Manual**—Available as an electronic file, the Instructor's Manual includes detailed lecture topics with teaching tips for each unit.

- **Sample Syllabus**—Prepare and customize your course easily using this sample course outline.

- **PowerPoint Presentations**—Each unit has a corresponding PowerPoint presentation that you can use in lecture, distribute to your students, or customize to suit your course.

- **Figure Files**—The figures in the text are provided on the Instructor Resources CD to help you illustrate key topics or concepts. You can create traditional overhead transparencies by printing the figure files. Or you can create electronic slide shows by using the figures in a presentation program such as PowerPoint.

- **Solutions to Exercises**—Solutions to Exercises contains files students are asked to create or modify in the lessons and end-of-unit material. Also provided in this section is a document outlining the solutions for the end-of-unit Concepts Review, Skills Review, and Independent Challenges.

- **Data Files for Students**—To complete the units in this book, your students will need Data Files. You can post the Data Files on a file server for students to copy. The Data Files available on the Instructor Resources CD are also included on a CD located at the front of the textbook.

Instruct students to use the Data Files List included on the CD found at the front of the book and the Instructor Resources CD. This list gives instructions on copying and organizing files.

- **ExamView**—ExamView is a powerful testing software package that allows you to create and administer printed and computer (LAN-based) exams. ExamView includes hundreds of questions that correspond to the topics covered in this text, enabling students to generate detailed study guides that include page references for further review. The computer-based testing components allow students to take exams at their computers, and also saves you time by grading each exam automatically.

CourseCasts – Learning on the Go. Always Available...Always Relevant.

Our fast-paced world is driven by technology. You know because you are an active participant—always on the go, always keeping up with technological trends, and always learning new ways to embrace technology to power your life.

Let CourseCasts, hosted by Ken Baldauf of Florida State University, be your guide into weekly updates in this ever-changing space. These timely, relevant podcasts are produced weekly and are available for download at *http://coursecasts.course.com* or directly from iTunes (search by CourseCasts).

CourseCasts are a perfect solution to getting students (and even instructors) to learn on the go!

Brief Contents

Contents

Dreamweaver CS4

Unit I: Collecting Data with Forms   213

Dreamweaver CS4

Appendix A: Maintaining and Publishing Your Web Site   241

Data Files List   257

Glossary   263

Index   271

Read This Before You Begin

Frequently Asked Questions

What are Data Files?

A Data File is a partially completed Web page, Web site, or another type of file that you use to complete the steps in the units and exercises to create the final document that you submit to your instructor. The Data Files that you need for each unit are listed in the back of the book.

Where are the Data Files?

Your instructor will provide the Data Files to you or direct you to a location on a network drive from which you can download them. Alternatively, you can follow the instructions on page xvi to download the Data Files from this book's Web page. As you download the files, select where to store them, such as a hard drive, a network server, or a USB storage device. The instructions in the lessons refer to "the drive and folder where your Data Files are stored" when referring to the Data Files for the book.

What software was used to write and test this book?

This book was written and tested on a computer with a typical installation of Microsoft Windows Vista. The browsers used for any steps that require a browser are Mozilla Firefox and Internet Explorer 7. If you are using this book on Windows XP, your dialog box title bars will look slightly different, but will work essentially the same.

This book is written for the Windows version and the Macintosh version of Adobe Dreamweaver CS4. The two versions of the software are virtually the same, but there are a few platform differences. When there are differences between the two versions of the software, steps written specifically for the Windows version end with the notation (Win) and steps for the Macintosh version end with the notation (Mac). In instances when the lessons are split between the two operating systems, a line divides the page and is accompanied by Mac and Win icons.

Also, in this book, Macintosh commands instruct users to press the [return] key to enter information. On some newer Macintosh keyboards, this key may be named [enter] or the keyboard may include both [return] and [enter].

Do I need to be connected to the Internet to complete the steps and exercises in this book?

Some of the exercises in this book assume that your computer is connected to the Internet. If you are not connected to the Internet, see your instructor for information on how to complete the exercises.

What do I do if my screen is different from the figures shown in this book?

This book was written and tested on computers with monitors set at a resolution of 1280 x 1024. If your screen shows more or less information than the figures in the book, your monitor is probably set at a higher or lower resolution. If you don't see something on your screen, you might have to scroll down or up to see the object identified in the figures. In some cases, the figures will not match your screen because the Dreamweaver windows have been resized or cropped in an effort to make the figures as easy to read as possible.

How do I create Web sites that have not been built through previous consecutive units? (Windows)

If you begin an assignment that requires a Web site that you did not create or maintain earlier in the text, you must perform the following steps:

1. Copy the Solution Files folder from the preceding unit for the Web site you wish to create onto the hard drive or USB storage device. For example, if you are working on Unit E, you need the Solution Files folder from Unit D. Your instructor will furnish this folder to you.
2. Start Dreamweaver.
3. Click **Site** on the Application bar, then click **Manage Sites**.
4. Click **New**, then click **Site**.

5. Click the **Advanced tab**, then type the name you want to use for your Web site in the Site Name text box. Spaces and upper-case letters are allowed in the Site name.

6. Click the **Browse for File icon** 🗀 next to the Local root folder text box.

7. Navigate to the location of the drive and folder of your newly copied folder to set the local root folder. The local root folder contains the name of the Web site you are working on. For example, the local root folder for The Striped Umbrella Web site is called striped_umbrella.

8. Double-click the local root folder, then click **Select**.

9. Click the **Browse for File icon** 🗀 next to the Default images folder text box. A message appears stating that the site cache is being updated. This scans the files in your site and starts tracking links as you change them.

10. Double-click the assets folder in your Web site, then click **Select**.

11. Verify that the **Links relative to: Document option** is checked.

12. Click **OK** to close the Site Definition dialog box.

13. Click **Done** to close the Manage Sites dialog box.

How do I create Web sites that have not been built through previous consecutive units? (Macintosh)

If you begin an assignment that requires a Web site that you did not create or maintain before this unit, you must perform the following steps:

1. Copy the Solution Files folder from the preceding unit for the Web site you wish to create onto the hard drive or USB storage device. For example, if you are working on Unit E, you need the Solution Files folder from Unit D. Your instructor will furnish this folder to you.

2. Start Dreamweaver, click **Site** on the Application bar, then click **Manage Sites**.

3. Click **New**, then click **Site**.

4. Click the **Advanced tab**, then type the name you want to use for your Web site in the Site name text box.

5. Click the **Browse for File icon** 🗀 next to the Local root folder text box, and then navigate to the location of the drive and folder of your newly copied folder to set the local root folder.

6. Click the local root folder, and then click **Choose**.

7. Click the **Browse for File icon** 🗀 next to the Default images folder text box. If necessary, click the drive and folder of your newly copied folder to locate the assets folder.

8. Click the assets folder, click **Choose**, then click **OK** to close the Site Definition dialog box.

9. Click **Done** to close the Manage Sites dialog box.

How do I use Dreamweaver on multiple computers?

If you are using Dreamweaver on multiple computers, such as one in the classroom and one at home or in a lab, you must define each Web site on each computer before you can access your Web site files on each computer. You only have to do this once for each Web site, but the root folder must be accessible from both machines. For instance, if you are storing your Web sites on a USB storage device and using it on a computer in a lab and your computer at home, you must define the Web site on each machine. Once you tell Dreamweaver where to find the files (the USB drive), it will find them automatically from that point forward.

What if I can't find some of the information in the exercises on the Internet?

This book uses the Internet to provide real-life examples in the lessons and end-of-unit exercises. Because the Internet is constantly changing to display current information, some of the links used and described in the book may be deleted or modified before the book is even published. If this happens, searching the referenced Web sites will usually locate similar information in a slightly modified form. In some cases, entire Web sites may move. Technical problems with Web servers may also prevent access to Web sites or Web pages temporarily. Patience, critical thinking, and creativity are necessary whenever the Internet is being used in the classroom.

What if my icons look different?

Symbols for icons, buttons, and pointers are shown in the steps each time they are used. Icons may look different in the Files panel depending on the file association settings on your computer.

What if I can't see my file extensions?

The learning process will be easier if you can see the file extensions for the files you will use in the lessons. To do this in Windows, open Windows Explorer, click Organize, click Folder and Search Options, click the View tab, then uncheck the box Hide Extensions for Known File Types. To do this on a Macintosh, go to the Finder, click the Finder menu, then click Preferences. Click the Advanced tab, then select the Show all file extensions check box.

What if I can't see Flash content in my browser?

To view objects such as Flash movies, you must set a preference in your browser to allow active content to run. Otherwise, you will not be able to view objects such as Flash buttons. To set this preference in Internet Explorer, click Tools, click Internet Options, click the Advanced tab, then check the box Allow active content to run in files on My computer (under Security). Your browser settings may be slightly different, but look for similar wording. When using Windows Internet Explorer 7, you can also click the information bar when prompted to allow blocked content.

What do I do if I see a Server Busy dialog box?

You may see a message that says "This action cannot be completed because the other program is busy. Choose 'Switch To' to activate the busy program and correct the problem." when you are attempting to import Word content. This is probably a memory problem. If it happens, click Word when the Start menu opens. Repeat again if necessary, then switch back to Dreamweaver. You should see the imported text.

Downloading Data Files for This Book

In order to complete many of the lesson steps and exercises in this book, you are asked to open and save Data Files. A **Data File** is a partially completed Web page, Photoshop image, InDesign page, Flash animation, or another type of file that you use as a starting point to complete the steps in the units and exercises. The benefit of using a Data File is that it saves you the time and effort needed to create a file; you can simply open a Data File, save it with a new name (so the original file remains intact), then make changes to it to complete lesson steps or an exercise. Your instructor will provide the Data Files to you or direct you to a location on a network drive from which you can download them. Alternatively, you can follow the instructions in this lesson to download the Data Files from this book's Web page.

1. Start Internet Explorer, type www.cengage.com/coursetechnology in the address bar, then press [Enter]

2. Click in the Enter ISBN Search text box, type 9781439035795, then click Search

3. When the page opens for this textbook, click the About this Product link for the Student, point to Student Downloads to expand the menu, and then click the Data Files for Students link

4. If the File Download – Security Warning dialog box opens, click Save. (If no dialog box appears, skip this step and go to Step 6)

5. If the Save As dialog box opens, click the Save in list arrow at the top of the dialog box, navigate to a folder on your USB drive or hard disk to download the file to, then click Save

6. Close Internet Explorer and then open My Computer or Windows Explorer and display the contents of the drive and folder to which you downloaded the file

7. Double-click the file 03579-5d.exe in the drive or folder, then, if the Open File – Security Warning dialog box opens, click Run

8. In the WinZip Self-Extractor window, navigate to the drive and folder where you want to unzip the files to, then click Unzip

9. When the WinZip Self-Extractor displays a dialog box listing the number of files that have unzipped successfully, click OK, click Close in the WinZip Self-Extractor dialog box, then close Windows Explorer or My Computer

You are now ready to open the required files.

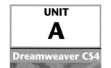

Getting Started with Adobe Dreamweaver CS4

Adobe Dreamweaver CS4 is a Web design program for creating media-rich Web pages and Web sites. Its easy-to-use tools let you incorporate sophisticated features, such as animations and interactive forms. In this unit, you learn to start Dreamweaver and examine the workspace. Next, you open a Web page and learn how to use the Help feature. Finally, you close the Web page and exit the program. You have recently been hired as a manager at The Striped Umbrella, a beach resort in Florida. You have been asked to develop the resort's Web site using Dreamweaver. You begin by familiarizing yourself with the Dreamweaver program.

OBJECTIVES

Define Web design software

Start Adobe Dreamweaver CS4

View the Dreamweaver workspace

Work with views and panels

Open a Web page

View Web page elements

Get help

View a Web page in a browser window

Close a Web page and exit
   Dreamweaver

Defining Web Design Software

Adobe Dreamweaver CS4 is a powerful **Web design program** that lets you create interactive Web pages containing text, images, animation, sounds, and video. You can create Web page objects in Dreamweaver, or you can import objects created in other programs. Dreamweaver creates files that have the .html extension. **HTML** is the acronym for **Hypertext Markup Language**, the language Web developers use to create Web pages. On your first day you learn some basic Dreamweaver features.

DETAILS

Using Dreamweaver you can:

- ### Create Web pages or Web sites
  Dreamweaver lets you create individual Web pages or entire Web sites, depending on your project needs. **Web pages** are collections of text in HTML format combined with images in special image formats. **Web sites** are collections of related Web pages. Web pages and Web sites are stored on **computer servers** connected to the Internet. Users can view Web pages and sites using a **Web browser**, which is software used to display pages in a Web site, such as Internet Explorer, Mozilla Firefox, or Netscape Navigator. You can also import Web pages created in other programs, then edit them in Dreamweaver and incorporate them into an existing Web site. The program provides predefined page layouts called **templates** that you can apply to existing pages or use as a basis for designing new ones.

- ### Add text, images, tables, and media files
  You can add text, images, tables, and media files to a Dreamweaver Web page by using the Insert panel. The **Insert panel** contains buttons for creating or inserting objects, such as tables, images, forms, and videos. Using the Insert panel, you can also insert objects made with other Adobe software programs, including Fireworks, Flash, and Photoshop. Table A-1 describes Insert panel categories and their corresponding buttons.

- ### Display Web pages as they will appear to users
  Pages you edit in Dreamweaver appear as **WYSIWYG**, which stands for "What You See Is What You Get." As you design a Web page in Dreamweaver, you see the page exactly as it will appear in a browser window.

- ### Use the Property inspector to view and edit page elements
  The **Property inspector** is a panel that displays the characteristics of a page's currently selected object. Figure A-1 shows a Web page open in Dreamweaver. The properties of the selected text appear in the Property inspector. The Property inspector changes as different types of page objects are selected. For example, when an image is selected, the Property inspector displays image properties. When text is selected, the Property inspector displays text properties with either the HTML Property inspector or the CSS Property inspector.

- ### Use Roundtrip HTML
  Because Dreamweaver utilizes **Roundtrip HTML**, HTML files created in other programs can be opened with no additional coding. Conversely, you can open and edit a file created in Dreamweaver in other software programs, such as Microsoft Expression Web. Your HTML code can "travel" between programs without coding problems.

- ### Manage Web sites
  Dreamweaver lets you manage Web site pages to ensure that all the **links**, or connections among the pages, work properly. As new pages are added to a Web site, this feature's importance increases. There are several types of reports that you can run to check for problems across the Web site. Dreamweaver also has special tools that help you manage a site when you are working with others on a site development team.

FIGURE A-1: Web page open in Dreamweaver

Tab displays filename of open file (Macintosh users will not see tabs unless multiple pages are open.)

Web page

Property inspector showing properties for selected text

Insert panel

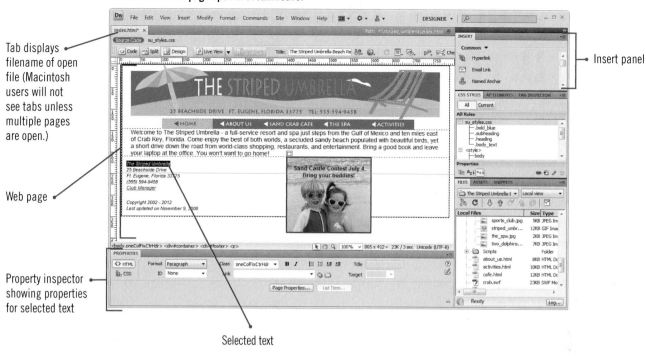

Selected text

TABLE A-1: Insert panel categories and corresponding buttons

category	buttons
Common	Commonly used buttons, such as images, media, and hyperlinks
Layout	Buttons for inserting div tags, tables, Spry objects, and frames
Forms	Buttons for inserting form objects, such as check boxes and radio buttons
Data	Buttons for inserting Tabular Data, Dynamic Data, and Recordsets
Spry	Buttons for inserting Spry data sets, Spry validations, and Spry panels
InContext Editing	Buttons for creating editable regions to allow others to add content
Text	Buttons for formatting text; for example, strong, headings, and lists
Favorites	Buttons you can add to, from among those you use most frequently

Starting Adobe Dreamweaver CS4

There are many ways to start Dreamweaver, depending on the type of computer you are using and the type of installation you have. Although the steps below start the program using the Start menu (Win) or the hard drive icon (Mac), and always work, the fastest way to start Dreamweaver is to place a shortcut (Win) or an alias (Mac) for Adobe Dreamweaver CS4 on your desktop or add it to the Quick Launch toolbar (Win). **Shortcuts** and **aliases** are icons that represent a software program stored on your computer system. When you double-click a shortcut (Win) or an alias (Mac), you do not need to use the Start menu (Win) or open submenus (Mac) to find your program. When Dreamweaver is open, the welcome screen appears. The welcome screen provides shortcuts you can click to open files or create new files or Web sites. You are given your first assignment and begin by starting Dreamweaver.

STEPS

WIN

1. **Click the Start button ⊕ on the taskbar**
   The Start button lets you open the Programs menu, which displays the names of the software programs installed on your computer.

2. **Point to All Programs, click Adobe Web Premium CS4 or Adobe Design Premium CS4 (if you have one of these suites of Adobe products), then click Adobe Dreamweaver CS4, as shown in Figure A-2**
   Dreamweaver opens, and the welcome screen appears.

3. **Click HTML in the Create New column on the Dreamweaver welcome screen**
   A new blank HTML document opens.

MAC

1. **Click Finder in the Dock, then click Applications**

2. **Click the Adobe Dreamweaver CS4 folder, then double-click the Dreamweaver CS4 application, as shown in Figure A-2**
   Dreamweaver opens, and the Start page appears.

3. **Click HTML in the Create New category on the Dreamweaver welcome screen**
   A blank document named Untitled-1 appears on the screen.

FIGURE A-2: Starting Dreamweaver (Windows and Macintosh)

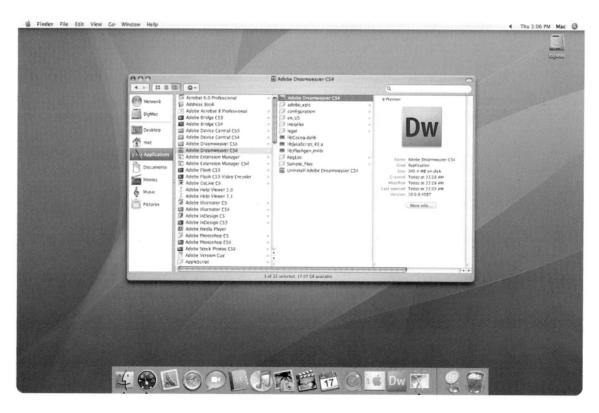

Viewing the Dreamweaver Workspace

The **workspace**, shown in Figure A-3, consists of the document window, the menu bar, toolbars, inspectors, and panels. The default layout in Dreamweaver is called the **Designer** layout. Other layouts include the **Coder** and **Dual Screen** layouts. The Designer and Coder layouts are built with an integrated workspace using the **Multiple Document Interface (MDI)**. This means that all document windows and panels are positioned within one large application window. In the Designer workspace layout, the panels are docked on the right side of the screen, and Design view is the default view. In the Coder layout, the panels are docked on the left side of the screen, and Code view is the default view. The Dual Screen layout is used with two monitors: one for the document window and Property inspector and one for the panels. Other views include App Developer, App Developer Plus, Classic, Coder Plus, and Designer Compact. You can change the workspace layout by using the **Workspace switcher**. **Panel Groups** are sets of related panels that are grouped together. **Inspectors** are panels that display the properties of the currently selected object. Inspectors allow you to make formatting changes quickly and easily, without having to open menus. You spend some time familiarizing yourself with the Dreamweaver workspace.

DETAILS

Use Figure A-3 to find many of the elements detailed below.

- When a document is maximized, the **title bar** displays the path of the active open file, with the filename displayed on a file tab. If the Document window is not maximized, the filename, path, and document type appear in the Document window title bar. The title bar also includes buttons for minimizing, resizing, and closing the window in the upper-left or upper-right corner, depending on which type of computer you are using.

- The Application bar (Win) or Menu bar (Mac), located above the title bar, lists the names of the **menus**, which contain Dreamweaver commands. You can also issue commands by using shortcut keys or by clicking corresponding buttons on the various panels.

TROUBLE

If you don't see the Insert panel, click Window on the Application bar (Win) or Menu bar (Mac), then click Insert.

- The **Insert panel** contains buttons that allow you to insert objects, such as images, tables, and horizontal rules. The buttons on the Insert panel change depending on what category is selected. You select categories using a drop-down menu. Each category contains buttons relating to a specific task. When you insert an object using one of the buttons, a dialog box opens, letting you choose the object's characteristics. The last button selected becomes the default button for that category until you choose another one.

- The **Document toolbar** contains buttons for changing the current Web page view, previewing and debugging Web pages, and managing files. The toolbar buttons are listed in Table A-2.

TROUBLE

If you do not see one of the toolbars, click View on the Application bar (Win) or Menu bar (Mac), point to Toolbars, then click the toolbar name. The Standard and the Style Rendering toolbars do not appear by default.

- The **Standard toolbar** contains buttons for some frequently used commands on the File and Edit menus.

- The **Style Rendering toolbar** contains buttons that can be used to display different media types.

- The **Coding toolbar** is useful when you are working with HTML code and can only be accessed in Code view.

- The **Related Files toolbar** dispays files related to an open and active file.

- The **Document window** is the large white area under the Document toolbar. Open Web pages appear in this area.

- The **Property inspector** displays the characteristics of the selected Web page object. You can change an object's properties using the text boxes, shortcut menus, and buttons in the Property inspector. The contents of the Property inspector vary according to the object currently selected.

- The **Status bar** appears at the bottom of the Dreamweaver window. The left end of the status bar displays the **tag selector**, which shows the HTML tags being used at the insertion point location. The right side displays the window size and estimated download time for the current page.

QUICK TIP

To collapse or expand a panel, double-click the panel tab.

- **Panels** are small windows containing program controls. Related panels appear together in **panel groups**, such as CSS and Files. Display a panel by choosing its name from the Window menu. You can dock panel groups on the right side of the screen, or undock them by dragging the panel tab. When two or more panels are docked together, you can access the panel you want by clicking its name tab to display its contents.

FIGURE A-3: The Dreamweaver CS4 workspace

Application bar (Win) or Menu bar (Mac)

Document toolbar (Depending on your resolution, you may not see the buttons on the far right side.)

Document window

Status bar

Property inspector

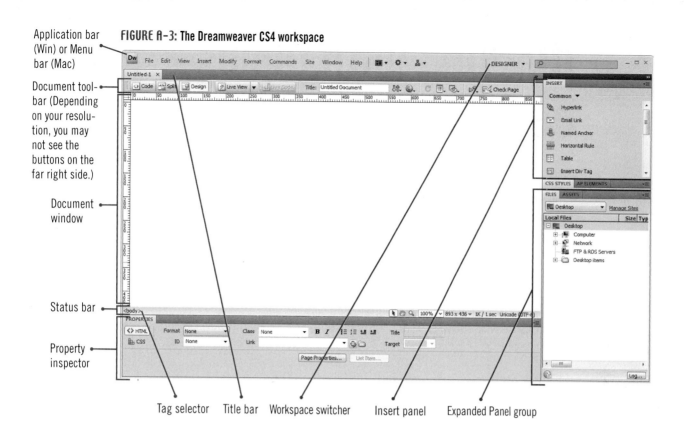

Tag selector   Title bar   Workspace switcher   Insert panel   Expanded Panel group

TABLE A-2: Document toolbar buttons

button	name	function
Code	Show Code view	Displays only the Code view in the Document window
Split	Show Code and Design views	Displays both the Code and Design views in the Document window
Design	Show Design view	Displays only the Design view in the Document window
Live View	Switch Design view to Live view	Displays the page with interactive elements active and functioning
Live Code	Show the Live View source in Code view	Displays the source code for the interactive content
	File management	Displays file management options
	Preview/Debug in browser	Activates the browser for viewing
	Refresh button	Forces Dreamweaver to reread the page to view changes made in Code view
	View options	Activates the View Options menu
	Visual Aids	Choices of visual aids to use as you design your pages
	Validate markup	Used to validate the active document or the entire site
Check Page	Check browser compatibility button	Displays information about potential problems in browsers

Working with Views and Panels

Dreamweaver has three ways you can view your Web pages. **Design view** shows a full-screen layout and is primarily used when designing and creating a Web page. **Code view** shows a full screen with the HTML code for the page; use this view to read or directly edit the code. **Code and Design views** is a combination of Code view and Design view in separate windows within the Document window. This view is the best for debugging or correcting errors because you can see both views simultaneously. Panels and panel groups appear on the right side of the screen, although you can move them and use them as "floating panels." **Panels** are individual windows that display information on a particular topic, such as Reference or History. **Panel groups**, sometimes referred to as Tab groups, are sets of related panels that are grouped together. The panels are listed by groups on the Window menu and are separated by horizontal lines (Win) or with space (Mac).  You spend some time experimenting with opening and closing panels.

STEPS

1. **Click the Show Code view button ⟨⟩ Code on the Document toolbar**

   The HTML code for the untitled, blank document appears, as shown in Figure A-4. Even though the page has no content, basic HTML code for a blank, untitled page appears. Notice in the first line of code that this is an XHTML document type, although the file extension is .html. **XHTML** is the most recent standard for HTML files and has slightly different tags and rules. Although XHTML files are more updated versions of HTML files, they still use the same file extension, and you still refer to the code as "HTML code."

2. **Click the Show Code and Design views button ⊞ Split on the Document toolbar**

   A split screen appears. The top half displays the HTML code, and the bottom half displays the page. The page is blank because there is no page content.

3. **Click the Show Design view button ☷ Design on the Document toolbar**

   The blank page appears.

4. **Double-click the CSS Styles panel tab**

   The CSS panel group expands and displays two panel tabs.

5. **Click each panel tab on the CSS Styles panel group to display the contents of each panel**

   As you click each panel tab, the panel tab changes color, and the panel contents appear. See Figure A-5.

6. **Double-click the CSS Styles panel tab**

   The panel group collapses.

7. **Double-click the panel tabs to view the panels in each of the other panel groups**

   You see how easy it is to access the views and panels in Dreamweaver.

8. **Collapse all panel groups except the Files panel group**

9. **Click File on the Application bar (Win) or Menu bar (Mac), then click Close to close the untitled document**

10. **If you are asked if you want to save the untitled page, click No**

FIGURE A-4: Code view for a blank document

Show Code
view button

Show Code
and Design
views button

Show Design
view button

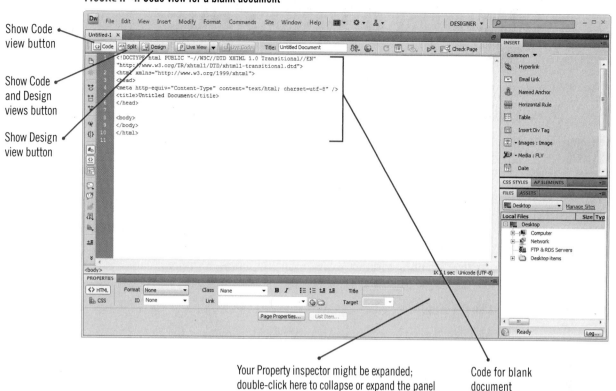

Your Property inspector might be expanded;
double-click here to collapse or expand the panel

Code for blank
document

FIGURE A-5: Displaying a panel group

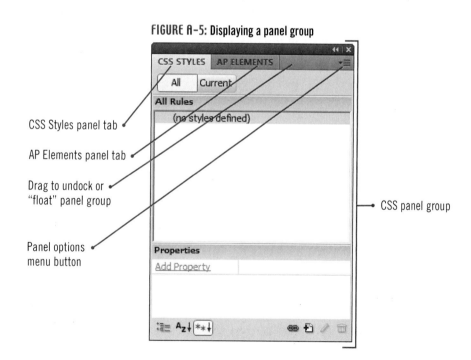

CSS Styles panel tab

AP Elements panel tab

Drag to undock or
"float" panel group

Panel options
menu button

CSS panel group

Using panel groups

By default, the Insert panel and two panel groups open when you first start Dreamweaver in Windows. These are CSS Styles and Files. The panels will retain their arrangement from one session to the next. For instance, if you open the Files panel and do not close it before exiting Dreamweaver, it will be open the next time you start Dreamweaver. To close a panel group, right-click (Win) or [ctrl]-click (Mac) its title bar, then click Close Tab Group. The **panel group title bar** is the dark gray bar at the top of each panel group. The Panel options menu button lets you choose commands related to the currently displayed panel.

Opening a Web Page

After opening Dreamweaver, you can create a new Web site, create a new Web page, or open an existing Web site or Web page. The first Web page that appears when users go to a Web site is called the **home page**. The home page sets the look and feel of the Web site and contains a navigation structure that directs the viewer to the rest of the pages in the Web site. 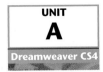 The resort's marketing firm has designed a new banner for The Striped Umbrella. You open The Striped Umbrella home page to view the new banner.

STEPS

1. **Click File on the Application bar (Win) or Menu bar (Mac), then click Open**
   The Open dialog box opens.

2. **Click the Look in list arrow ▾ (Win) or click the Current file location list arrow ⬍ (Mac), navigate to the drive and folder where your Data Files are stored, then double-click the unit_a folder (Win) or click the unit_a folder (Mac)**
   See Figure A-6.

> **QUICK TIP**
> You can also double-click a file in the Open dialog box to open it. Or click File on the Application bar, then click one of the recently opened files listed at the bottom of the menu (Win).

3. **Click dwa_1.html, then click Open**
   The document named dwa_1.html opens in the document window in Design view.

4. **If your Document window is not maximized, click the Maximize button on the Document window title bar**

5. **Click the Show Code view button** `◄► Code`
   The HTML code for the page appears.

6. **Scroll through the code, click the Show Design view button** `▣ Design` **to return to Design view, then scroll to display the top of the page if necessary**

Design Matters

Opening or creating different document types with Dreamweaver

You can use either the welcome screen or the New command on the File menu to open or create several types of files. For example, you can create HTML documents, XML documents, style sheets, and text files. You can create new documents from scratch, or base them on existing pages. The predesigned CSS page layouts make it easy to design Web pages based on Cascading Style Sheets without an advanced level of expertise in writing HTML code. Pre-designed templates save you time and promote consistency across a Web site. As you get to know Dreamweaver, you will find it worthwhile to explore each category to understand what is available to you as a designer.

FIGURE A-6: Open dialog box (Windows and Macintosh)

Click this file

Look in list arrow

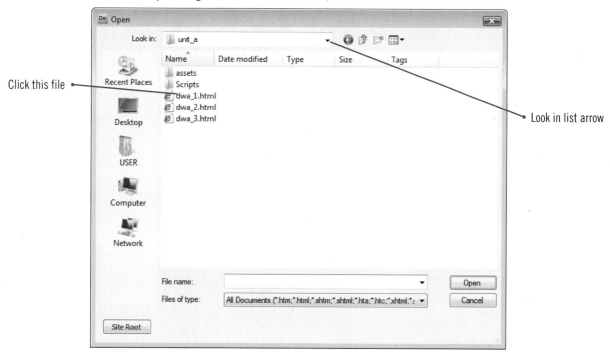

File dwa_1.html

Current file location list arrow

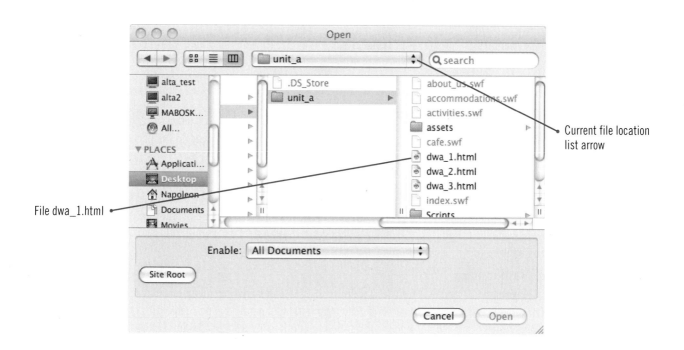

Docking panel groups

You can move panel groups to a different area on the screen by dragging the panel group title bar. To dock a panel group, drag the panel group back to the right side of the screen. A heavy bar indicates the position it will take when you release the mouse button. This position is called the **drop zone**.

Viewing Web Page Elements

There are many elements that make up Web pages. Web pages can be very simple, designed primarily with text, or media-rich with text, images, sound, and movies. You can use the programs shown in Table A-3 to create many Web page elements. Web page elements can be placed directly on the page, or pages can be designed with elements placed in table cells or specially defined areas called div tags to provide for exact placement. While working through the exercises in this book, do not be concerned if your screen shows a larger or smaller area of the document. Differences in monitor size and settings affect the size of the program and document windows. ▄▄▄▄▄ You examine the various elements on the page you have open in the Document window.

DETAILS

Compare your screen to Figure A-7 as you examine the following:

- **Text**

  Text is the most basic element on a Web page. Most information is presented with text. You type or import text onto a Web page and then format it with the Property inspector so it is easy to read. Text should be short and to the point so that viewers can easily skim through it as they browse through Web sites.

- **Images**

  Images add visual interest to a Web page. However, "less is more" is certainly true with images. Too many images cause the page to load too slowly and discourage viewers from waiting. Many pages today have **banners**, images that appear across the top of the screen and incorporate the company's logo, contact information, and navigation bars.

- **Hyperlinks**

  Hyperlinks, also known as **links**, are graphic or text elements on a Web page that users click to display another location on the page, another Web page on the same Web site, or a Web page on a different Web site.

- **Tables**

  Tables, grids of rows and columns, can be used either to hold tabular data on a Web page or as a basic design tool for page layout. When used as a design tool, they can be made invisible to the viewer. Elements are then placed in table cells to control the placement of each element on the page.

- **Div tags and AP Elements**

  Div tags and AP Elements are also important page layout tools because they allow you to "draw" or insert blocks of content on a page. These "content containers" can then be used to hold page elements, such as text or images. Because AP elements can "float" over any page element, they are easier to reposition than table cells and are more flexible tools. Many designers use a combination of tables, div tags, and AP Elements for page design.

- **Flash movies**

  Flash movies are low-bandwidth animations and interactive elements created using Adobe Flash. These animations use a series of vector-based graphics that load quickly and merge with other graphics and sounds to create short movies. Some Web sites are built entirely by using Flash. Some sites may have Flash movies in the form of buttons placed on individual pages. Most browsers today include the Flash player as part of the software. The Flash player is required to play these animations.

- **Flash video**

  Flash videos are videos that have been converted from a digital video file format to an .flv file using Adobe Flash. These videos can be **streamed**, which means that they begin playing before the entire file has been downloaded.

FIGURE A-7: Viewing Web page elements

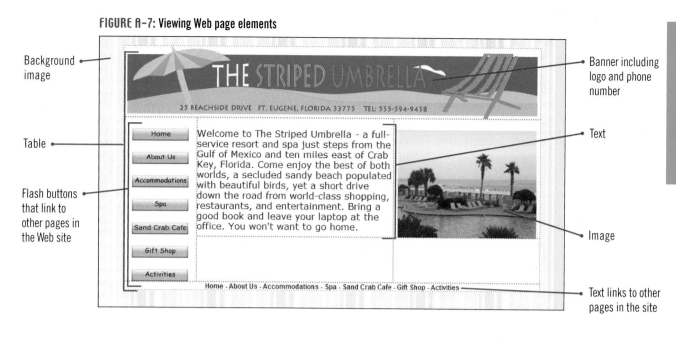

Background image

Table

Flash buttons that link to other pages in the Web site

Banner including logo and phone number

Text

Image

Text links to other pages in the site

TABLE A-3: Programs used to create Web page elements

source program	elements created
Adobe Illustrator	Used to draw or edit original images for the Web
Adobe Fireworks	Used to draw or edit original images for the Web
Adobe Flash	Used to create animation and vector graphics
Adobe Photoshop	Used to edit and enhance images
Java	Used to create small applications (applets) that can be embedded on Web pages

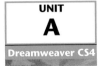

Getting Help

Dreamweaver has an excellent Help feature that is comprehensive and easy to use. When questions or problems arise, you can use the Adobe Help and Support window that contains two links that you can use to search for answers in different ways. Clicking the Dreamweaver Help command opens the Dreamweaver Help and Support page that contains a list of topics and subtopics by category. The Search text box at the top of the window lets you enter a keyword to search for a specific topic. You can see context-specific help by clicking the Help button in the Property inspector (Win). You decide to access the Help feature to learn more about Dreamweaver.

STEPS

1. **Click Help on the Application bar (Win) or Menu bar (Mac)**

   The Help menu appears, displaying the Help categories. See Figure A-8.

2. **Click Dreamweaver Help**

   The Dreamweaver Help and Support window opens.

QUICK TIP

If you don't see the link, enlarge or maximize the window.

3. **Click the Dreamweaver help (web) link in the top right corner of the Dreamweaver Help and Support window, as shown in Figure A-9**

TROUBLE

Be sure that Dreamweaver CS4 is the selected program at the top of the page.

4. **Click the plus sign next to Workspace in the left column, click the plus sign next to Working in the Document window, then click Switch between views in the Document window**

   The topic opens on the right side of the Help window, as shown in Figure A-10, and the plus signs change to minus signs, indicating that the topics are expanded.

5. **Read the text in the content side of the Help window, then close the Help window**

TROUBLE

Macintosh users may see slightly different search results; if so, click the topic of your choice.

6. **Type CSS Property inspector in the search text box in the Dreamweaver Help and Support window, then press [Enter] (Win) or [Return] (Mac)**

   A list of topics opens in the bottom of the window.

7. **Click one of the links to read information about one of the topics of your choice**

   You can either search the Adobe Web site, the Support Center, or the Community Help by clicking each link under the Search text box.

8. **Close the Dreamweaver Help and Support window**

   The Help window closes, and you return to the Dreamweaver workspace.

FIGURE A-8: Help menu

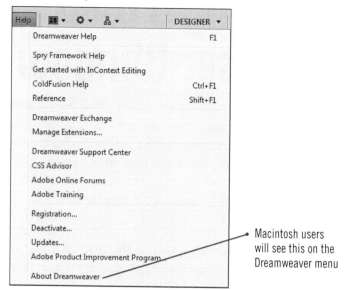

Macintosh users will see this on the Dreamweaver menu

FIGURE A-9: Dreamweaver Help and Support Web page

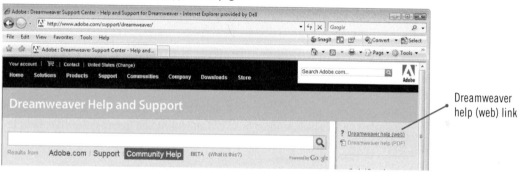

Dreamweaver help (web) link

FIGURE A-10: Displaying Help content

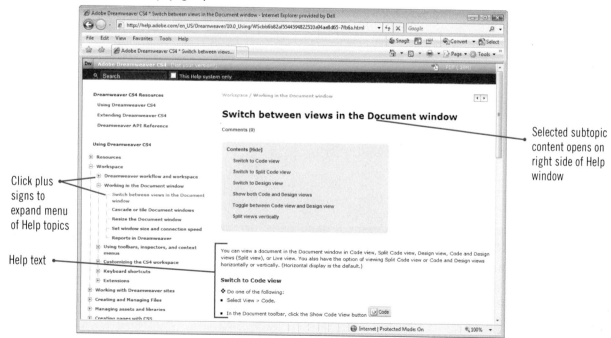

Click plus signs to expand menu of Help topics

Help text

Selected subtopic content opens on right side of Help window

Viewing a Web Page in a Browser Window

During the process of creating and editing a Web page, it is helpful to frequently view the page in a Web browser. Viewing the page in a browser provides visual feedback of what the page will look like when it is published on the Internet. It is best to view the page using different browsers and different screen sizes and resolutions to ensure the best view of your page on all types of computer equipment. It is important to remember that you cannot print a Web page in Dreamweaver except in Code view. You must go to the browser window to print the page. You decide to view The Striped Umbrella home page in your default browser.

STEPS

TROUBLE
On a Windows computer, your menu options will be dimmed if your document window is maximized.

1. **Click the Restore Down button** ⬜ **(Win), click the Window Size shortcut menu on the right side of the status bar, shown in Figure A-11, then click** 760 × 420 (800 × 600, Maximized)

   (You may need to collapse the Property inspector to see the Window Size pop-up menu.) The screen size is set to 760 × 420, which translates to a monitor set at an 800 × 600 screen resolution. When you choose your screen size, it is important to consider the equipment your audience is using. The most common screen sizes that designers use today are 800 × 600 and 1020 × 768, so check your pages using those settings. See Table A-4 for window size options.

TROUBLE
Because you are opening a single sample page that is not in a Web site with access to the other pages, the links will not work. You'll work with links in the rest of the book.

2. **Click the Preview/Debug in browser button** 🌐 **on the Document toolbar, then click Preview in [your browser name]**

   The browser window opens, and the page appears in the browser, as shown in Figure A-12. If you are using Internet Explorer 7 and see a security message when the page opens, click the Information bar when prompted and then click Allow Blocked Content. If you have a different default browser on your computer, your screen may differ.

TROUBLE
If you are using Internet Explorer 7, you may not see the menu bar. To display it, right-click any other toolbar displayed, then click Menu bar.

3. **Click File on the browser's menu bar, click Print, then click Print**

   A copy of the Web page prints. The background stripes on the page will not print unless you have chosen the print background option in your printer settings.

Design Matters

Choosing a window size

The 640 × 480 window size is not used by many viewers today. The 800 × 600 window setting is used on 15-inch monitors and some 17-inch monitors. Most consumers today use a 1024 × 768 or higher screen size, but many viewers restore down individual program windows to a size comparable to 800 × 600 to be able to have more windows open simultaneously on their screen. People use their "screen real estate" according to their personal work style.

FIGURE A-11: Window Size pop-up menu

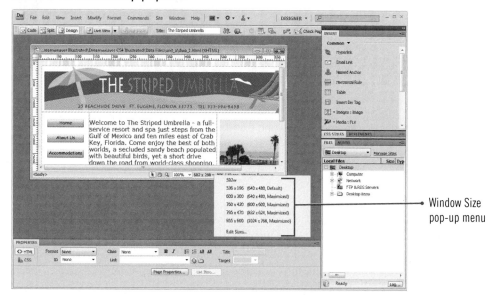

Window Size
pop-up menu

FIGURE A-12: Preview in browser

Your path
may differ

TABLE A-4: Window size options

window size (inside dimensions of browser window without borders)	corresponding resolution
592	(Fixed width, variable height)
536 × 196	640 × 480, Default
600 × 300	640 × 480, Maximized
760 × 420	800 × 600, Maximized
795 × 470	832 × 624, Maximized
955 × 600	1024 × 768, Maximized

Closing a Web Page and Exiting Dreamweaver

When you are ready to stop working with a file in Dreamweaver, it is a good idea to close the current page or pages you are working on and exit the program. This should prevent data loss if power is interrupted. In some cases, power outages can corrupt an open file and make it unusable. ▰▰▰▰▰ You are finished for the day, so you close the browser, then close The Striped Umbrella home page, and exit Dreamweaver.

STEPS

1. **In the browser, click** File **on the Menu bar, then click** Exit **(Win), or click** Safari **on the Menu bar, then click** Quit Safari **(Mac)**

   The browser closes, and your finished project is again visible in the Dreamweaver window, as shown in Figure A-13. In this book, screenshots of finished projects feature enlarged windows to display as much content as possible. You may have to scroll to see the same content.

QUICK TIP
You may need to click the Dreamweaver CS4 title bar to activate the program.

2. **In Dreamweaver, click** File **on the Application bar, then click** Exit **(Win) or click** Dreamweaver **on the Menu bar, then click** Quit Dreamweaver **(Mac)**

   Dreamweaver closes.

Saving and closing Dreamweaver files

It is wise to save a file as soon as you begin creating it and to save frequently as you work. A quick glance at the title bar shows whether you have saved your file. If you haven't saved the file initially, the filename shows "untitled" rather than a filename. This does not refer to the page title, but the actual filename. After you save the file and make a change to it, an asterisk appears at the end of the filename until you save it again. It is always wise to save and close a page on which you are not actively working. Keeping multiple files open can cause confusion, especially when you are working with multiple Web sites that have similarly named pages. Each open page has a tab at the top of the page with the filename. You use these tabs to switch between each open page to make it the active page.

FIGURE A-13: The finished project

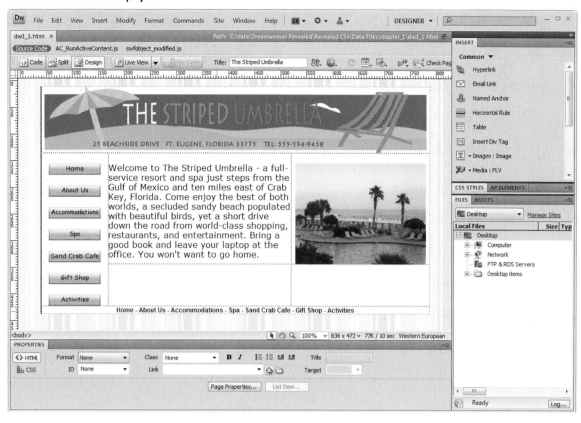

Using Adobe Community Help

When you access the Help feature in Dreamweaver, you have a choice of using offline help (which is similar to searching in a Dreamweaver manual) or using online help. The online help feature is called Adobe Community Help. Adobe Community Help is a collection of materials such as tutorials, published articles, or blogs, in addition to the regular help content. All content is monitored and approved by the Adobe Community Expert program.

Practice

▼ CONCEPTS REVIEW

Label each element in the Dreamweaver window as shown in Figure A-14.

FIGURE A-14

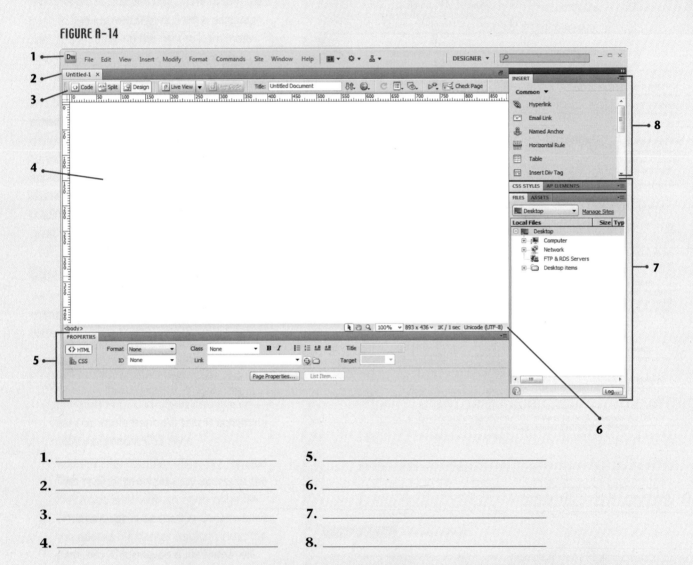

1. _____   5. _____

2. _____   6. _____

3. _____   7. _____

4. _____   8. _____

Match each of the following terms with the statement that best describes its function.

9. **Standard toolbar**

10. **Document toolbar**

11. **Code view**

12. **Tag selector**

13. **Workspace**

14. **Design view**

15. **Insert panel**

16. **Menu bar**

a. The Document window, the menu bar, toolbars, inspectors, and panels

b. Allows you to choose program commands

c. Shows the page layout

d. Contains buttons that allow you to insert objects, such as images

e. Contains buttons for some of the more commonly used options under the File and Edit menus

f. Shows the HTML code

g. Contains buttons for changing the current viewing mode of Dreamweaver

h. Shows the HTML tags being used at the current insertion point

Select the best answer from the list of choices.

17. You display panels using the _____ menu.
    a. Window
    b. Edit
    c. Panel
    d. View

18. The tool that allows you to show the characteristics of a selected page element is the:
    a. Tool inspector.
    b. Element inspector.
    c. Insert panel.
    d. Property inspector.

19. Most information on a Web page is presented in the form of:
    a. Text.
    b. Images.
    c. Links.
    d. Video.

20. The view that is best for designing and creating a Web page is:
    a. Code view.
    b. Design view.
    c. a combination of both Code and Design views.
    d. any of the above.

21. On a Windows computer, which of the following is one of the Dreamweaver default panel groups?
    a. History
    b. Design
    c. Application
    d. Files

▼ SKILLS REVIEW

1. **Define Web design software.**
    a. Write a short paragraph describing at least three features of Dreamweaver; use paper or your word processing software.
    b. Add your name to the top of the page.

2. **Start Adobe Dreamweaver CS4.**
    a. Start Dreamweaver.
    b. Write a list of the panels that currently appear on the screen.

3. **View the Dreamweaver workspace.**
    a. Locate the title bar.
    b. Locate the Application bar (Win) or Menu bar (Mac).
    c. Locate the Document toolbar.
    d. Locate the Insert panel.
    e. Locate the Property inspector.

4. **Work with views and panels.**
    a. Switch to Code view.
    b. Switch to Code and Design views.
    c. Switch to Design view.
    d. Expand the CSS Styles panel group.
    e. Collapse the CSS Styles panel group.

5. Open a Web page.

a. Open dwa_2.html from the drive and folder where your Data Files are stored. Maximize the window if necessary. Your screen should resemble Figure A-15, except the panels are not displayed in the figure.

b. Display the page in Code view.

c. Display the page in Design view.

6. View Web page elements.

a. Locate a banner.

b. Locate text.

c. Locate an image.

7. Get Help.

a. Use the Dreamweaver Help (web) command to search for topics relating to the Assets panel.

b. Display Help information on one of the topics.

c. Print the topic information.

d. Close the Help window.

8. View a Web page in a browser window.

a. Note the view that is currently selected in Dreamweaver.

b. Change the window size to a different setting.

c. Preview the page in your Web browser. If you are using Internet Explorer 7 and see a security message when the page opens, click the Information bar when prompted and then click Allow Blocked Content.

d. Print the page.

e. Close the browser window.

9. Close a Web page and exit Dreamweaver.

a. Close the Web page file.

b. Exit the Dreamweaver program.

FIGURE A-15

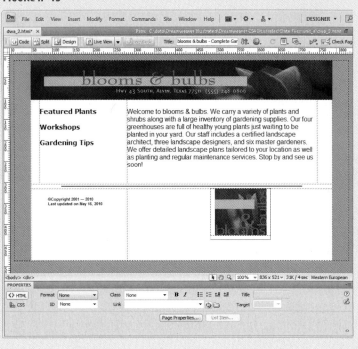

▼ INDEPENDENT CHALLENGE 1

You have recently purchased Adobe Dreamweaver CS4 and are eager to learn to use it. You open a Web page and view it using Dreamweaver.

a. Start Dreamweaver.

b. Open the file dwa_3.html from the drive and folder where your Unit A Data Files are stored. Your screen should resemble Figure A-16, except the panels are not displayed in the figure. (*Hint*: The file will open in the window size last selected. You can change it by using the Window Size menu.)

c. Change to Code view.

d. Change back to Design view.

e. Collapse the Files panel group.

f. Expand the Files panel group.

FIGURE A-16

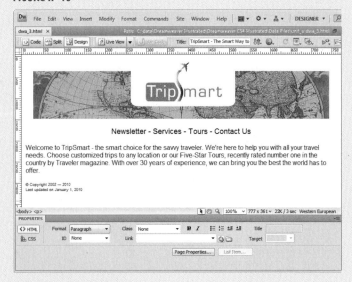

▼ INDEPENDENT CHALLENGE 1 (CONTINUED)

g. Change the window size, then preview the page in your browser. If you are using Internet Explorer 7 and see a security message when the page opens, click the Information bar when prompted and then click Allow Blocked Content.

h. Close the browser, then close the file and exit the Dreamweaver program.

▼ INDEPENDENT CHALLENGE 2

When you work in Dreamweaver, it is important to organize your panels so that you have the information you need where you can access it quickly.

a. Start Dreamweaver.

b. Use the Dreamweaver Help (web) link to locate information on how to collapse or expand panel groups.

c. Read the information, using the Previous and Next buttons in the top right corner of the Help window to advance or back up in the screens.

d. Print the information.

e. Close the Help window, then exit the Dreamweaver program.

▼ INDEPENDENT CHALLENGE 3

The Adobe Web site has a feature called Customer Showcase. Customer Showcase includes links to Web sites that were created using Adobe software, such as Dreamweaver, Flash, and Fireworks. The Customer Showcase feature includes the Site of the Day and Customer Showcase Features. The Customer Showcase Features links provide information about the company being showcased, the challenge that was presented to the design team, the solution, and the resulting benefits to the company.

a. Connect to the Internet and go to the Adobe Web site at www.adobe.com.

b. Point to the Company link near the top of the screen, then click Customer Showcase. Scroll down and click one of the companies listed under Customer Showcase Features.

c. Read the information about the company and print the page from the browser window.

d. Close your browser window.

e. Using a word processing program or paper, write a short summary (two paragraphs) of the Web site you visited, then list three things that you learned about the Adobe software used to create the site. For example: "I learned that Flash animation files can be inserted into Dreamweaver."

▼ REAL LIFE INDEPENDENT CHALLENGE

You are about to begin work on an original Web site. This site can be about anything you are interested in developing. It can be about you and your family, a hobby, a business, or a fictitious Web site. There will be no data files supplied. This site will build from unit to unit, so you must do each Real Life Independent Challenge to complete your Web site.

a. Decide what type of Web site you would like to build.

b. Find sites on the Internet that are similar to the one you would like to design to gather some ideas.

c. Evaluate what works on these sites and what doesn't work.

d. Write down at least three ideas for your new site.

e. Write down the screen size you will use for designing your pages.

▼ VISUAL WORKSHOP

Open Dreamweaver and use the Window menu to open the panels and windows, as shown in Figure A-17. If necessary, collapse or expand the panels into the position on the screen shown in Figure A-17. Exit (Win) or Quit (Mac) the Dreamweaver program.

FIGURE A-17

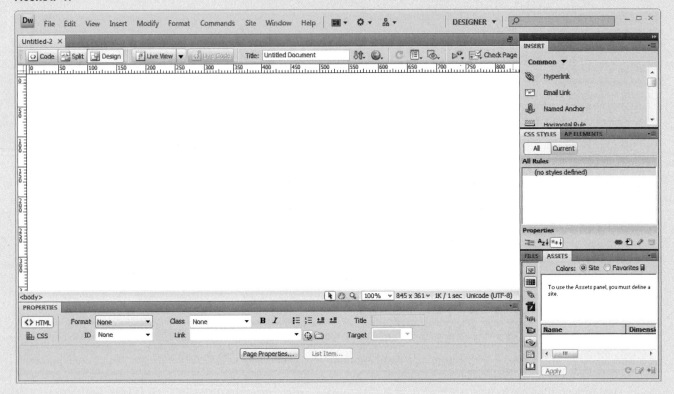

Creating a Web Site

Creating a Web site requires a lot of thought and careful planning. Adobe Dreamweaver CS4 has many tools to help you plan, create, and manage your sites. In this unit, you use these tools to plan and design a new Web site. The owners of The Striped Umbrella meet with you to discuss their ideas for a new and improved Web site. You assure them that you can create a great site for them, using Dreamweaver.

OBJECTIVES

Plan a Web site

Create a folder for Web site management

Define a Web site

Add a folder to a Web site

Save a Web page

Copy a new image to a Web site

Add new pages to a Web site

Planning a Web Site

Developing a Web site is a process that begins with careful planning and research. Planning is an essential part of creating an effective Web site. You should plan all development phases before you begin. Figure B-1 illustrates the steps involved in Web site planning. Your plan should include how you will organize and implement your site. It should also encompass testing your pages on different types of computers and modifying the pages to handle any problems. Careful planning of your Web site may prevent mistakes that would be costly and time-consuming to correct. ██████ After consulting with the lead member of the Web development team, you review the steps described below to help you create a plan for the The Striped Umbrella site.

DETAILS

- **Research site goals and needs**

  When you research your Web site, you determine the site's purpose and requirements. Create a checklist of questions and answer them before you begin. For example, "What are the company's or client's goals for the Web site? What software will I need to construct the site? Will the site require animations? If so, who will create them?" The more questions that you can answer about the site, the more prepared you will be to begin development. Once you have gone through your checklist, create a timeline and a budget for the site.

QUICK TIP

You can easily create a storyboard on a computer using a software program, such as Microsoft PowerPoint, Adobe Illustrator, or Adobe Fireworks. A computer-created storyboard is easier to change than one created on paper.

- **Create a storyboard**

  A **storyboard** is a small sketch that represents every page in a Web site. Like a flowchart, a storyboard shows the relationship of each page to the other pages in the site. Storyboards, like the one shown in Figure B-2, are helpful when planning a Web site because they allow you to visualize how each page in the site is linked to others.

- **Create folders**

  Before you create your Web site, you should create a system of folders for all of the elements you will use in the site. Decide where on your computer you will store your site. Start by creating a folder for the Web site with a descriptive name, such as the name of the company. Then create a subfolder called **assets** to store all of the files that are not Web pages; for example, images, audio files, and video clips. An organized folder system makes it easy to find files quickly as you develop and edit your Web site. Figure B-3 shows the folder structure of the Striped Umbrella site.

- **Collect the page content and create the Web pages**

  This is the fun part. After studying your storyboard, gather the files you need to create the pages; for example, text, images, buttons, videos, and animations. Some of these elements will come from other software programs, and some will be created in Dreamweaver. For example, you can create text in a word processing program and import it into Dreamweaver, or you can create and format it directly in Dreamweaver.

- **Test the pages**

  It is important to test your Web pages using different browser software. The two most common browsers are Microsoft Internet Explorer and Mozilla Firefox. You should also test your Web site using different versions of each browser, a variety of screen resolutions, and various connection speeds. Today, most people are using cable modems or DSL (Digital Subscriber Line); however, a few still use slower dial-up modems. Like Web site development, testing is a continuous process, so you should allocate plenty of time for it as you plan your site.

- **Modify the pages**

  After you create a Web site, you'll find that you need to change it, especially when information in the site needs updating. Each time you modify a Web site element, it is wise to test the site again.

- **Publish the site**

  To **publish** a Web site means to make it available for viewing on the Internet or on an **intranet**, an internal Web site without public access. Many companies have intranets to enable them to share information within their organizations. You publish a Web site to a **Web server**, a computer that is connected to the Internet with an **IP (Internet Protocol) address**. Until a Web site is published, you can only view the site on the storage device that contains it.

FIGURE B-1: Steps in Web site planning

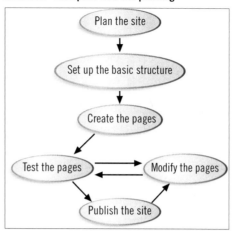

FIGURE B-2: The Striped Umbrella Web site storyboard

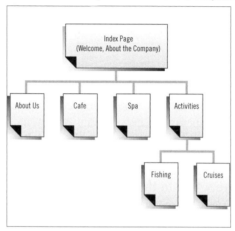

FIGURE B-3: Folder structure for The Striped Umbrella Web site

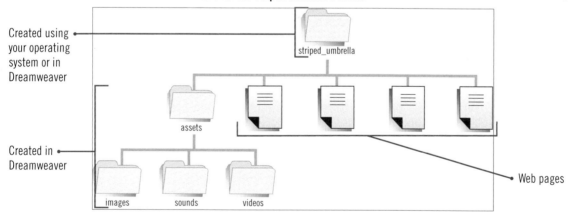

IP addresses and domain names

To make a Web site accessible over the Internet, you must publish it to a Web server with a permanent IP address. An **IP address** is an assigned series of numbers, separated by periods, that designates an address on the Internet. To access a Web page, you can enter either an IP address or a domain name in the address box of your browser window. A **domain name** is expressed in letters instead of numbers, and it usually reflects the name of the business represented by the Web site. An example would be the Adobe Web site. The domain name is www.adobe.com, but the IP address is 192.150.20.61. Because domain names use descriptive text instead of numbers, they are much easier to remember. Compare an IP address to your Social Security number and a domain name to your name. Both your Social Security number and your name are used to refer to you as a person, but your name is much easier for your friends and family to use than your Social Security number.

Creating a Folder for Web Site Management

After composing your checklist, creating storyboards, and gathering the files and resources you need for your Web site, you set up the site's folder structure. The first folder you should create for the Web site is called a local root folder. A **local root folder** is a folder on your hard drive, USB drive, or network drive that will hold all the files and folders for the Web site. You can create this folder using Windows Explorer (Win), the Finder (Mac), or the Files panel in Dreamweaver. The **Files panel** is a file management tool similar to Windows Explorer (Win) or Finder (Mac), where Dreamweaver stores and manages your Web site files and folders. When naming folders, avoid using spaces, special characters, or uppercase characters to prevent problems when you publish your Web site. When you publish the Web site, you transfer a copy of the root folder contents to a remote computer, usually hosted by an Internet Service Provider (ISP). You create the root folder for The Striped Umbrella Web site and name it striped_umbrella.

STEPS

1. **Start Dreamweaver**

   If your Dreamweaver Welcome Screen opens, you can close it if you prefer to not use it. If you don't want it to open each time you start Dreamweaver, you can click the "Don't show again" check box on the Welcome Screen. If you change your mind later and want it to open by default, use the Edit, Preferences, menu to select the "Show Welcome Screen" check box in the General category.

2. **Open or expand the Files panel if necessary to view its contents**

3. **Click the list arrow next to the Site list box in the Files panel**

   The pop-up menu displays the drives on your computer. See Figure B-4.

4. **Click to select the drive, folder, or subfolder in the list where you will store your folders and files for your Web sites**

   Dreamweaver will store all of the folders and files you create inside this drive or folder. After you select the drive or folder, the name appears in the Files panel list box. When you see a drive or folder in the list box in the pop-up menu, you do not have a Web site open.

5. **With the drive or folder in the Files panel selected, right-click (Win) or control-click (Mac), then click New Folder**

6. **Type striped_umbrella to rename the folder, then press [Enter]**

   The folder is renamed striped_umbrella, as shown in Figure B-5. You'll use this folder to store the folders and files for The Striped Umbrella Web site.

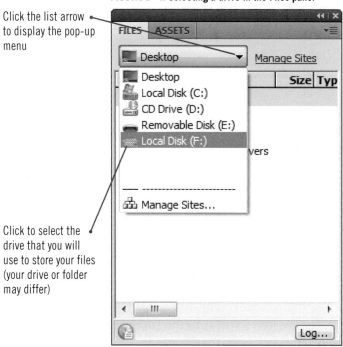

FIGURE B-4: Selecting a drive in the Files panel

Click the list arrow to display the pop-up menu

Click to select the drive that you will use to store your files (your drive or folder may differ)

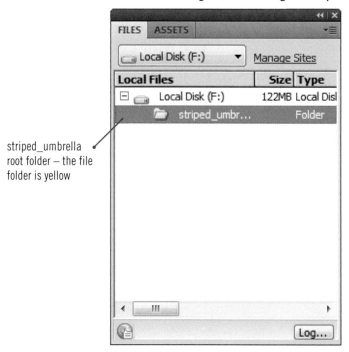

FIGURE B-5: Creating a root folder using the Files panel

striped_umbrella root folder — the file folder is yellow

Design Matters

Managing files

It is imperative that you understand the basics of good file management before you can master Dreamweaver. You should be able to create new folders and new files in a specified location. You should also learn the basic file naming conventions for Web content. To ensure that your files are available to all viewers regardless of their operating system, do not use uppercase letters or spaces in filenames. Although files with uppercase letters or spaces in their names may look fine on your screen, they might not when they are published on a Web server and might appear as broken links. If you do not have a basic understanding of file management, a quick review will pay big dividends and shorten your Dreamweaver learning curve.

Defining a Web Site

After you create a local root folder, the next step is to define your Web site. When you **define** a Web site, you specify the site's local root folder location to help Dreamweaver keep track of the links among your Web pages and supporting files. After you define the site, the program displays the local root folder in the **Files panel**. The Files panel contains a listing of all the folders and files in your Web site. The Files panel also helps you publish your Web site to a remote computer; see the Appendix for more information on publishing your site. ▓▒▒▓▓▓ You define The Striped Umbrella site.

STEPS

QUICK TIP

You can also create a new site by clicking Dreamweaver Site under Create New on the Welcome Screen.

1. **Click Site on the Application bar (Win) or Menu bar (Mac), click New Site, then click the Advanced tab (Win) or Advanced button (Mac), shown in Figure B-6, in the Site Definition dialog box if it's not already selected**

   The Site Definition for Unnamed Site 1 dialog box opens. If you have created another new site since you have opened Dreamweaver, your Unnamed Site number could be different.

2. **Type The Striped Umbrella in the Site name text box, replacing the existing text**

QUICK TIP

It is acceptable to use uppercase letters in the site name because it is not the name of a file or folder.

3. **Click the Browse for File icon 📁 next to the Local root folder text box, click the Select list arrow ▾ (Win) or ▲▼ (Mac) from the Choose local root folder for site The Striped Umbrella dialog box, click the drive and folder where you created your root folder, double-click (Win) or click (Mac) the striped_umbrella folder, then click Select (Win) or Choose (Mac)**

   The local root folder, striped_umbrella, is designated as the location for the Web site files and folders.

4. **Click the Document option next to "Links relative to:", if necessary**

   The Document option will make all links document-relative. This will prevent broken links as you create new pages and import images as you work through the lessons.

5. **Verify that the Enable cache check box is checked, as shown in Figure B-7, then click OK**

   Enable cache means that you want the computer system to use space on the hard drive as temporary memory, or **cache**, while you are working. The Site Definition is complete. You can use the Advanced tab (Win) or Advanced button (Mac) at any time to edit your settings. Your Files panel should resemble Figure B-8. Notice that the striped_umbrella folder is green. In Dreamweaver, this indicates that it is a Web site folder. Non-Web site folders are displayed as yellow folders.

Design Matters

Using the Web as your classroom

Throughout this book, you are asked to evaluate real Web sites. You learn basic design principles parallel to the new skills you learn using Dreamweaver. Learning a new skill, such as inserting an image, will not be very useful if you do not understand how to use images efficiently and effectively on a page.

The best way to learn is to examine how real Web sites use page elements, such as images, to convey information. Therefore, you are encouraged to complete the Design Quest Independent Challenges to gain a practical understanding of the skills you learn.

FIGURE B-6: Site Definition for Unnamed Site 1 dialog box

Click Advanced tab

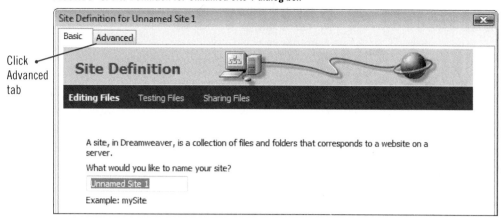

FIGURE B-7: Site Definition for The Striped Umbrella

Site name

The Striped Umbrella local root folder (your path may differ)

Links relative to: Document

Enable cache should be checked

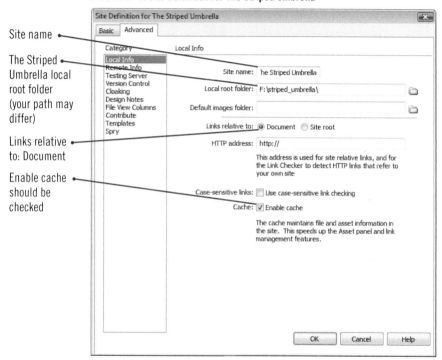

FIGURE B-8: Files panel

The Striped Umbrella local root folder (your path will vary); the file folder is now green, rather than yellow

Macintosh Files panel will vary slightly

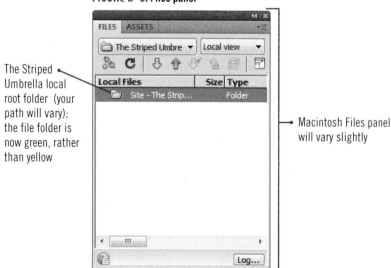

Adding a Folder to a Web Site

After defining your Web site, you need to create folders to contain the non-HTML files that will add content to the site. Creating a folder called assets is a good beginning. Complex Web sites with many types of media files or text files may have organizing subfolders within the assets folder. For example, you might have folders for text files, image files, sound files, or video clips. You should create these folders in Dreamweaver, not in Windows Explorer or Macintosh Finder. Once you have a site defined, let Dreamweaver perform all of the file management tasks. ▰▰▰▰ You create a folder called assets for The Striped Umbrella Web site.

STEPS

1. **If necessary, expand the Files panel and click the striped_umbrella folder in the Files panel**

   The folder is now highlighted, indicating that the site is selected.

   TROUBLE

   If you are using a Macintosh, you may not see the new folder if the striped_umbrella folder is collapsed. To expand it, click the triangle ▶ to the left of the striped_umbrella folder.

2. **Click the Files panel Options menu button 🔳 , point to File, then click New Folder, as shown in Figure B-9**

   This is an alternative way to add a new folder to the Files panel. A new untitled folder appears.

3. **Type assets in the folder text box, then press [Enter] (Win); or click the triangle ▶ to the left of the striped_umbrella folder to open it; if necessary, click untitled on the new folder, type assets as the folder name, then press [return] (Mac)**

   See Figure B-10. You will use the assets folder to store images and other elements used in the Web site. Next, you set the assets folder to be the default folder for the images you save in the Web site.

4. **Click Site on the Application bar (Win) or Menu bar (Mac), click Manage Sites, then click Edit**

   The Site Definition for The Striped Umbrella dialog box opens.

5. **Click the Browse for File icon 🗀 next to the Default images folder text box, click the Select list arrow ▾ (Win) or ⬍ (Mac)**

   QUICK TIP

   Your striped_umbrella folder may already be selected. If it is, you only need to select the assets folder and click Open.

6. **Navigate to display the striped_umbrella folder, double-click (Win) or click (Mac) the striped_umbrella folder (if necessary), click the assets folder, then click Open (Win)**

7. **Click Select (Win) or Choose (Mac), click OK, then click Done**

   The assets folder is now set as the default location for saving all images and other multimedia elements. This will save steps when you copy image files to the Web site.

Design Matters

Why name the folder assets?

There is no particular significance to the word "assets" for the name of the folder you will use to store non-HTML files in your Web sites. Some Web design programs use the term "images" instead. You can name the folder anything you want, but the term assets is a good descriptive word for a folder that can be used to store other types of graphic or media files besides images for your site, such as photographs or sound files. The main point is to organize your files by separating the HTML files from the non-HTML files by using a folder structure with appropriate folder names according to the content that they store.

FIGURE B-9: Creating a new folder in the Files panel

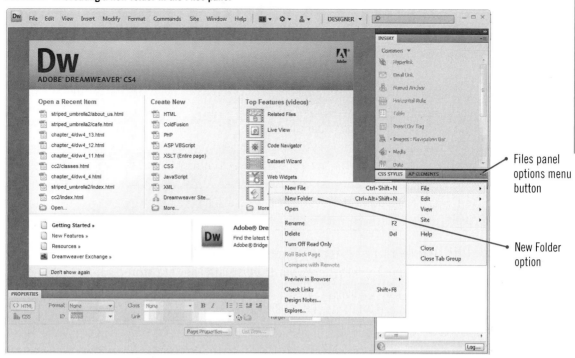

Files panel options menu button

New Folder option

FIGURE B-10: The Striped Umbrella Site window with assets folder created

Assets folder

Using the Files panel for file management

You can use the Files panel to add, delete, move, or rename files and folders in a Web site. *It is very important that you perform these file maintenance tasks in the Files panel rather than in Windows Explorer (Win) or the Finder (Mac). If you make changes to the folder structure outside the Files panel, you may experience problems.* You should only use Windows Explorer (Win) or the Finder (Mac) to create the original root folder or to move or copy the root folder of a Web site to another location. However, you can create the root folder in the Files panel. If you move or copy the root folder to a new location, you must define the Web site again in Dreamweaver, as you did in the lesson on defining a Web site.

Saving a Web Page

It is wise to save your work frequently. A good practice is to save every five or ten minutes, before you attempt a difficult step, and after you successfully complete a step. This ensures that you do not lose any work in the event of a power outage or computer problem. To save your work, you use the Save command. In this book, you are instructed to use the Save As command after you open each Data File. The Save As command duplicates the open document and allows you to give the new document a different name. By duplicating the Data Files, you can repeat an exercise or start a lesson over if you make a mistake. ▰▰▰ You open a copy of The Striped Umbrella home page and save it to the Web site before you continue working. You save the renamed file in your striped_umbrella folder. Because it will be the home page for your site, you save it using the name index.html, the usual name for a site's home page.

STEPS

1. **Click File on the Application bar (Win) or Menu bar (Mac), click Open, navigate to the drive and folder where your Unit B Data Files are stored, then double-click dwb_1.html**

    The page opens in the Document window in Design View. This is the home page, the page viewers see when they first visit The Striped Umbrella Web site.

2. **Click File on the Application bar (Win) or Menu bar (Mac), click Save As, click the Save in list arrow ▼ (Win) or ⬍ (Mac) to navigate to the striped_umbrella root folder, then double-click (Win) or click (Mac) the striped_umbrella folder**

QUICK TIP

You can just type the filename "index"; the program automatically adds the .html file extension to the filename after you click Save As.

3. **Highlight the existing filename if necessary, type index.html in the File name text box (Win) or Save As text box (Mac) of the Save As dialog box, as shown in Figure B-11, click Save, click No in the Update Links dialog box, then maximize the document window (if necessary)**

    If a filename already appears in the File name text box (Win) or the Save As text box (Mac), typing the new name replaces the current one. The path to the root folder and the filename (Win) are displayed to the right of the document tab, as shown in Figure B-12 if you are not viewing the page in a separate window. If you are viewing the page in a separate window, this information appears on the document title bar. The information within the parentheses is called the **path**, or location of the open file in relation to any folders in the Web site. The page banner does not appear and is replaced by a gray box, indicating the link is broken. This means the program cannot link to the image, which is in the Data Files folder. You must identify the image source file so Dreamweaver can copy it to the Web site assets folder. This will repair the link, and the image will then appear. You will do this in the next lesson.

4. **Click the dwb_1.html file tab to switch to the dwb_1.html file, then click the Close button on the file tab to close the dwb_1.html page**

Design Matters

Choosing filenames

When you name a file, you should use a descriptive name that reflects the file's contents. For example, if the page is about a company's products, you could name it "products." You must also follow some general rules for naming Web pages. For example, the home page should be named "index." Most file servers look for the file named index to use as a Web site's initial page. Do not use spaces, special characters, or punctuation in Web page filenames or in the names of any images that will be inserted in your Web site. Spaces in filenames can cause errors when a browser attempts to read a file, and they may cause your images to load incorrectly. Another rule is not to use a number for the first character of a filename. To ensure that everything loads properly on all platforms, including UNIX, assume that filenames are case sensitive and use lowercase characters.

FIGURE B-11: The Save As dialog box (Windows and Macintosh)

Save in the striped_umbrella root folder

Type index.html in the File name text box

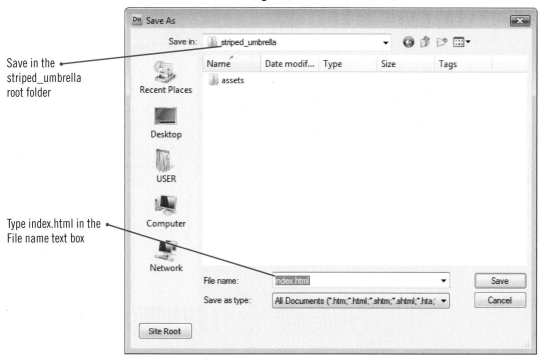

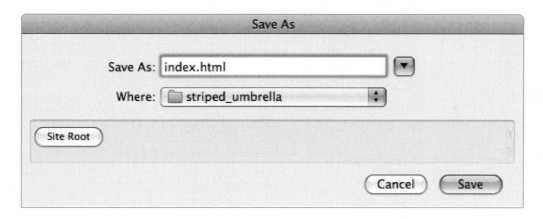

FIGURE B-12: The Striped Umbrella home page

Click the "x" on a file tab to close the file

Banner link is broken because the image file has not been copied into the Web site assets folder

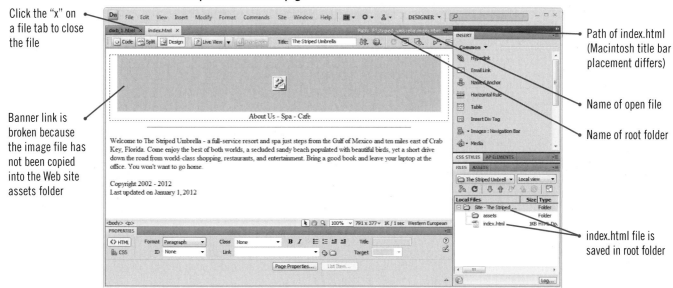

Path of index.html (Macintosh title bar placement differs)

Name of open file

Name of root folder

index.html file is saved in root folder

Copying a New Image to a Web Site

The home page is usually the first page viewers see when they visit a Web site. Sometimes a "welcome" page precedes it. When sites use a welcome page, it will include a link to the home page, and, in some cases, automatically open the home page after a few seconds. Most Web sites contain many other pages that all connect to the home page. On your home page, The Striped Umbrella banner is currently located in the unit_b Data Files assets folder; you'll need to identify its source so Dreamweaver can copy it to the site assets folder. You identify The Striped Umbrella banner source file to copy it to the site's assets folder.

STEPS

TROUBLE
If your index.html page does not appear in the Files panel, click the Refresh button ⟳ on the Files panel toolbar.

1. **Click the gray box representing the broken image on the index page**

   The Striped Umbrella banner is currently in the assets folder inside the unit_b folder. You need to tell Dreamweaver to copy it to the assets folder in the striped_umbrella folder so that the program can locate it the next time it opens the home page. Selection handles appear on the lower and right edges of the broken image. The Property inspector displays the banner's properties. The Src (Source) text box in the Property inspector displays the location where Dreamweaver is looking for and finding The Striped Umbrella banner, which is the source (the unit_b assets folder). You need to navigate to the Data Files and select the source file. Then Dreamweaver will know to automatically copy it to the site's assets folder, because you have set it as the default for images in your site.

QUICK TIP
If the path for an image or a link begins with the word "file," you can be sure you will have linking problems. Delete all extraneous path information in the Src text box or the browser will not be able to find the image when the Web site is published. A good practice is to go to Code view and search for the word "file." If you find "file" in your code, you must evaluate each occurrence to see if you need to remove unnecessary code.

2. **Expand the Property inspector if necessary, click the Browse for file icon 📁 next to the Src text box on the Property inspector, click the Look in list arrow ▾ (Win) or ⬍ (Mac) if necessary to locate the drive and folder where your Data Files are stored, double-click the unit_b folder, double-click the assets folder, then double-click striped_umbrella_banner.gif**

   Now that you have identified the source of the image, the file is automatically copied to the site assets folder. The Src text box in the Property inspector now reads assets/striped_umbrella_banner.gif without any extra path designation in front of it.

3. **Click anywhere on the page outside of the banner, if necessary, to display the image, select the image again to display the image settings in the Property inspector, then compare your screen to Figure B-13**

   The banner now appears correctly on the page because the source file has been copied to the Web site assets folder. The Property inspector displays the properties of the selected image.

Design Matters

Planning the page layout

When you begin developing the content for your Web site, you must decide what to include and how to arrange each element on each page. You must also design the content with the audience in mind. What is your audience's age group? What reading level is appropriate? Should pages be simple, containing mostly text, or rich with images and media files? To ensure that viewers do not get "lost" in your Web site, make sure all the pages have a consistent look and feel. This can be accomplished easily through the use of templates. **Templates** are Web pages that contain the basic layout for each page in the site.

FIGURE B-13: Property inspector showing properties of The Striped Umbrella banner

Selected Striped Umbrella banner

Lower Selection handle

Property Inspector provides details about the selected image

Source is pointing to Web site assets folder

Click folder to open the Select Image Source dialog box

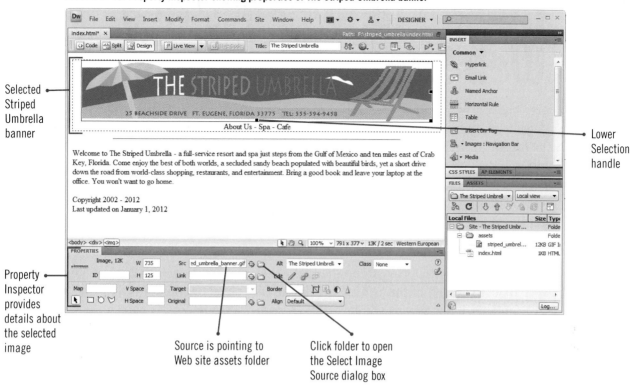

Design Matters

Making a good first impression

Since the home page is the first page viewers see as they enter a Web site, it is important to make a good first impression. When you enter a store, you immediately notice the way the merchandise is displayed, whether the staff is accessible and friendly, and the general overall appearance and comfort of the interior. The same is true of a Web site. If you see pleasing colors and images; friendly, easy-to-understand text; and a simple navigation system;

you are favorably impressed and want to explore the site. If you see poorly organized content, misspelled words, and confusing navigation, you will probably leave the site. It is much faster and easier to leave a Web site than to leave a store, so you have less time to correct a bad first impression. Have others evaluate your home page before you finalize it so you understand how others see your page.

Adding New Pages to a Web Site

Web sites may be as small as one page or contain hundreds of pages. In Dreamweaver, you can add new pages to the Web site, then add content, such as text and images. The blank pages serve as placeholders for pages that you anticipate designing. That way you can set up the navigation structure of the Web site and view how each page is linked to others. When you are satisfied with the overall structure, you can then create the content for the pages. You add new pages by using the Files panel. After consulting your storyboard, you create new Web pages to add to The Striped Umbrella Web site. You create new pages called about_us, spa, cafe, activities, cruises, and fishing, and place them in the root folder.

STEPS

1. **Click the Refresh button** ⟳ **on the Files Panel, click the plus sign (Win) or the triangle (Mac) to the left of the assets folder in the Files panel to open the folder and view its contents, if not already visible**

   The striped_umbrella_banner.gif file is in the assets folder, as shown in Figure B-14.

   QUICK TIP

   When you create a new file in the Files panel, you must type the filename extension manually.

2. **Click the root folder to select it, right-click in the Files panel, click New File, type about_us.html in the filename text box to replace untitled.html, then press [Enter] (Win) or [return] (Mac)**

   The about us page is added to the Web site. You can also click the Files panel Options menu ▼≡, point to File, then click New File to create a new file.

3. **Repeat Step 2 to add five more blank pages to The Striped Umbrella Web site, and name the new files spa.html, cafe.html, activities.html, cruises.html, and fishing.html**

   The new pages appear in the striped_umbrella root folder.

   TROUBLE

   If the site listing does not refresh, click the Files panel Options menu button ▼≡, point to Site, then click Recreate Site Cache.

4. **Click the Refresh button** ⟳ **on the Files panel toolbar to refresh the file listing**

   The files are now sorted in alphabetical order, as shown in Figure B-15.

5. **Click File on the Application bar, then click Exit (Win) or click Dreamweaver on the Menu bar, then click Quit Dreamweaver (Mac)**

FIGURE B-14: Files panel showing striped_umbrella_banner.gif in the assets folder

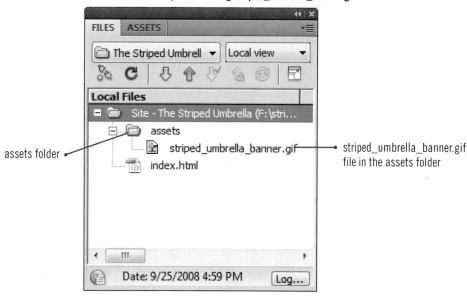

assets folder

striped_umbrella_banner.gif file in the assets folder

FIGURE B-15: New pages added to The Striped Umbrella Web site and sorted

Refresh icon

Your image icon for striped_umbrella_banner.gif may differ

New pages added to the striped_umbrella root folder and sorted

Macintosh Files panel will vary slightly

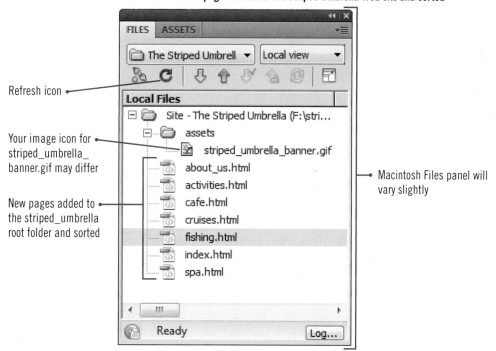

Practice

▼ CONCEPTS REVIEW

Label each element in the Site window in Figure B-16.

FIGURE B-16

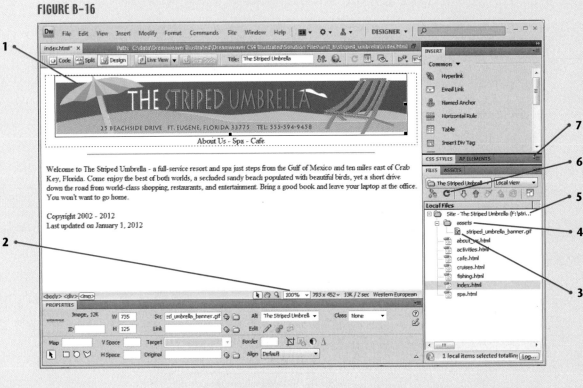

1. _____
2. _____
3. _____
4. _____

5. _____
6. _____
7. _____

Match each of the following terms with the statement that best describes its function.

8. Domain name
9. Storyboard
10. Assets
11. IP address
12. Web server
13. Root folder
14. Cache
15. Home page
16. Publish a Web site

a. An address on the Web expressed in numbers
b. Computer connected to the Internet with a permanent IP address
c. Temporary memory used to increase the speed of site management tasks
d. To make a Web site available for viewing on the Internet
e. A folder that holds all the files and folders for the Web site
f. Usually the first page viewers see when they visit a Web site
g. A folder that contains non-HTML files
h. A diagram of a Web site's folder structure showing links
i. An address on the Web expressed in letters

Select the best answer from the following list of choices.

17. **An internal Web site without public access is called a(n):**
    a. Internet.
    b. Intranet.
    c. Domain.
    d. Extension.

18. **The first step in designing a Web site should be:**
    a. Setting up Web server access.
    b. Testing the pages.
    c. Planning the site.
    d. Creating the pages and developing the content.

19. **Which icon do you click to refresh the Files panel after you have changed files listed there?**
    a. [Code]
    b. [C]
    c. [icon]
    d. [folder icon]

20. **Web pages that contain the basic layout for each page in a Web site are called:**
    a. Templates.
    b. Examples.
    c. Shells.
    d. Forms.

▼ SKILLS REVIEW

1. **Plan a Web site.**
   a. Sketch a storyboard with five pages for a company called blooms & bulbs.
   b. Name the pages **index**, **plants**, **classes**, **newsletter**, and **tips**. (The plants, classes, newsletter, and tips pages will be links from the index page.)

2. **Create a folder for Web site management.**
   a. Start Dreamweaver, then open or expand the Files panel if necessary.
   b. Select the drive or folder in the Site list box where you will store your Web site files.
   c. Create a new folder with the name **blooms** to store your Web site files.

3. **Define the Web site.**
   a. Create a new site using the Site, New Site command. Name the site **blooms & bulbs**.
   b. In the Local root folder text box, browse to the root folder you created for the Web site.

4. **Add a folder to the Web site.**
   a. Use the Files panel to create an assets folder for the Web site.
   b. Use the Site Definition dialog box to set the assets folder as the default images folder for storing your image files. Set the Links relative to: to Document and select Enable cache.

5. **Copy a new image to a Web site.**
   a. Open dwb_2.html from the drive and folder where your Data Files are stored.
   b. Save the file as **index.html** in the blooms & bulbs Web site, and do not update the links.
   c. Close the dwb_2.html file.
   d. Select the gray box representing the broken banner image link on the page.
   e. Using the folder icon next to the Src text box on the Property inspector if necessary, navigate to the assets folder inside the unit_b folder where your Data Files are stored, then select blooms_banner.jpg.
   f. Refresh the Files panel, click on the page to deselect the banner, then verify that the banner was copied to the assets folder in your blooms & bulbs site.

6. Add new pages to a Web site.

    a. Using the Files panel, create a new page called **plants.html**.

    b. Create three more pages, called **classes.html**, **tips.html**, and **newsletter.html**.

    c. Use the Refresh button to sort the files in alphabetical order, then compare your screen to Figure B-17.

    d. Close the index page, then exit Dreamweaver.

FIGURE B-17

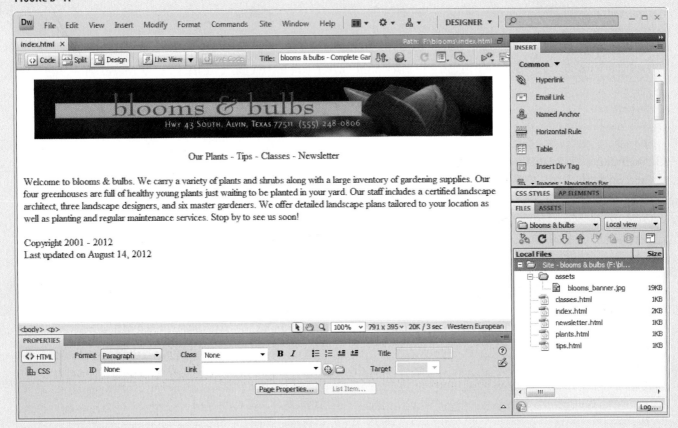

▼ INDEPENDENT CHALLENGE 1

You have been hired to create a Web site for a river expedition company named Rapids Transit, located on the Buffalo River in Arkansas. In addition to renting canoes, kayaks, and rafts, they have several types of cabin rentals for overnight stays. River guides are available, if requested, to accompany clients on float trips. The clients range from high school and college students to families to vacationing professionals. Refer to Figure B-18 as you work through the following steps:

a. Create a Web site plan and storyboard for this site.

b. Create a folder named **rapids** in the drive and folder where you save your Web site files.

c. Define the Web site with the name **Rapids Transit**, setting the rapids folder as the root folder for the Web site.

d. Create an **assets** folder and set it as the default images folder.

e. Open dwb_3.html from the drive and folder where your Data Files are stored, then save it in the root folder of the Web site as **index.html**. Do not update the links.

f. Close dwb_3.html.

g. Save the rapids_banner.jpg image in the assets folder for your site. (*Hint*: Navigate to the Unit B assets folder to locate the source for the image.) Refresh the Files panel and verify that the rapids_banner.jpg image was copied to the assets folder.

h. Create four additional files for the pages in your site plan, and give them the following names: **guides.html**, **rentals.html**, **lodging.html**, and **before.html**. Refresh the Files panel to display the files in alphabetical order.

i. Exit Dreamweaver, saving your changes.

FIGURE B-18

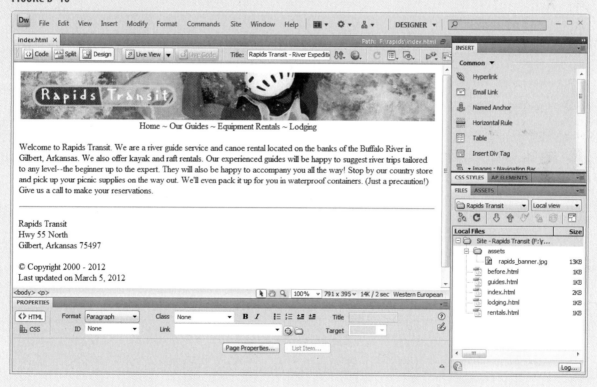

▼ INDEPENDENT CHALLENGE 2

Your company is designing a new Web site for a travel outfitter named TripSmart. TripSmart specializes in travel products and services. In addition to selling travel products, such as luggage and accessories, they sponsor trips and offer travel advice. Their clients range from college students to families to vacationing professionals. The owner, Thomas Howard, has requested a dynamic Web site that conveys the excitement of traveling. Refer to Figure B-19 as you work through the following steps:

a. Create a Web site plan and storyboard for this site to present to Thomas.

b. Create a folder named **tripsmart** in the drive and folder where you save your Web site files.

c. Define the Web site with the name **TripSmart**, setting the tripsmart folder as the root folder for the Web site.

d. Create an assets folder and set it as the default images folder, then verify that Enable cache is selected and the links are set to document relative.

e. Open the file dwb_4.html from the drive and folder where your Data Files are stored, then save it in the root folder of the Web site as **index.html**, remembering to choose not to update the links.

f. Close dwb_4.html.

g. Save the tripsmart_banner.jpg image in the assets folder for the site and refresh the Files panel to display the image file in the assets folder.

h. Create four additional files for the pages in your plan, and give them the following names: **catalog.html**, **newsletter.html**, **services.html**, and **destinations.html**. Refresh the Files panel to display the files in alphabetical order.

i. Exit Dreamweaver.

FIGURE B-19

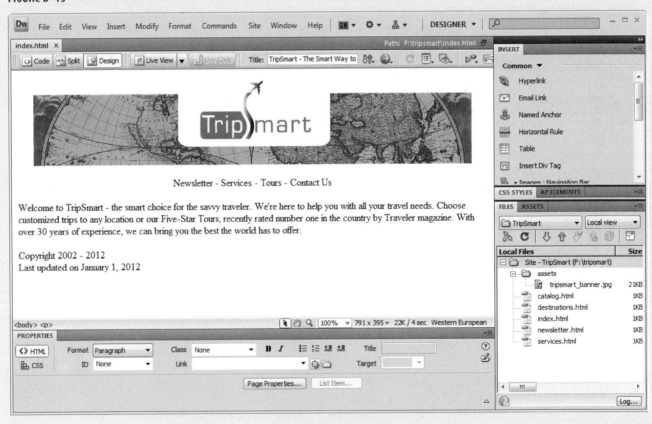

▼ INDEPENDENT CHALLENGE 3

Patsy Broers would like to buy a new car. She is considering many different makes and models, but is concentrating today on an Audi. She is looking for information on the environmental commitment of Audis in general, and for information on retail financing. Record your answers to the questions below on paper or in your word processing software. Refer to Figure B-20 as you work.

a. Connect to the Internet and go to Audi at www.audiusa.com.

b. Click the Audi Worldwide link at the bottom of the page, then click the Sitemap link. What do you think is the purpose of the site map?

c. How has Audi organized information to help you navigate its Web site?

d. Can you find the information that Patsy needs?

e. Did you feel that the site map helped you navigate the Web site?

f. Do you feel that this is a definite benefit for viewers?

g. Close your browser.

FIGURE B-20

Audi Web site used with permission from Audi AG–www.audiusa.com

▼ INDEPENDENT CHALLENGE 4

In this assignment, you create a personal Web site entirely on your own. There will be no Data Files supplied. Each Your Site Independent Challenge will build from unit to unit, so you must do each Your Site assignment in each unit to complete your Web site.

a. Decide what type of Web site you would like to build. It can be a personal Web site about you and your family, a business Web site if you have a business you would like to promote, or a fictitious Web site. Your instructor may direct your choices for this assignment.

b. Create a storyboard for your Web site and include at least four pages.

c. Create a root folder where you store your Web site files and name it appropriately.

d. Define the Web site with an appropriate name, using the root folder that you created.

e. Create an assets folder and set it as the default location for images.

f. Begin planning the content you would like to use for the home page and plan how you would like to organize it on the page.

g. Use the Files panel to create the pages you listed in your storyboard.

h. Collect information to use in your Web site, such as pictures or text. Store these in a folder (paper, not electronic) that you can bring with you to class as you develop your site.

i. Exit Dreamweaver.

▼ VISUAL WORKSHOP

Your company has been selected to design a Web site for a catering business called Carolyne's Creations. In addition to catering, Carolyne's services include cooking classes and daily specials available as take-out meals. She also has a retail shop that stocks gourmet treats and kitchen items. Create the Web site pictured in Figure B-21, using the files dwb_5.html for the index (home) page and cc_banner.jpg for the banner. Name the site Carolyne's Creations and name the root folder cc. The files are located in the drive and folder where your Data Files are stored.

FIGURE B-21

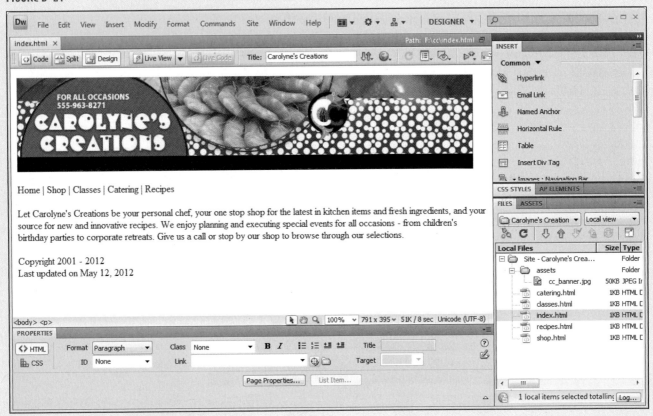

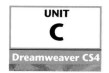

Developing a Web Page

When you begin developing Web pages, you should choose the page content with the audience in mind. A Web site designed for a large professional corporation is designed quite differently from an educational Web site for children. You can use colors, font types and sizes, and images to set a formal or casual tone. In this unit, you learn about planning a Web site, modifying a Web page, and linking it to other pages. Finally, you'll use Code view to modify some of the page code, and test the links to make sure they work.  The Striped Umbrella Web site should appeal to families, singles, and maturing baby boomers with leisure time and money to spend. You improve the design and content of the home page to attract this broad target audience.

OBJECTIVES

Plan the page layout

Create the head content

Set Web page properties

Create and format text

Add links to Web pages

Use the History panel

View HTML code

Test and modify Web pages

Planning the Page Layout

When people visit your Web site, you want them to feel "at home," as if they know their way around the pages in your site. You also want to ensure that viewers will not get "lost" due to layout inconsistencies. When you plan your Web site, consider the layout of all of the Web site pages so that they have a consistent look and feel. To help maintain a common look for all pages, you can use templates. **Templates** are Web pages that contain basic layouts you can apply to your Web site pages, such as the location of a company logo or a menu of buttons. As you will learn in Units D and G, **Cascading Style Sheets (CSS)** provide a way to easily format objects or entire pages by providing common formatting characteristics that can be applied to multiple objects. And, as you will learn in Unit H, many designers use **tables**, simple grids of cells in rows and columns, as a page layout tool to position elements on the page easily. Tables can contain headings, text, and/or images, and you can adjust their layout to provide exact placement on the page. Before you begin working on The Striped Umbrella home page, you identify key concepts that govern good page layout.

When planning the layout of your Web pages, remember the following guidelines:

- **Use white space effectively**

  Too many text blocks, links, and images can confuse viewers, and actually make them feel agitated. Consider leaving some white space on each page. **White space**, which is not necessarily white, is a Web page area that is not filled with text or graphics. Using white space effectively creates a harmonious balance on the page. Figure C-1 shows how white space can help emphasize strong visual page elements, yet still achieve a simple, clean look for the page.

- **Limit media objects**

  The expression "less is more" is especially true of Web pages. Too many media objects, such as graphics, video clips, or sounds, may result in a page that takes too long to load. Viewers may tire of waiting for these objects to appear and leave your site before the entire page finishes loading. In addition, placing an unnecessary media object on your page may make your Web site seem unprofessional.

- **Keep it simple**

  Often the simplest Web sites are the most appealing. Plus, Web sites that are simple in layout and design are the easiest to create and maintain. A simple Web site that works is far superior to a complex one with errors.

- **Use an intuitive navigation structure**

  A Web site's navigational structure should be easy to use. It can be based on text links or a combination of text and graphic links. Viewers should always know where they are in the Web site, and be able to find their way back to the home page quickly. If viewers get "lost" in your Web site, they may leave the site rather than struggle to find their way around.

- **Apply a consistent theme using templates**

  A theme can be almost anything—from the same background color on each page to common graphics, such as buttons or icons that reflect a nautical, western, automotive, or literary theme. Common design elements, such as borders, can also be considered a theme. Templates are a great way to easily incorporate consistent themes in Web sites.

- **Use tables or CSS for page layout**

  When you use tables or CSS as the basis for page layout, you can control both how the entire page appears in the browser window and how the various page elements are positioned on the page in relation to each other. This allows a page to look the same, regardless of the size of a viewer's screen.

- **Be conscious of accessibility issues**

  There are several techniques you can use to ensure that your Web site is accessible to individuals with disabilities. These techniques include using alternate text with images, avoiding certain colors on Web pages, and supplying text as an alternate source for information that is presented in an audio file. Dreamweaver can display Accessibility dialog boxes to prompt you to insert accessibility information for the page objects, as shown in Figure C-2.

FIGURE C-1: An effective Web page layout

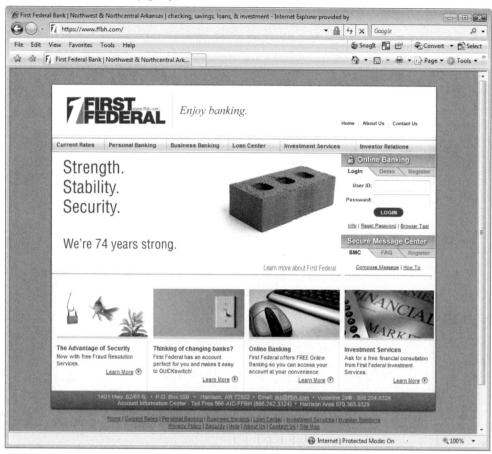

First Federal Bank Web site used with permission from First Federal Bank—www.ffbh.com

FIGURE C-2: Accessibility attributes for page design

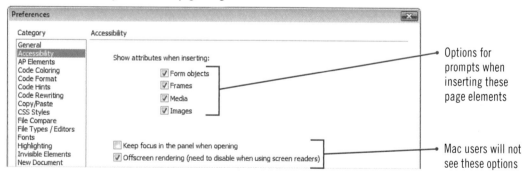

Options for prompts when inserting these page elements

Mac users will not see these options

Design Matters

Designing for accessibility

It is extremely important to design your Web site so that individuals with disabilities can successfully navigate the Web site and read the page content. In fact, government Web sites must be made accessible pursuant to Section 508 of the Workforce Investment Act of 1998, based on the Americans with Disabilities Act (ADA). On May 5, 1999, the Web Content Accessibility Guidelines were published by the World Wide Web Consortium (W3C). For more information, go to

http://www.w3.org. Adobe also provides much information about Web site compliance with Section 508 accessibility guidelines. For more information, visit the accessibility page at the Adobe Accessibility Resource Center Web site: http://www.adobe.com/accessibility/. Here you will find suggestions for creating accessible Web sites, an explanation of Section 508, and information on how people with disabilitites use assistive devices to navigate the Internet.

Creating the Head Content

A Web page consists of two sections: the head section and the body. The **body** contains all the page content viewers see in their browser window, such as text, graphics, and links. The **head section** contains the **head content**, including the page title that is displayed in the browser title bar, as well as some very important page elements that are not visible in the browser. These items are called meta tags. **Meta tags** are HTML codes that include information about the page, such as keywords and descriptions. **Keywords** are words that relate to the content of the Web site. Search engines find Web pages by matching the title, description, and keywords in the head content of Web pages with keywords viewers enter in search text boxes. A **description** is a short summary of Web site content. **Before** you work on page content for the home page, you modify the page title and add a description and keywords that will draw viewers to The Striped Umbrella Web site.

STEPS

TROUBLE
If you don't see the index.html file listed, click the plus sign (Win) or triangle (Mac) next to the striped_umbrella folder to expand the folder contents.

1. **Start Dreamweaver, click the Site list arrow ▾ (Win) or ▾ (Mac) on the Files panel, then click The Striped Umbrella, if it isn't already selected**

2. **Double-click index.html in the Files panel, make sure the Document window is maximized, click View on the Application bar (Win) or Menu bar (Mac), then click Head Content, if it isn't already checked**

   The head content section appears at the top of The Striped Umbrella home page, as shown in Figure C-3. The head content section includes the Title icon ⬚ and the Meta tag icon ⬚.

QUICK TIP
You can also change the page title using either the Title text box on the Document toolbar or the Page Properties dialog box.

3. **Click the Title icon ⬚ in the head section, place the insertion point after the current title in the Title text box in the Property inspector, press [spacebar], type beach resort and spa, Ft. Eugene, Florida, then press [Enter] (Win) or [return] (Mac)**

   The new title replaces the old title. See Figure C-4. (To read the title without the highlighting, click inside the title.) The new title uses the words beach and resort, which are words that potential customers may use as keywords when using a search engine.

4. **Click the Common category on the Insert panel (if necessary), click the Head list arrow, as shown in Figure C-3, then click Keywords**

   Some buttons on the Insert panel include a list arrow, indicating that there is a menu of choices beneath the current button. The button that was selected last appears on the Insert panel until you select another.

5. **Type beach resort, spa, Ft. Eugene, Florida, Gulf of Mexico, fishing, dolphin cruises (including the commas) in the Keywords text box, as shown in Figure C-5, then click OK**

   The Keywords icon ⬚ appears in the head section, indicating that keywords have been created for the Web page. Keywords should always be separated by commas.

6. **Click the Head list arrow on the Insert panel, click Description, then type The Striped Umbrella is a full-service resort and spa just steps from the Gulf of Mexico in Ft. Eugene, Florida., as shown in Figure C-6, then click OK**

   The Description icon ⬚ appears in the head section, indicating that a description has been entered. The Description icon appears with a blue background when it is selected.

7. **Click the Show Code view button ⬚ Code, on the Document toolbar, click anywhere in the code, view the head section code, as shown in Figure C-7, click the Show Design view button ⬚ Design, then save your work**

   The title, keywords, and description appear in the HTML code.

FIGURE C-3: Viewing the head content

Page title icon

Head content section

Meta tag icon

Head list arrow (the button may look different according to which option was last selected)

FIGURE C-4: Property inspector displaying new page title

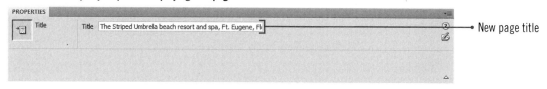

New page title

FIGURE C-5: Entering keywords

Keywords separated by commas

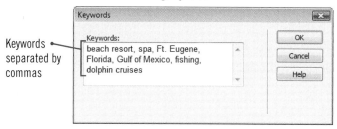

FIGURE C-6: Entering a page description

Description

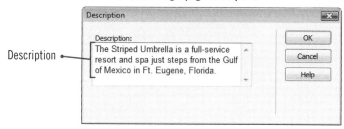

FIGURE C-7: Code View displaying the head content

Title

Keywords

Description

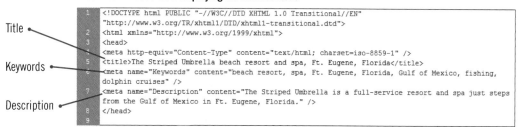

Design Matters

Entering titles, keywords, and descriptions

Search engines use titles, keywords, and descriptions to find pages after the user enters search terms. Therefore, it is important to anticipate what your potential customers will use for search terms, and to try to include those in the keywords, description, or title. Many search engines print the page titles and descriptions when they list pages in their search results. Some search engines limit the number of keywords that they will index. Keep your keywords and description short and to the point to avoid being ignored by search engines that limit the number of words you can use. It is usually sufficient to enter keywords and a description only for the home page or any other page you want viewers to find, rather than for every page on the Web site.

Setting Web Page Properties

One of the first design decisions that you should make is the background color of your Web page. The **background color** is the color that fills the entire Web page. This color should complement the colors used for text, links, and images you place on the page. A strong contrast between the text and background colors makes it easier for viewers to read the text. You can choose a light background color and a dark text color, or a dark background color and a light text color. A white background, though not terribly exciting, is the easiest to read for most viewers, and provides good contrast in combination with dark text. The next step is to choose the default text color. The **default text color** is the color the browser uses to display text. Settings such as the page background color and the default text color are specified using Cascading Style Sheets, or CSS. **Cascading Style Sheets** are sets of formatting rules that define styles used to format Web page elements. You will learn more about Cascading Style sheets in Unit D. You set the background color and the default text color for The Striped Umbrella home page.

STEPS

QUICK TIP

You can also open the Page Properties dialog box by clicking the Page Properties button in the Property inspector. The

1. **Click Modify on the Application bar (Win) or Menu bar (Mac), then click Page Properties**

   The Page Properties dialog box opens. This dialog box is where you set page properties, such as the background color and default text color.

2. **Click the Background color box , as shown in Figure C-8**

   The color picker opens, and the pointer changes to an eyedropper . Initially, the color boxes are set to gray, which represents the default colors. This does not mean that the color gray will be applied. After you select a color, it appears in the appropriate color box.

3. **Click the blue color swatch, #6CF, the next to the last color in the sixth row, as shown in Figure C-8**

   Each color is assigned a **hexadecimal value**, a value that represents the amount of red, green, and blue in the color. For example, white, which is made of equal parts of red, green, and blue, has a hexadecimal value of FFFFFF. Each pair of numbers represents the red, green, and blue values. The hexadecimal number system is based on 16, rather than 10 as in the decimal number system. Since you run out of digits after you reach the number 9, you begin using letters of the alphabet. The letter A represents the number 10, and F represents the number 15 in the hexadecimal number system. The hexadecimal values can be entered in the code using a form of shorthand that shortens the six characters to three characters. For instance: 0066CC becomes 06C. The number value for a color is preceded by a pound sign (#) in the HTML code.

4. **Click Apply in the Page Properties dialog box**

   The background color of the Web page changes to blue. The text color is set to the default color, which is black. The Apply button allows you to see changes that you have made to the page without having to close the Page Properties dialog box. You decide to change the page background back to white.

QUICK TIP

Background color box appears blue (the last color selected) until you click the white color swatch.

5. **Click the Background color box , click the white color swatch, the rightmost color in the bottom row, then click Apply**

6. **Click the Text color box, shown in Figure C-9, use to select a shade of blue for the color of the text on the home page, then click Apply to see the change**

   You decide that blue text is not quite as easy to read as black text.

7. **Click the Text color box again, then click the Default Color button at the top of the color picker**

   The color for text is set back to the default color. Your dialog box should resemble Figure C-9. The Default Color button returns the text to the default color.

8. **Click OK to close the Page Properties dialog box, then save your work**

   The colors for the page have been set. You don't have to click Apply this time, since you clicked OK. Clicking OK automatically applies the changes to the page. A new icon, the CSS icon has been added to the head content. Macintosh users will see the Properties icon .

FIGURE C-8: Color picker

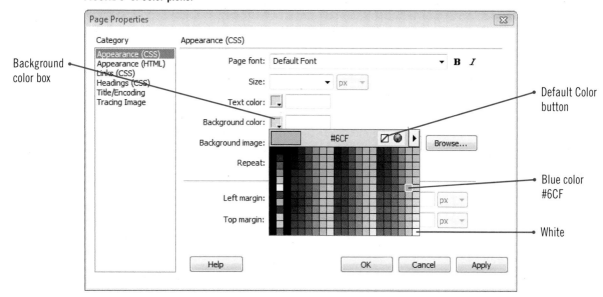

Background color box

Default Color button

Blue color #6CF

White

FIGURE C-9: Page Properties dialog box

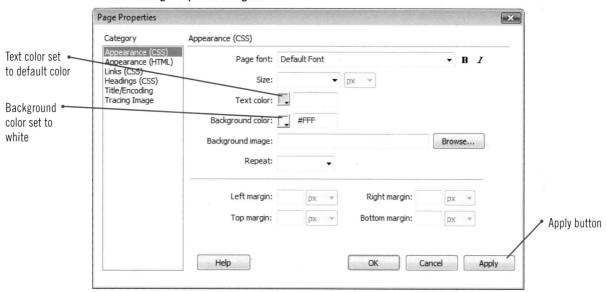

Text color set to default color

Background color set to white

Apply button

Design Matters

Using Web-safe colors

Prior to 1994, colors appeared differently on different types of computers. In 1994, Netscape developed the first **Web-safe color palette**, a set of colors that appears consistently in all browsers and on Macintosh, Windows, and UNIX platforms. The evolution of video cards has made this less relevant today, although understanding Web-safe colors may still prove important given the limitations of other online devices, such as cell phones and PDAs. If you want your Web pages to be viewed across a wide variety of computer platforms, choose Web-safe colors for all your page elements. Dreamweaver has two Web-safe color palettes: Color Cubes and Continuous Tone. Each palette contains the 216 Web-safe colors. Color Cubes is the default color palette; however, you can choose another one by clicking Modify on the Application bar (Win) or

Menu bar (Mac), clicking Page Properties, clicking the Appearance (CSS) or (HTML) category, clicking the Background or Text color box, clicking the color palette list arrow, then clicking the desired color palette. Figure C-10 shows the list of color palette choices. See the Adobe Help files for more information about Web-safe colors.

FIGURE C-10: Color Palettes

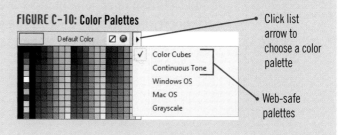

Click list arrow to choose a color palette

Web-safe palettes

Dreamweaver CS4

Creating and Formatting Text

Text is an important part of any Web page. You can type text directly in Dreamweaver, import text (Win) only, or copy and paste text from another document. You can format text in Dreamweaver by changing the font, size, and color of the text, just as in other software programs. Each time you press [Enter] (Win) or [return] (Mac) on the keyboard, you create a new paragraph in the HTML code. Each paragraph is surrounded by <p> </p> tags. Anything is considered a paragraph if it is preceded and followed by a paragraph return. Once you enter or import text, you can format it using HTML text styles. For example, **headings** are six different HTML text styles that you can apply to text: Heading 1 (the largest size) through Heading 6 (the smallest size). A **style** is a named group of formatting characteristics. While you can set some formatting characteristics with HTML styles, the preferred practice is to use Cascading Style Sheets (CSS). You revise the current text links on The Striped Umbrella home page and format them using an HTML heading style. You also apply the Italic setting to selected text on the page using the HTML Property inspector.

STEPS

QUICK TIP

Be careful with selected text or objects on the page because the next keystroke will replace the selected items, and you may inadvertently delete page elements that you want to keep.

1. **Position the insertion point to the left of A in About Us, then drag to select** About Us - Spa - Cafe, **as shown in Figure C-11**

   You select text in order to delete it. If text is not selected, you can use [Backspace] or [Delete]. You may see an icon next to the selected text. If you click this icon, you will bring up the Code Navigator, a small window that opens with code for the selected page element. You will learn more about the Code Navigator in Unit D.

2. **Type** Home - About Us - Spa - Cafe - Activities, **using spaces on either side of the hyphens**

   The text you typed forms the page's new navigation bar. A **navigation bar** is a set of text or graphic links that viewers use to navigate to other pages in your Web site.

3. **Position the insertion point to the left of H in Home, then drag to select** Home - About Us - Spa - Cafe - Activities

4. **Click the** HTML button <> HTML **on the Property inspector to switch to the HTML Property inspector if necessary, click the** Format list arrow **in the HTML Property inspector, then click** Heading 4

   The Heading 4 format is applied to the line of text, as shown in Figure C-12.

5. **Position the insertion point after the period following** ...want to go home, **as shown in Figure C-12, press [Enter] (Win) or [return] (Mac), then type** The Striped Umbrella

QUICK TIP

Line breaks are useful when you want to apply the same formatting to text but place it on separate lines. The HTML code for a line break is <br>, which stands for break.

6. **Press and hold [Shift], press [Enter] (Win) or [return] (Mac) to create a line break, then enter the following information, using a line break at the end of each line**

   25 Beachside Drive
   Ft. Eugene, Florida 33775
   (555) 594-9458

   A **line break** places text on separate lines without creating new paragraphs. You are now ready to format the address and telephone number.

QUICK TIP

The Italic button is located in both the CSS and HTML Property inspectors.

7. **Position the pointer to the left of** The Striped Umbrella, **click and drag until the entire address and telephone number are selected, click the** Italic button *I* **in the HTML Property inspector to italicize the text, click anywhere to deselect the text, compare your screen to Figure C-13, then save your work**

FIGURE C-11: Deleting the current navigation bar

Click insertion point here, then drag to select the text

Click indicator to bring up the Code Navigator

FIGURE C-12: Formatting the new navigation bar

New navigation bar with Heading 4 format applied

Depending on your monitor, your text may wrap differently

Format list arrow

HTML button

Place insertion point here, then press [Enter] (Win) or [return] (Mac)

HTML Property Inspector

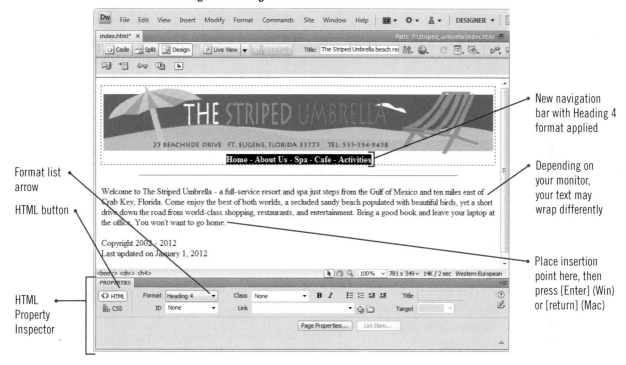

FIGURE C-13: Creating and formatting the address and telephone number

Address and telephone number with italic format applied

Italic button

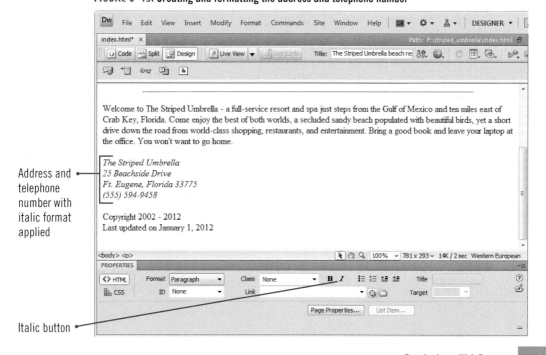

Adding Links to Web Pages

Hyperlinks, or links, are specially formatted text or images that users click to navigate, or move, through the pages in Web sites. Viewers are more likely to return to Web sites that have a user-friendly navigation system. Viewers also enjoy Web sites that have interesting links to other Web pages or other Web sites. After a link has been clicked in a browser window, it is called a **visited link**, and changes by default to a purple color in the browser window. The default color for links that have not yet been clicked in a browser window is blue. When creating Web pages it is important to avoid **broken links**, links that cannot find the intended destination file. You should also provide a **point of contact**, a place on a Web page that gives viewers a means of contacting the company if they have questions or problems. A **mailto: link**, an e-mail address for viewers to contact someone at the Web site's headquarters, is a common point of contact. You enter the links for the navigation bar for The Striped Umbrella home page. You also create an e-mail link for viewer inquiries, which will be sent to the club manager at The Striped Umbrella.

STEPS

1. **Double-click Home to select it**
   You must select the text that you want to use to make a link.

> **TROUBLE**
> If your Browse for File icon is behind the Panel Groups window, drag the border between the document window and the panels to resize as necessary.

2. **Click the Browse for File icon ▣ next to the Link text box in the HTML Property inspector, as shown in Figure C-14, then navigate to the striped_umbrella root folder if necessary**
   The Select File dialog box opens, showing the striped_umbrella root folder contents for The Striped Umbrella Web site.

3. **Click index.html, as shown in Figure C-15, verify that Document is selected next to Relative to, then click OK (Win) or Choose (Mac)**
   The Select File dialog box closes.

> **QUICK TIP**
> When text is selected, you cannot see the text color.

4. **Click anywhere on the home page to deselect Home**
   Home is underlined and blue, the default color for links, indicating that it is linked to the index.html page in The Striped Umbrella Web site. When users click the Home link in a browser window, the index.html page opens.

5. **Repeat Steps 1-4 to create links for About Us, Spa, Cafe, and Activities, using about_us.html, spa.html, cafe.html, and activities.html as the corresponding files, then click anywhere on the page**
   All five links are now created for The Striped Umbrella home page. Your screen should resemble Figure C-16.

> **QUICK TIP**
> If you don't put the insertion point immediately after the last digit in the telephone number, you will not retain the formatting.

6. **Position the insertion point immediately after the last digit in the telephone number, press and hold [Shift], then press [Enter] (Win) or [return] (Mac)**

7. **Click the Insert panel list arrow, click Common if it's not already selected, then click the Email Link button on the Insert panel**
   The Email Link dialog box opens.

8. **Type Club Manager in the Text text box, press [Tab], then type manager@thestripedumbrella.com in the E-Mail text box, as shown in Figure C-17, click OK, then italicize the Club Manager link text if necessary**
   You must enter the correct e-mail address in the E-Mail text box for the link to work; however, you can use a descriptive name, such as Customer Service, in the Text text box.

FIGURE C-14: Creating a link using the Property inspector

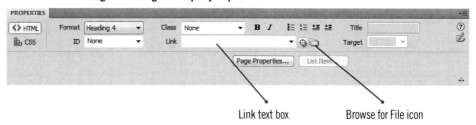

Link text box   Browse for File icon

FIGURE C-15: Select File dialog box

striped_umbrella root folder

index page

Make sure that Relative to is set to Document

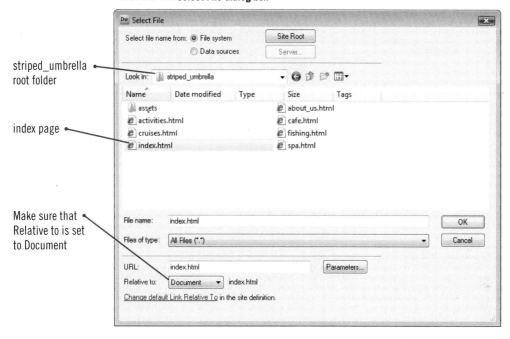

FIGURE C-16: Links added to navigation bar

Links to Home, About Us, Spa, Cafe, and Activities pages

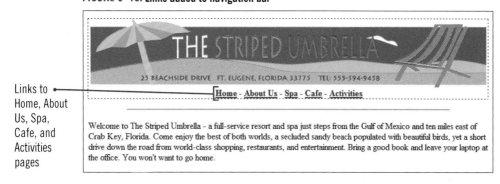

FIGURE C-17: Email Link dialog box

Text for e-mail link on the page

Link information

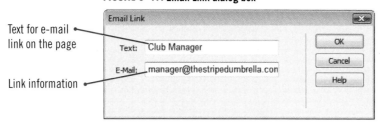

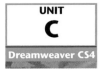

Using the History Panel

The **History panel** shows the steps that you have performed while editing and formatting a particular document in Dreamweaver. To **edit** a page means to insert, delete, or change page content by, for example, inserting a new image, adding a link, or correcting spelling errors. Remember that formatting means to change the appearance of page elements. The History panel records all tasks that you perform and displays them in the order in which you completed them. You can undo steps by dragging the slider up next to the step you want to revert to, as shown in Figure C-18. It is a more efficient way to undo steps than the Edit, Undo command. You open the History panel by using the Window, History command. You insert, and then format, a horizontal rule, and then use the History panel to undo these actions.

STEPS

1. **Click Window on the Application bar (Win) or Menu bar (Mac), then click History to open the History panel**

   The History panel opens, and the steps you have already performed are displayed in the panel window.

2. **Click the Options menu button ▾ on the History panel title bar, click Clear History, as shown in Figure C-18, then click Yes in the warning box**

   The History panel is empty.

3. **Position the insertion point to the left of the words The Striped Umbrella in the first address line, click Insert on the Application bar (Win) or Menu bar (Mac), point to HTML, then click Horizontal Rule**

   A horizontal rule, or line, appears on the page above the address and remains selected.

4. **Click the list arrow next to pixels in the Property inspector, click % if necessary, type 90 in the W text box, then press [Enter] (Win) or [return] (Mac)**

   The width of the horizontal rule is 90% of the width of the page. When you set the width of a horizontal rule as a percentage of the page rather than in pixels, it resizes itself proportionately when viewed on different-sized monitors.

5. **Click the Align list arrow in the Property inspector, then click Center**

   Your horizontal rule is centered on the page. Compare your Property inspector settings to those shown in Figure C-19.

6. **Using the Property inspector, change the width of the rule to 80% and the alignment to Left**

   The rule is now 80% of the width of the window and is left aligned. You prefer the way the rule looked when it was centered, so you decide to undo the last two steps.

7. **Drag the slider on the History panel up until it is pointing to Set Alignment: center, as shown in Figure C-20, then release the mouse button**

   The bottom two steps in the History panel appear gray, indicating that these steps have been undone, and the horizontal rule returns to the centered, 90% width settings.

8. **Save your work**

Checking your screen against book figures

To show as much of the Document window as possible, most figures appear with the Standard toolbar hidden. Keep in mind that Dreamweaver will "remember" the screen arrangement from the last session when it opens each time. This may mean that you must open, close, collapse, or expand the various panels, toolbars, and inspectors to match your screens to the figures in the book. The rulers may also be displayed in figures in Design view. To turn this feature on or off, use the View, Rulers, Show command.

FIGURE C-18: History panel

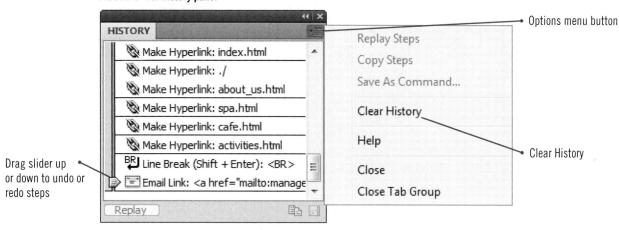

Options menu button

Drag slider up
or down to undo or
redo steps

Clear History

FIGURE C-19: Property inspector settings for rule

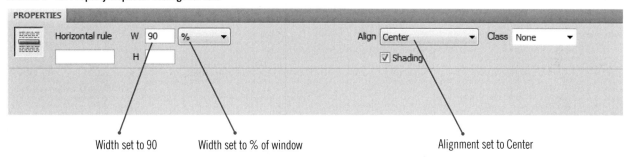

Width set to 90   Width set to % of window   Alignment set to Center

FIGURE C-20: Undoing steps using the History panel

Slider

Center alignment,
90% settings remain

Steps that have
been undone

Using the History panel

Dragging the slider up and down in the History panel is a quick way to undo or redo steps. However, the History panel offers much more. It can "memorize" certain steps and consolidate them into one command. This is a useful feature for steps that you need to perform repeatedly. However, some Dreamweaver features, such as steps performed in the Files panel, cannot be recorded in the History panel. The default number of steps that the History panel will record is 50, unless you specify otherwise in the General Preferences dialog box. Setting this number higher requires additional memory, and may affect the speed at which Dreamweaver functions.

Viewing HTML Code

Although the default files created in Dreamweaver are XHTML files, the file extension is .html, and the code is referred to as "HTML." XHTML is the newest standard for HTML code. It is often helpful to view the code while editing or formatting a Web page. Some designers prefer to make changes to their pages by typing directly into the code, rather than working in Design view. Some features, such as JavaScript functions, are often added to pages by copying and pasting code into the existing page's HTML code. **JavaScript** is code that adds interaction between the user and the Web page, such as rollovers or interactive forms. **Rollovers** are screen elements that change in appearance as the pointer rests on them. You can view the HTML code in Dreamweaver by using Code view or Code and Design view. In these views, you can view the HTML code and the page content in different colors, highlight HTML code that contains errors, and **debug**, or correct, HTML errors. You can use the **Reference panel** to find answers to coding questions covering topics such as HTML, JavaScript, and accessibility. Dreamweaver also has a feature that tells you the last date that changes were made to a Web page. ▰▰▰▰ You view the home page HTML code in Code view, use the HTML Reference panel to find out how to change the color of a rule, and then insert the date.

STEPS

1. **Click** Window **on the Application bar (Win) or Menu bar (Mac), click** History **to close the History panel, then click the** top horizontal rule **to select it**

   After you select an object, you can format it.

2. **Click the** Show Code view button ⟨⟩ Code **on the Document toolbar**

   The highlighted HTML code represents the selected horizontal rule on the page. The Coding toolbar is docked along the left side of the document window.

3. **Click the** View options button ▦▾ **on the Document toolbar, then click** Word Wrap, **if necessary, to select it**

   The code appears within the width of the window, making it easier to read.

4. **Click** ▦▾ **again and check all options that are unchecked except Hidden Characters, as shown in Figure C-21**

   If Syntax Coloring is not checked, the color of the HTML code and the text on the Web page are both black, making it harder to differentiate between the two. Next, you would like to find out how to change the color of the horizontal rule. You'll use one of the built-in electronic reference books supplied with Dreamweaver.

5. **Click** Window **on the Application bar (Win) or Menu bar (Mac), point to** Results, **click** Reference, **choose the** O'REILLY HTML Reference **in the Book list if necessary, click the** Tag list arrow, **then scroll to and click** HR **in the Tag text box if necessary, as shown in Figure C-22**

   HR is the HTML code for horizontal rule. You find out that the color of rules can be changed by using style sheets, then decide to leave the horizontal rule alone. (Style sheets will be covered in the next unit.)

6. **Click the** Options button ▤ **on the Results panel toolbar, then click** Close Tab Group **to close the Results tab group**

7. **Highlight** January 1, 2012 **at the bottom of the Code window, press** [Delete], **click the** Date button **in the Common category on the Insert panel, click** March 7, 1974 **if necessary, in the Date format options, click the** Update automatically on save check box **to select it, as shown in Figure C-23, then click** OK

   Dreamweaver lets you insert a date that updates automatically each time you save the file. March 7, 1974 is an example of a date format. The manually entered date on the page is replaced with a date that will automatically update each time the page is opened and saved. The HTML code for the date has changed.

8. **Click the** Show Design view button ▧ Design **to return to Design view, then save your work**

FIGURE C-21: Code view options

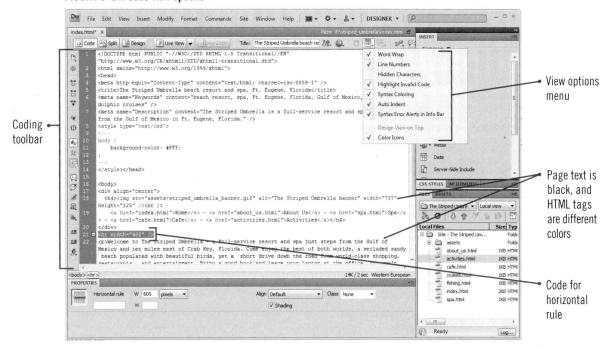

Coding toolbar

View options menu

Page text is black, and HTML tags are different colors

Code for horizontal rule

FIGURE C-22: Viewing the Reference panel

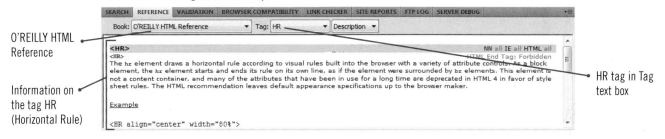

O'REILLY HTML Reference

Information on the tag HR (Horizontal Rule)

HR tag in Tag text box

FIGURE C-23: Insert Date dialog box

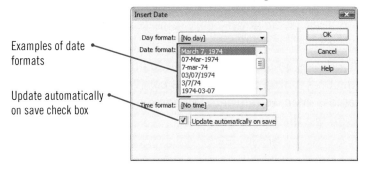

Examples of date formats

Update automatically on save check box

Understanding XHTML vs. HTML

You can save Dreamweaver files in many different file formats, including XHTML, HTML, JavaScript, CSS, or XML, to name a few. XHTML is the acronym for eXtensible HyperText Markup Language, the current standard language used to create Web pages. XHTML, which is based on XML (eXtensible Markup Language), is an extension of HTML 4. Using XHTML rather than HTML combines the advantages of both HTML and XML content and is the next step in the evolution of the Internet. You can still use HTML (HyperText Markup Language) in Dreamweaver; however, it is no longer considered the standard language. In Dreamweaver CS4 you can easily convert existing HTML code to XHTML-compliant code. Although the default files created in Dreamweaver CS4 are XHTML files, the file extension is .html, and the code is still referred to as "HTML code."

Testing and Modifying Web Pages

As you develop your Web pages, you should test them frequently. The best way to test a Web page is to preview it in a browser window to make sure it appears the way you expect it to. You should also check to see that the links work properly, that there are no typographical or grammatical errors, and that you have included all of the necessary information for the page. ░░░░ You view The Striped Umbrella home page in Dreamweaver, preview it using your default browser, and make adjustments to the page.

STEPS

TROUBLE

(Win) You cannot resize a document in the Document window if it is maximized. Click the Document window Restore Down button before attempting to resize the window. If, due to your monitor size, you cannot see the status bar, try hiding some toolbars or the Property inspector.

1. **Restore down your Document window if necessary, click the Window Size list arrow on the Status bar, click 760 x 420 (800 x 600, Maximized), as shown in Figure C-24, then view the page in the Document window**

   Although the most common screen size that designers use today is 1024 x 768 or higher, many viewers restore down individual program windows to a size comparable to 800 x 600 to be able to have more windows open simultaneously on their screen. It is strictly a matter of personal preference.

2. **Click the Preview/Debug in browser button 🌐 on the Document toolbar, then click Preview in [your default browser]**

   The page opens in the browser window. If you see a message asking if you want to allow blocked content, click the Information bar, then click Yes in the Security Warning dialog box that asks if you want to run active content. You decide to replace the period after "...go home" with an exclamation point.

3. **Close your browser, highlight the period after "...go home." then type ! (an exclamation point)**

   You now decide that the horizontal rules need adjusting to better balance the page.

4. **Click the top horizontal rule to select it, type 55 in the W text box of the Property inspector, click the Width list arrow, then click %**

5. **Select the second horizontal rule and set its width to 100%**

   The horizontal rules look more balanced on the page with the rest of the page objects.

QUICK TIP

It is a good idea to make a back-up copy of the Web site fairly frequently. Save the back-up copy to a different drive or folder other than the one where the original Web site is stored.

6. **Save the file, then use 🌐 to view the changes in your browser**

   You can also press the F12 key to preview a page in the default browser. With your finishing touches, the home page should resemble Figure C-25.

7. **Click the About Us link on the navigation bar to display the blank page you created earlier, click the Back button on the Address bar (Win) or the Back button on the Navigation toolbar (Mac) to return to the home page, then click the Spa, Cafe, and Activities links to test them**

   Each link should open a blank page in the browser since you haven't placed any text or images on them yet.

TROUBLE

If you are asked to configure your default e-mail client, answer the questions in the series of dialog boxes that appears.

8. **Click the Club Manager link, then close the Untitled message window that appears**

   The default mail program on your computer opens with a message addressed to The Striped Umbrella club manager.

9. **Close the browser, click View on the Application bar (Win) or Menu bar (Mac), then click Head Content to hide the head content icons, close the file, then Exit (Win) or Quit (Mac) the Dreamweaver program**

FIGURE C-24: Using the Window Size menu

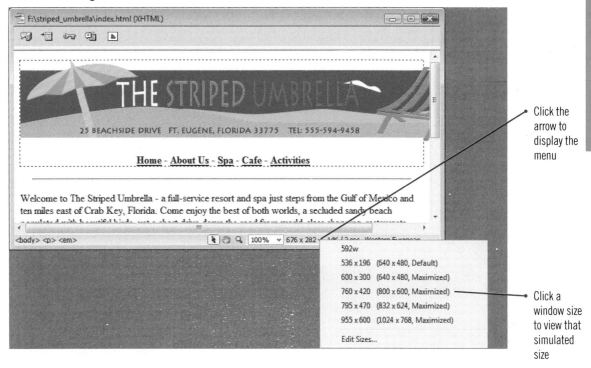

Click the arrow to display the menu

Click a window size to view that simulated size

FIGURE C-25: The finished page

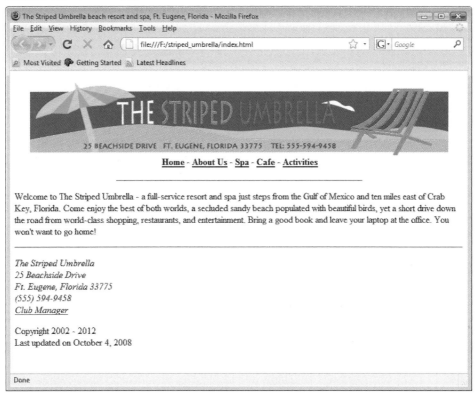

Publishing finished work

You want to make the best possible impression on your viewing audience. It is considered unprofessional to publish a Web page that has links to unfinished or blank pages. Some people feel that marking pages "Under construction" is acceptable for publishing unfinished pages, but this can irritate your viewing audience. If you don't have time to complete a page before publishing it, provide at least enough information on it to make it "worth the trip" for your audience. Then complete it as soon as you can.

Practice

▼ CONCEPTS REVIEW

Label each element in the Dreamweaver window shown in Figure C-26.

FIGURE C-26

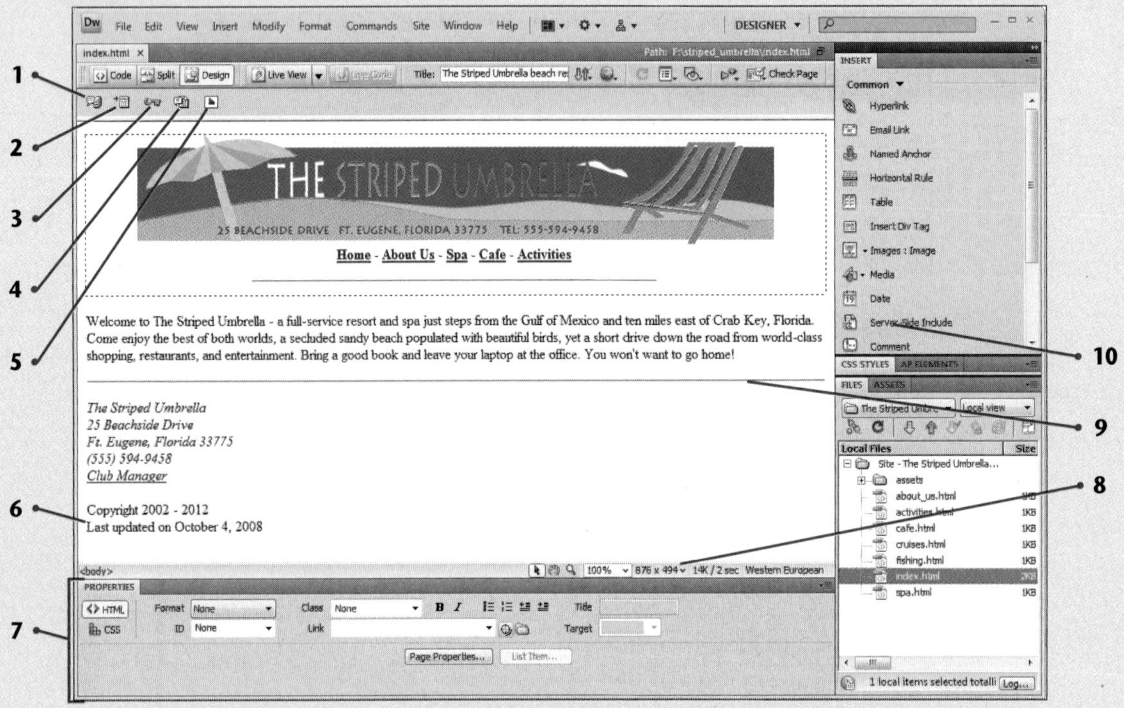

1. _____   6. _____

2. _____   7. _____

3. _____   8. _____

4. _____   9. _____

5. _____   10. _____

Match each of the following terms with the statement that best describes its function.

11. **Style**
12. **Head section**
13. **Body section**
14. **Page Properties dialog box**
15. **Heading 1**
16. **Heading 6**
17. **Edit a page**
18. **Format a page**

a. The part of a Web page that includes text, graphics, and links

b. A named group of formatting characteristics

c. Includes the default Web page settings

d. The smallest heading size

e. Make adjustments in the appearance of page elements

f. Insert, delete, or change page content

g. The largest heading size

h. The part of a Web page that includes the page title and meta tags

Select the best answer from the following list of choices.

19. **The head section of a Web page can include:**
    a. Keywords.
    b. Descriptions.
    c. Meta tags.
    d. All of the above.

20. **Links that have been previously clicked are called:**
    a. Active links.
    b. Links.
    c. Visited links.
    d. Broken links.

21. **A Websafe palette contains _____ colors.**
    a. 256
    b. 216
    c. 125
    d. 250

22. **The _____ on the History panel is used to undo or redo several steps.**
    a. Scroll bar
    b. Pointer
    c. Slider
    d. Undo/Redo Tool

23. **An example of a point of contact is a:**
    a. Heading.
    b. Title.
    c. Mailto: link.
    d. Keywords.

24. **The Dreamweaver default color palette is the:**
    a. Continuous Tone.
    b. Color Cubes.
    c. Windows OS.
    d. Mac OS.

▼ SKILLS REVIEW

Important: If you did not create the Web sites used in the preceding exercises in Unit B, you need to create a root folder for each Web site and define the Web sites using files your instructor provides. See the "Read This Before You Begin" section for more detailed instructions.

1. **Plan the page layout.**
   a. Using a word processor or a piece of paper, list three principles of good page design that you have learned, and list them in order of most important to least important to you, based on your experiences.
   b. Explain why you chose these three concepts and why you selected the order you did.

2. **Create the head content.**
   a. Start Dreamweaver.
   b. Use the Files panel to open the blooms & bulbs Web site.
   c. Open the index page and view the head content.
   d. Insert the following keywords: **garden, plants, nursery, flowers, landscape,** and **greenhouse.**
   e. Insert the description **blooms & bulbs is a premier supplier of garden plants for both professional and home gardeners.**
   f. Switch to Code view to view the HTML code for the head section.
   g. Switch to Design view.
   h. Save your work.

3. **Set Web page properties.**
   a. View the page properties.
   b. Change the background color to a color of your choice and apply it to the page, leaving the dialog box open.
   c. Change the background color to white.
   d. Save your work.

4. **Create and format text.**
   a. Replace the hyphens in the current navigation bar with a split vertical bar (the top of the backslash key) separated by a space on either side to separate the items.
   b. Using the HTML Property inspector, apply the Heading 4 tag to the navigation bar.
   c. Place the insertion point at the end of the last sentence and add a paragraph break.
   d. Type the following text, inserting a line break after each line. (*Hint*: To create a line break, press and hold [Shift], then press [Enter] (Win) or [return] (Mac).)
   blooms & bulbs
   Hwy 43 South
   Alvin, Texas 77511
   (555) 248-0806
   e. Delete the date in the "Last updated" line and replace it with a date that will update automatically each time the page is saved, using the March 7, 1974 format.
   f. Using the HTML Property inspector, italicize the copyright statement and last updated statement.
   g. Save your work.

5. **Add links to Web pages.**
   a. Add the word "Home" to the beginning of the navigation bar and link it to index.html.
   b. Link Our Plants to plants.html.
   c. Link Tips to tips.html.
   d. Link Classes to classes.html.
   e. Link Newsletter to newsletter.html.
   f. Using the Insert panel, create an e-mail link under the telephone number using a line break; type **Customer Service** in the Text text box and **mailbox@blooms.com** in the E-Mail text box.

6. **Use the History panel.**

   a. Open and clear the History panel.

   b. Using the Insert menu, insert a horizontal rule under the paragraph about blooms & bulbs.

   c. Using the Property inspector, center the rule and set the width to 80% of the width of the window.

   d. Use the History panel to return the horizontal rule to its original width.

   e. Set the horizontal rule width to 75% of the window width.

   f. Close the History panel.

   g. Save your work.

7. **View HTML code.**

   a. Use Code view to examine the code for the horizontal rule properties, the e-mail link, and the date in the "Last updated" statement.

   b. Return to Design view.

8. **Test and modify Web pages.**

   a. Using the Window Size pop-up menu on the status bar, view the page at two different sizes. (*Hint:* Recall that if you select a size that is larger than your monitor, you may need to hide toolbars or the Property inspector to see your status bar.)

   b. Preview the page in your browser.

   c. Verify that all links work correctly, then close the browser.

   d. Add the text **We are happy to ship your orders by FedEx.** to the end of the paragraph.

   e. Save your work, preview the page in your browser, compare your screen to Figure C-27, then close your browser.

   f. Close the page, then exit Dreamweaver.

FIGURE C-27

Important: *If you did not create the Web sites used in the preceding exercises in Unit B, you need to create a root folder for each Web site and define the Web sites using files your instructor provides. See the "Read This Before You Begin" section for more detailed instructions.*

▼ INDEPENDENT CHALLENGE 1

You have been hired to create a Web site for a river expedition company named Rapids Transit, located on the Buffalo River in Arkansas. In addition to renting canoes, kayaks, and rafts, they have several types of cabin rentals for overnight stays. River guides are available, if requested, to accompany clients on float trips. The clients range from high school and college students, to families or vacationing professionals. The owner's name is Mike Andrew.

  a. Use the Files panel to open the Rapids Transit Web site.

  b. Open the index page in the Rapids Transit Web site.

  c. Create the following keywords: river, rafting, Buffalo, Arkansas, kayak, canoe, and float.

  d. Create the following description: Rapids Transit is a river expedition company located on the Buffalo River in Arkansas.

  e. Change the page title to Rapids Transit – Buffalo River Outfitters.

  f. Edit the navigation bar below the Rapids Transit banner by changing Our Guides to River Guides.

  g. Apply the Heading 4 tag to the navigation bar.

  h. Enter the telephone number (555) 365-5228 below the address, with a line break between the lines.

  i. Italicize the company copyright and last updated statements, then, after the phone number, enter a line break and create an e-mail link, using Mike Andrew for the text and mailbox@rapidstransit.com for the e-mail link.

  j. Add links to the entries in the navigation bar, using the files index.html, guides.html, rentals.html, and lodging.html in the rapids root folder. (Recall that these files don't have any content yet, but you can still link to them. You will add content to the pages as you work through the remaining units of the book.)

  k. Delete the horizontal rule.

  l. Delete the date in the last updated statement and change it to a date that will be automatically updated when the page is saved, using the March 7, 1974 data format. Reformat the date to match the rest of the line if necessary.

  m. View the HTML code for the page, noting in particular the code for the head section.

  n. View the page in Design view in two different window sizes, save your work, then test the links in your browser window, as shown in Figure C-28.

  o. Close the browser, close the page, and exit Dreamweaver.

FIGURE C-28

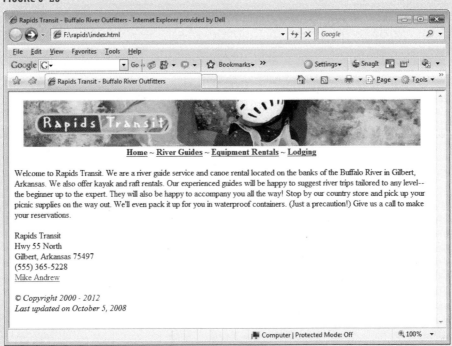

▼ INDEPENDENT CHALLENGE 2

Your company is designing a new Web site for a travel outfitter named TripSmart. TripSmart specializes in travel products and services. In addition to selling travel products, such as luggage and accessories, they sponsor trips and offer travel advice. Their clients range from college students to families to vacationing professionals. The owner, Thomas Howard, has requested a dynamic Web site that conveys the excitement of traveling. Refer to Figure C-29 as you work through the following steps.

a. Open the TripSmart Web site, then open its index page.

b. Create the following keywords: travel, traveling, tours, trips, vacations.

c. Create the following description: TripSmart is a comprehensive travel store. We can help you plan trips, make the arrangements, and supply you with travel gear.

d. Change the page title to read TripSmart: Serving all your travel needs.

e. Change the navigation bar below the banner to read Home - Destinations - Newsletter - Services - Catalog.

f. Apply a heading tag of your choice to the text links in the navigation bar.

g. Add links to the navigation bar entries, using the files index.html, destinations.html, newsletter.html, services.html, and catalog.html. (Recall that these files don't have any content yet, but you can still link to them. You will add content to the pages as you work through the remaining units of the book.)

h. Replace the date in the "Last updated" statement with a date that will update automatically when the file is saved, then apply the italic setting to the copyright and last updated statements.

i. Add the following contact information between the paragraph and copyright statement using line breaks after each line: TripSmart, 1106 Beechwood, Fayetteville, AR 72604, (555) 848-0807.

j. Immediately beneath the telephone number, place an Email link using Contact us as the text and associate@tripsmart.com for the link.

k. View the HTML code for the page, noting in particular the head section code.

l. View the page in two different window sizes, save your work, then test the links in your browser window.

m. Close the page and exit Dreamweaver.

FIGURE C-29

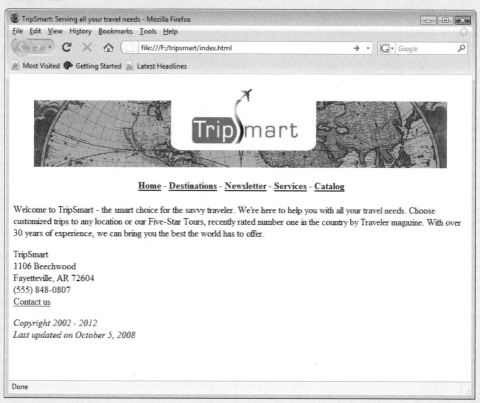

▼ INDEPENDENT CHALLENGE 3

Angela Lou is a freelance photographer. She is searching the Internet for a particular type of paper to use in printing her digital images. She knows that Web sites use keywords and descriptions to receive "hits" with search engines. She is curious as to how keywords and descriptions work with search engines. Write your answers to these questions on paper or using your word processor.

a. Connect to the Internet, then go to www.snapfish.com to see the Snapfish Web site's home page, as shown in Figure C-30.

b. View the page source by clicking View on the menu bar, then clicking Source (Internet Explorer) or Page Source (Netscape Navigator or Mozilla Firefox).

c. Can you locate a description and keywords?

d. How many keywords do you find?

e. How many words are in the description?

f. In your opinion, is the number of keywords and words in the description about right, too many, or not enough?

g. Use a search engine such as Google at www.google.com, then type the words **photo quality paper** in the Search text box, then press [Enter] (Win) or [Return] (Mac).

h. Choose a link in the list of results and view the source code for that page. If you see a message asking if you want to allow blocked content, click Allow. Do you see keywords and a description? Do any of them match the words you used in the search? (You may have to scroll down quite a bit to find the keywords. Try using the Find feature to quickly search the code.)

i. If you don't see the search words in keywords or descriptions, do you see them in the body of the pages?

j. Save your work and exit all programs.

FIGURE C-30

Snapfish Web site used with permission from Snapfish—www.snapfish.com

▼ REAL LIFE INDEPENDENT CHALLENGE

This assignment will continue to build on the personal Web site that you created in Unit B. In this lesson, you will work with your home page.

   a. Insert a brief description and a list of meaningful keywords for your home page in the appropriate locations.

   b. Insert an effective title for your home page.

   c. Format the home page attractively, creating a strong contrast between your page background and your page content.

   d. Add links from the home page to your other pages.

   e. Insert an e-mail link.

   f. Insert a "Last updated" statement that includes a date that updates automatically when you save the file.

   g. Preview the home page in your browser, verifying that each link works correctly.

   h. Check the page for errors in content or format and edit as necessary.

   i. Save your work, close the page, and exit the program.

▼ VISUAL WORKSHOP

Your company has been selected to design a Web site for a catering business named Carolyne's Creations. You are now ready to add content to the home page and apply formatting options to improve the page appearance, using Figure C-31 as a guide. Open your Carolyne's Creations Web site and modify the index page to duplicate Figure C-31. (*Hint*: Remember to add an appropriate description and keywords, and revise the last updated statement so it will automatically update when the page is saved. Also, have the e-mail link create an e-mail addressed to carolyne@carolynescreations.com.)

FIGURE C-31

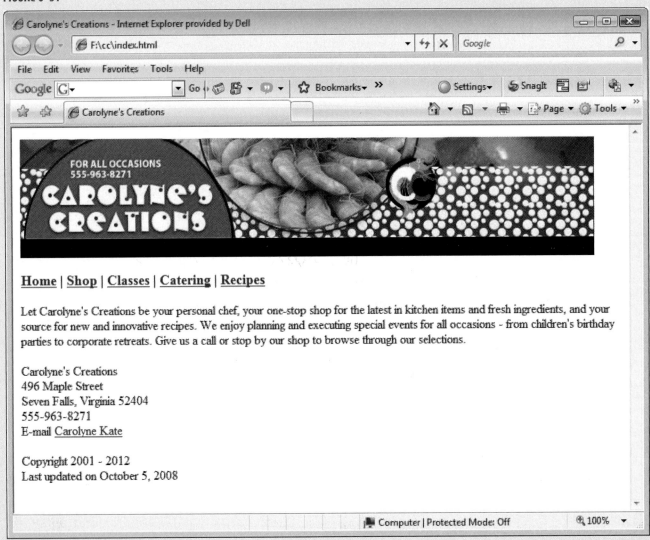

Formatting Text Using HTML and CSS Styles

The content of most Web pages is based on text. Because text on a computer screen is more tiring to read than text on a printed page, you should strive to make your Web page text attractive and easy to read. Dreamweaver has many options for enhancing text, including HTML properties for fonts, paragraphs, and lists, as well as Cascading Style Sheets (CSS). Cascading Style Sheets are used to assign sets of common formatting characteristics to page elements, such as text and tables. ▄▄▄▄ Your current focus is on the spa page for The Striped Umbrella Web site. You have decided to use lists to group content on the page to make the page more readable. You will use CSS styles to make the formatting throughout the Web site consistent.

OBJECTIVES

Import text

Set text properties

Create an unordered list

Understand Cascading Style Sheets

Create a style in a new Cascading
Style Sheet

Apply and edit a style

Add styles to a Cascading Style Sheet

Attach a Cascading Style Sheet to
a page

Check for spelling errors

Importing Text

Entering text in Dreamweaver is as easy as entering text in a word processing program. The Dreamweaver text editing features, listed in Table D-1, are similar to those in word processing programs. If you have text that you want to place on a Dreamweaver page, you can either copy and paste it, or save the file in the source program and then import it into Dreamweaver. Keep in mind that viewers must have the same fonts installed on their computers as the fonts that you apply to your text; otherwise, the text may appear incorrectly. Some software programs, such as Adobe Photoshop and Adobe Illustrator, can convert text into graphics, which eliminates this problem. When text is converted to a graphic, it retains the same appearance, but is no longer editable. ██████ The Striped Umbrella has given you a list of the services they want to include on their Web page. The document, which contains a list of spa services and descriptions, was created in Microsoft Word, then saved as a Word document. You open the spa Web page, import the text, and format it.

STEPS

1. **Start Dreamweaver, open** The Striped Umbrella Web site, **open** dwd_1.html **from the drive and folder where your Unit D Data Files are stored, save it as** spa.html **in the striped_umbrella root folder, overwriting the existing file and not updating links, then close dwd_1.html**

   The small image under the banner appears as a broken link. The source of this file, named the_spa.jpg, is in the unit_d Data Files folder. You must copy it to the assets folder in the striped_umbrella root folder by selecting the original image source in the Property inspector. Then Dreamweaver automatically copies it to the Web site's assets folder and displays the image file correctly. The banner at the top of the page is already displayed correctly since it resides in the Web site assets folder.

TROUBLE
You may have to refresh your screen by pressing [F5] or changing views to see the image on the page.

2. **In Design view, click the** gray image box, **click the** Browse for File icon 🗁 **next to the Src text box in the Property inspector, navigate to the drive and folder where your Unit D Data Files are stored, double-click** the_spa.jpg **in the assets folder, then click on the page to deselect the image**

   The file is now copied to the assets folder of The Striped Umbrella Web site. This image is an example of text that has been converted to a graphic. You are ready to import the Word text file into the Web site to place the text onto the spa page.

QUICK TIP
You may need to maximize your spa.html window to match the figure.

3. **Expand the assets folder on the Files panel if necessary, then if the newly copied file is not visible, click the** Refresh button **C̰ on the Files panel**

   You see two images saved in the assets folder, striped_umbrella_banner.gif and the_spa.jpg, as shown in Figure D-1.

4. **(Win) Click to the right of** The Spa **logo on the page, press** [Enter], **click** File **on the Application bar, point to** Import, **click** Word Document, **navigate to the drive and folder where your Unit D Data Files are stored, then double-click** spa.doc

   (Mac) Navigate to the drive and folder where your Unit D Data Files are stored, double-click spa.doc, **click** Edit, **click** Select All, **click** Edit, **click** Copy, **close** spa.doc, **click to the right of** The Spa **logo, press** [return], **then paste the copied text on the spa page in Dreamweaver**

   The text from the Word file is copied to the page, as shown in Figure D-2.

5. **(Win) Click** Commands **on the Application bar, then click** Clean Up Word HTML; **in the Clean Up Word HTML dialog box, click** OK, **then click** OK **again**

6. **Click** File **on the Application bar (Win) or Menu bar (Mac), then click** Save

Saving a Word file for importing into Dreamweaver

When you create text in Microsoft Word that you know will eventually be used on a Web page, you should not spend time formatting the text. Formatting should be applied *after* the text is imported into Dreamweaver. Some formatting, such as creating new paragraphs, is OK; however, you should avoid applying styles to the text or aligning it. Creating text, importing it into Dreamweaver, and then applying styles for formatting is a much better plan. This practice will save both time and unnecessary frustration.

FIGURE D-1: The Striped Umbrella Web site with two image files in the assets folder

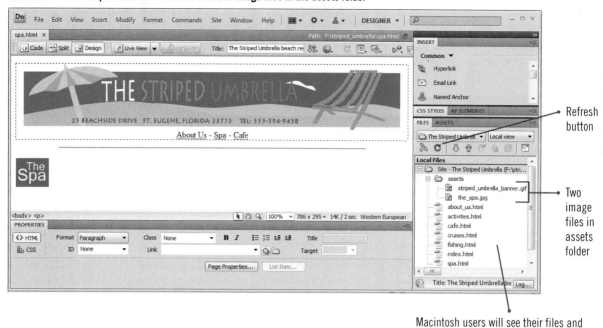

Refresh button

Two image files in assets folder

Macintosh users will see their files and folders listed together in alphabetical order

FIGURE D-2: Imported Word text

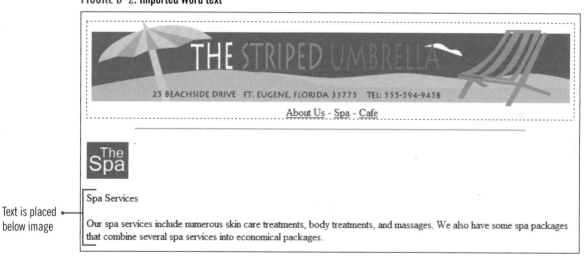

Text is placed below image

TABLE D-1: Dreamweaver text editing features

feature	menu	function	feature	menu	function
Find and Replace	Edit	Finds and replaces text on the current Web page, the entire Web site, or in selected files	**Font**	Format	Sets font combinations to be used by a browser
Indent and Outdent	Format	Indents selected text to the right or left	**Style**	Format	Sets various styles, such as bold and italic
Paragraph Format	Format	Used to set paragraph (H1 through H6) and preformatted text	**CSS Styles**	Format	Gives you the choice of applying a style, creating a new CSS style, attaching a style sheet, converting or moving rules, and applying Design-Time Style Sheets
Align	Format	Aligns text with the left or right margin, justifies it, or centers it on the page	**Color**	Format	Sets text color
List	Format	Creates unordered, ordered, or definition list settings	**Check Spelling**	Commands	Runs a spell check on the page

Setting Text Properties

You can format text on a Web page in many ways to enhance its appearance. Text formatting attributes, such as paragraph formatting, heading formatting, fonts, size, color, alignment, indents, and styles, are easy to change using either the HTML Property inspector or the CSS Property inspector. Some formatting options appear on both of them, and some are specific to either the HTML or CSS Property inspector. Using fonts within the default settings is wise because fonts set outside the default settings may not be available on all viewers' computers. To apply formatting to text, you must select it first. When formatting paragraphs, you can simply position the insertion point anywhere inside the paragraph that you want to format. Avoid mixing too many different fonts or formatting attributes on a Web page. This can lead to pages that are visually confusing and may be difficult to read. ▰▰▰ Now that you have the text on the spa page, you decide to apply some formatting to improve its appearance.

STEPS

1. **Click to place the insertion point anywhere within the words** Spa Services

   Spa Services is a paragraph; therefore you can format it with a paragraph format by clicking the insertion point within it instead of selecting the text. (Character formats such as bold and italic, on the other hand, require you to select the text.) The Property inspector shows the settings for the paragraph with the insertion point.

QUICK TIP

Even a single word is considered a paragraph if there is a hard return or paragraph break after it.

2. **Click the** HTML **button** `<> HTML` **on the Property inspector if necessary, click the** Format **list arrow, then click** Heading 4

   The Heading 4 format is applied to the paragraph.

3. **Click** Format **on the Application bar (Win) or Menu bar (Mac), point to** Align, **then click** Center

   The paragraph is centered on the page, as shown in Figure D-3.

TROUBLE

Mac users may notice that Design view and Code view do not scroll together as shown in Figure D-4.

4. **Click the** Show Code and Design views **button** `Split` **to view the HTML code, as shown in Figure D-4**

   The HTML code for a Heading 4 tag is <h4>. The tag is then closed with </h4>. When the paragraph is centered, the HTML code 'align="center"' is added to the <h4> tag. HTML code is built from a series of **tags**, or individual code references surrounded by < > symbols. Tags instruct the browser how to display the page elements between each opening and closing tag. It is always helpful to learn what the HTML code means. As you edit and format your pages, read the code frequently for each element to see how it is written. The more familiar you are with the code, the more comfortable you will feel with Dreamweaver and Web design.

5. **Click the** Show Design view **button** `Design` **to return to Design view**

6. **Save your work, click the** Preview/Debug in browser **button** 🌐 **on the Document toolbar, click** Preview in [your browser name], **examine the page, then close the browser**

FIGURE D-3: Property inspector

Text is centered with the Heading 4 tag applied

Format list arrow

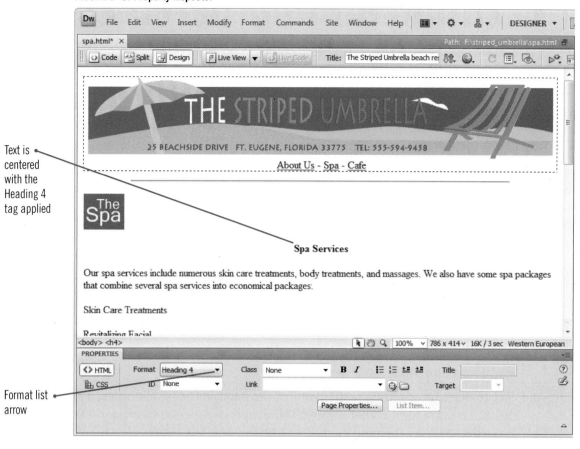

FIGURE D-4: Show Code and Design views

Code that center-aligns the heading

The code that is displayed in Code view reflects the position of the insertion point on the page

Insertion point is placed in heading

Show Code and Design views button

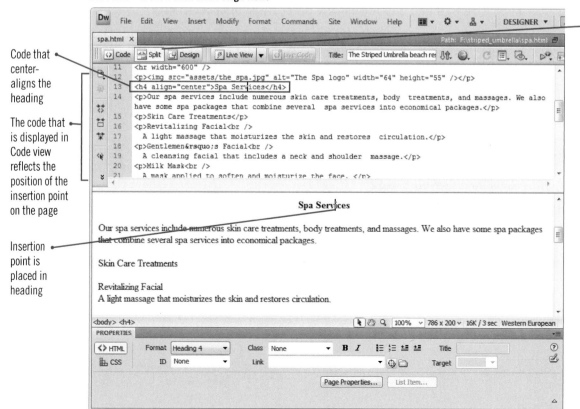

Creating an Unordered List

You may need to create a list of products or services on your Web pages. Dreamweaver provides three types of lists: bulleted lists, numbered lists, and definition lists. **Bulleted lists**, or unordered lists, are lists of items that do not need to be placed in a specific order. Each item is usually preceded by a **bullet**, a small filled circle, or a similar icon. Bullets make lists easier to read than unformatted text. Numbered lists, or **ordered lists**, are lists of items that must be placed in a specific order, and each item is preceded by a number or a letter. Definition lists are similar to unordered lists, but do not use numbers or bullets. ▰▰▰ You decide to create an unordered list from the spa service items, to make them easier to read.

STEPS

1. **Select the three items and their descriptions under the Skin Care Treatments heading**
   The three items are selected.

2. **Click the Unordered List button** ▤ **on the HTML Property inspector to create an unordered list**
   The list of items becomes an unordered list. As you type page text, you can extend the list to add more bullets by pressing [Enter] (Win) or [return] (Mac) once at the end of an unordered list. To end an unordered list, press [Enter] (Win) or [return] twice (Mac).

3. **Repeat Steps 1 and 2 to create unordered lists of the items under the Body Treatments, Massages, and Spa Packages headings**

4. **Click to place the insertion point in any of the items in the first unordered list, double-click the bottom-right corner of the HTML Property inspector to expand the Property inspector (Win) if necessary, then click List Item**
   The List Properties dialog box opens.

5. **Click the Style list arrow, click Square, as shown in Figure D-5, then click OK**
   The bullets now appear as squares rather than circles.

6. **Repeat Steps 4 and 5 to format the other three unordered lists**

7. **Click to place the insertion point before the first item in the first unordered list, click the Show Code view button** ▣ Code **on the Document toolbar to view the code for the unordered list, click the View options button** ▤▾ **on the Document toolbar, then uncheck the Hidden Characters option if necessary**
   The HTML codes, or tags, surrounding the unordered list are <ul> and </ul>. Each of the items is surrounded by a <li> and </li> tag, as shown in Figure D-6. The first tag in each pair begins the code, and the last tag ends the code.

8. **Click the Show Design view button** ▣ Design **on the Document toolbar to return to Design view, then save your work**

FIGURE D-5: List Properties dialog box

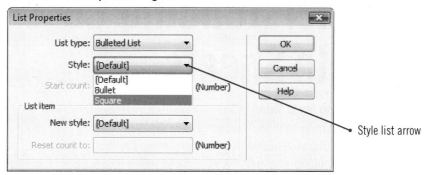

Style list arrow

FIGURE D-6: Code view

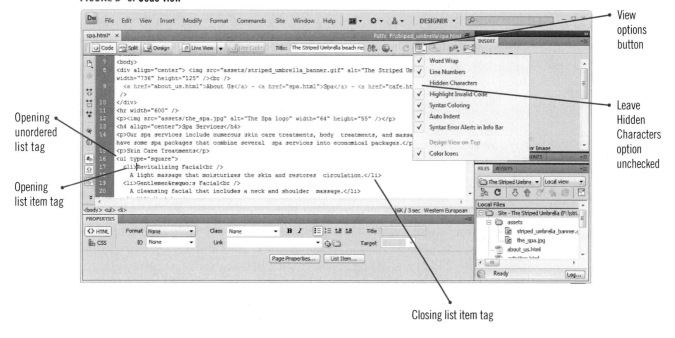

View options button

Leave Hidden Characters option unchecked

Opening unordered list tag

Opening list item tag

Closing list item tag

Ordered lists

Numbered lists, or ordered lists, contain numbered or lettered items that should appear in a particular order, such as listing the steps to accomplish a task. For example, if you followed directions to drive from point A to point B, each step would have to be executed in order or you would not successfully reach your destination. For sequential items such as this, ordered lists can add more emphasis than bullets. Dreamweaver uses several options for number styles, including Roman and Arabic.

Understanding Cascading Style Sheets

A **Cascading Style Sheet (CSS)** consists of sets of formatting rules that create **styles** that can be used to format Web page content. You create CSS styles when you want to apply the same formatting attributes to page elements, such as text, objects, and tables. Cascading style sheets can contain many different styles, such as heading or body text, that are saved with a descriptive name. You can apply CSS styles to any element in a document or to all of the documents in a Web site. If you edit an existing CSS style, all the page elements you have formatted with that style will automatically update. ▰▰▰▰▰ You decide to learn how CSS styles will save you time and give a more consistent look to your site.

As you plan to use CSS styles in a Web site, keep in mind the following guidelines:

- **Advantages of using CSS styles**

  Cascading Style Sheets (CSS) are made up of individual **rules**, or sets of formatting attributes such as font-family and font-size. These rules create styles that are applied to individual page elements, such as text or horizontal rules. Cascading Style Sheets are great time savers and are an efficient way to provide continuity across site content. After you apply styles, you can edit the rules definition, and every item to which you've applied that style will then be automatically updated to reflect the changes. You can provide continuity across a Web site by applying styles to all similar elements such as headings or subheadings.

- **CSS styles classified by location**

  For most people who are beginning to learn about Cascading Style Sheets, the terms are confusing. One way to categorize style sheets is by the location where they are stored. An **External Cascading Style Sheet** is a single, separate file with a .css file extension that can be attached to a page in a Web site and determines the formatting for various page elements. This file can contain many individual styles. If you have a Cascading Style Sheet with ten styles, you would only have one file with ten styles defined within it, rather than ten separate style sheet files. You can then attach the style sheet file to all of the pages in the same Web site (or to pages in other Web sites) so the pages can use the styles the Cascading Style Sheet contains. The ability to attach one style sheet to multiple Web pages makes them a powerful tool. **Internal style sheets** are contained in the code for an individual Web page and can be embedded or inline styles. An **embedded style** consists of code that is stored in a page's head content; an **inline style** is stored in a page's body content.

- **CSS styles classified by function**

  Another way to classify CSS styles is by their function. A **Class style** can be used to format any page element, such as a paragraph of text or an image. An **HTML style** is used to redefine an HTML tag, such as changing the color of a horizontal rule. An **Advanced**, or **Compound style** is used to format combinations of page elements. For example, you could define a style that determines how all images are displayed when they are inside a div tag.

- **The CSS Styles panel**

  You use the CSS Styles panel to create, edit, and apply rules. The panel has two views: All (Document) Mode and Current Selection Mode. The CSS Styles panel in Figure D-7 is in All (Document) Mode, which lists all attached and embedded rules. When you select a rule in the All Rules pane, that rule's properties appear in the Properties pane at the bottom of the panel. Figure D-8 shows the CSS Styles panel in Current Selection mode, which shows the properties for the page element at the current position of the insertion point. You can edit the properties for the rule in the Properties pane. The small pane between the Summary for selection pane and the Properties pane in Current mode is called the Rules pane, which shows the location of the current selected rule in the open document.

FIGURE D-7: CSS Styles panel in All Document Mode

Switch to All (Document) Mode button

External CSS styles

Embedded CSS styles

Properties for selected style are displayed in Properties pane

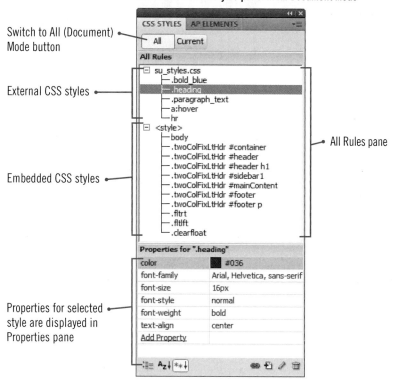

All Rules pane

FIGURE D-8: CSS Styles panel in Current Selection Mode

Switch to Current Selection Mode button

The insertion point on the page is in a paragraph with the paragraph_text rule applied

Properties for selected style are displayed in Properties pane

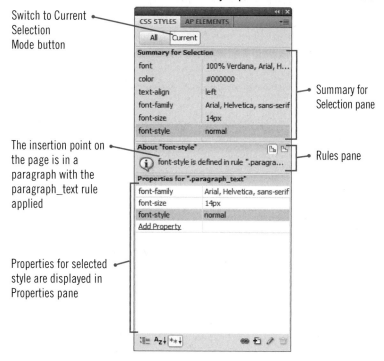

Summary for Selection pane

Rules pane

Using the CSS and HTML Property inspector

You apply CSS styles using the CSS or HTML Property inspector. First you select the element on the page, then you apply a style from the Property inspector. In the HTML Property inspector, you select a style from the Class list box. In the CSS Property inspector, you select a style from the Targeted Rule list box. You change back and forth between the two Property inspectors by clicking the HTML button <> HTML or CSS button 🔓 CSS .

Creating a Style in a New Cascading Style Sheet

The steps for creating the first style in a new Cascading Style Sheet are different from the steps for creating additional styles in an existing style sheet. Creating the first style in a new CSS is a two-step process. When you create the first style, you have not yet created the style sheet, so you must first name the style sheet file in which you want to save the first style. After you have named and saved the style sheet file, you then simply add new styles to it. ▰▰▰ You decide to apply the same formatting to the names of each spa service. Instead of formatting each item one at a time, you create a Cascading Style Sheet and apply the style to each item. That way, if you decide to change it later, you only have to change the CSS rule, and all the items will update automatically.

STEPS

1. **Click Window on the Application bar (Win) or Menu bar (Mac), then click CSS Styles if necessary, to open the CSS tab group**
   The CSS Styles panel opens in the CSS tab group. This panel is where you can add, delete, edit, and apply styles.

2. **Click the New CSS Rule button 🖻 on the CSS Styles panel, if necessary, click the Selector Type list arrow, click Class (can apply to any HTML element) then type bold_blue in the Selector Name text box**
   The Class option creates a new custom style that can apply to any HTML tag and will place it in the CSS Styles panel.

3. **Click the Rule Definition list arrow, click (New Style Sheet File), compare your screen to Figure D-9, then click OK**
   The Save Style Sheet File As dialog box opens, prompting you to name the Cascading Style Sheet file and store it in the Web site's root folder. The name of the new rule is bold_blue. You will save the rule bold_blue in the Cascading Style Sheet file called su_styles.css. The New Style Sheet File option makes the CSS style available to use in the entire Web site, not just the current document.

4. **Type su_styles.css in the File name text box (Win) or the Save As text box (Mac), then click Save**
   The CSS Rule Definition for .bold_blue in su_styles.css dialog box opens. The .css extension stands for Cascading Style Sheet. This dialog box allows you to choose attributes, such as font color and font size, for the CSS rule.

5. **Click the Font-family list arrow, then click Arial, Helvetica, sans-serif**

6. **Click the Font-size list arrow, click 14, leave the size measurement unit as px, click the Font-style list arrow, click normal, click the Font-weight list arrow, then click bold**
   Using a measurement of pixels rather than points will help keep the text from distorting in browser windows.

7. **Click the Color box to open the color picker, 🔲 as shown in Figure D-10, click #006, then click OK**
   The CSS rule named bold_blue appears in the CSS Styles panel as a style for The Striped Umbrella Web site, preceded by a period in the name. Notice, also, that the style sheet file name is listed in the **Related Files toolbar**, the toolbar under the file tab (Win) or file title bar (Mac) that displays the names of files related to the open document file. You can view and edit files in the Related Files toolbar by clicking the file name.

8. **Click the Refresh button 🔁 on the Files panel if necessary to view the su_styles CSS file**
   The su_styles.css file appears in the file listing for the Web site, as shown in Figure D-11, with a different file extension from the HTML files.

9. **Click the Show Code view button 🔲 Code on the Document toolbar to view the HTML code linking to the su_styles.css file, click File on the Application bar (Win) or Menu bar (Mac), then click Save All to save your changes to both the page and the style sheet file**
   The code linking to the su_styles.css file appears in the Head section, shown in Figure D-12, and the bold_blue rule appears indented under the file su_styles.css in the CSS Styles panel.

FIGURE D-9: New CSS Rule dialog box

Class option for Selector Type

Enter name of rule here

Location of rule definition

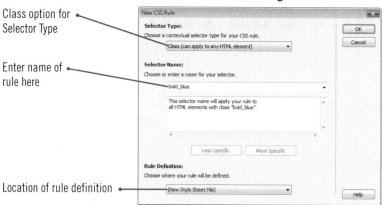

FIGURE D-10: CSS Rule Definition for .bold_blue in su_styles.css dialog box

Font-family list arrow

Font-weight list arrow

Font-size list arrow

Font-style list arrow

Color picker

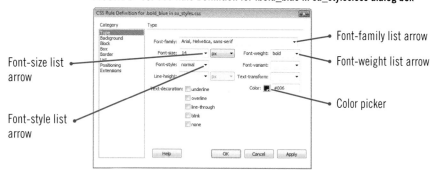

FIGURE D-11: The Striped Umbrella site with the su_styles.css file listed

su_styles.css style sheet file

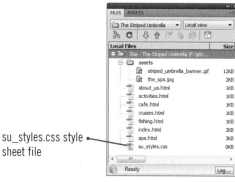

FIGURE D-12: Code view showing link to style sheet file

Related Files toolbar

Head section

HTML code linking su_styles.css

The plus sign changes to a minus sign (Win) or the right-pointing triangle changes to a down-pointing triangle (Mac) when the styles are visible

bold_blue rule

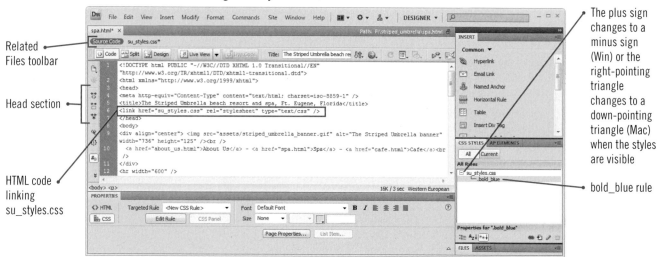

Applying and Editing a Style

After creating a Cascading Style Sheet, it is easy to apply the styles to Web page elements. If, after applying a style, the results are not satisfactory, you can edit the rule to change the formatting of all items to which that style applies. To apply a CSS style, you select the text or page element to which you want to apply the style, remove any manual formatting, and then select the CSS style from the Property inspector. You are ready to apply the bold_blue style to each item in the list of spa services, to emphasize them and to make them easier to read. Then you modify the rule and see its effect on the items.

STEPS

1. **Click the Show Design view button [Design] on the Document toolbar to return to Design view**

   You are ready to apply the new CSS style to the list of bulleted items.

2. **Select Revitalizing facial, as shown in Figure D-14, click the Targeted Rule list arrow on the CSS Property inspector, then click bold_blue**

   The bold_blue style is applied to the Revitalizing Facial text. The Font-family, Font-size, Font-weight, Color, and Font-style text boxes all reflect the bold_blue settings. You apply it to the rest of the items in the list.

3. **Repeat Step 2 to apply the bold_blue style to the names of each of the remaining spa services**

   The bold_blue style is now applied to each item name. You decide that the text is too small.

4. **Click the bold_blue style in the CSS Styles panel, then click the Edit Rule button [pencil] on the CSS Styles panel**

   The CSS Rule Definition for .bold_blue in su_styles.css dialog box opens, as shown in Figure D-15. You can use this dialog box to edit a .css file. This is the same dialog box you used to create the original rule.

5. **Click the Font-size arrow, click 16, click OK, then deselect the text**

   The bold_blue rule now includes a larger text size, as shown in Figure D-16, and all the text on the page with that style applied appears larger.

6. **Save your work using the Save All command**

   This saves both the changes to the Web page and the changes to the style sheet.

Understanding CSS Style Sheet code

You can also use Cascading Style Sheets to format page content other than text. For example, you can use them to format a background, borders, lists, and images. A CSS style consists of two parts: the selector and the declaration. The **selector** is the name or the tag to which the style declarations have been assigned. The **declaration** consists of the property and the value. An example of a property would be font-family. An example of a value would be Arial. Figure D-13 shows the coding for two CSS Styles in a style sheet file.

FIGURE D-13: Code for two styles in a style sheet file

Code for .bold_blue style

Code for .heading style

```
1   .bold_blue {
2       font-family: Arial, Helvetica, sans-serif;
3       font-size: 16px;
4       font-style: normal;
5       font-weight: bold;
6       color: #006;
7   }
8   .heading {
9       font-family: Arial, Helvetica, sans-serif;
10      font-size: 18px;
11      font-weight: bold;
12      color: #006;
13      text-align: center;
14  }
```

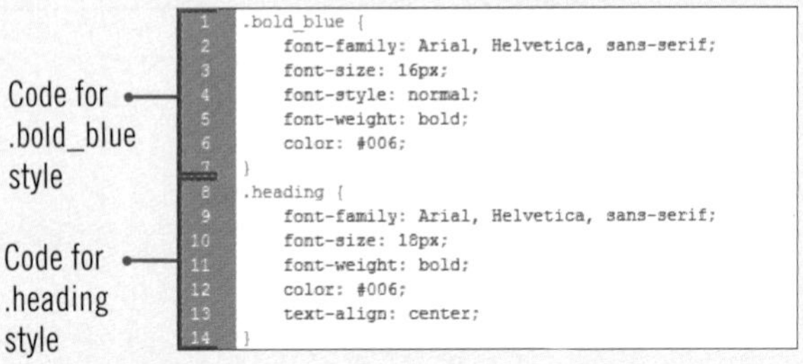

FIGURE D-14: Applying a CSS style to text

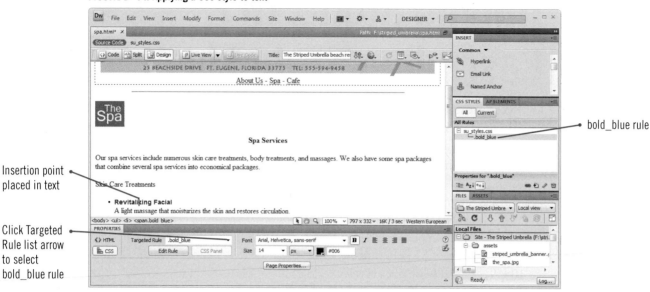

bold_blue rule

Insertion point placed in text

Click Targeted Rule list arrow to select bold_blue rule

FIGURE D-15: CSS Rule Definition for .bold_blue in su_styles.css

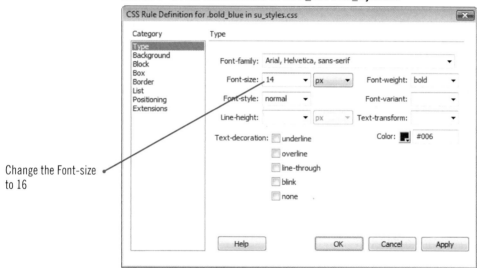

Change the Font-size to 16

FIGURE D-16: Viewing text with .bold_blue style applied to it

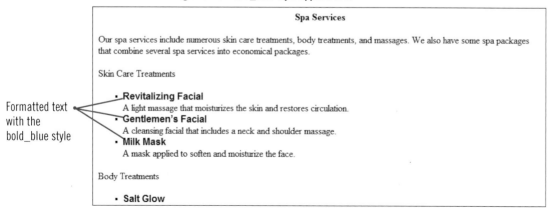

Formatted text with the bold_blue style

Adding Styles to a Cascading Style Sheet

Once you have created a Cascading Style Sheet, it is easy to add styles to it. Generally, the more styles you have defined in a Style Sheet, the more time you can save in formatting text. You add styles by using the New CSS Rule button in the CSS Styles panel. When you have several pages in a Web site, you will probably want to use the same style sheet for each page to ensure that all your elements have a consistent appearance. 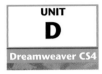 You decide to add two new styles in the su_styles.css file, one for the Spa Services heading and one for the service categories.

STEPS

1. **Click the New CSS Rule button** 🖼 **on the CSS Styles Panel**
   The New CSS Rule dialog box opens.

2. **Click the Selector Type list arrow, click Class (can apply to any HTML element), type heading in the Selector Name text box, click the Rule Definition list arrow, click su_styles.css, as shown in Figure D-17, then click OK**
   The CSS Rule Definition for .heading in su_styles.css dialog box opens.

3. **Click the Font-family list arrow, then click Arial, Helvetica, sans-serif**

4. **Click the Font-size list arrow, then click 18, click the Font-weight list arrow, then click bold**

5. **Click the Color picker 🖼, then select color #006**
   The color for the heading style is set to navy blue.

6. **Click the Block category in the Category list, click the Text-align list arrow, click center, as shown in Figure D-18, then click OK**
   You have defined the heading style and are ready to apply it to the page headings. Two styles are now listed in the CSS Styles panel.

7. **Select the heading Spa Services, click the Format list arrow in the HTML Property inspector, then click Paragraph**
   For the align format to work correctly, you must designate the text as a paragraph.

8. **Click the Class list arrow on the Property inspector, click heading, then click once inside the heading to deselect it**
   See Figure D-19. If you click the insertion point in text or select text that has an applied CSS style, that style appears in the Class list box in the HTML Property inspector, or the Targeted Rule list box in the CSS Property inspector.

9. **Repeat Steps 1–5 to add another class style called subheading in the su_styles.css style sheet with the following settings: Font-family, Arial, Helvetica, sans-serif; Font-size, 16 px, Font-style, normal; and Color, #006**

10. **Apply the subheading style to each category of spa services, then save your work using the File, Save All command**

Using font combinations in styles

When you are setting rule properties for text, you apply font combinations, rather than a single font, so that if one font is not available, the browser will use a similar one. For instance, with the font family Arial, Helvetica, sans-serif, the browser will first look on the viewer's system for the Arial font, then the Helvetica font, then a sans-serif font to apply to the text.

FIGURE D-17: New CSS Rule dialog box

Class Selector Type

Name of new style

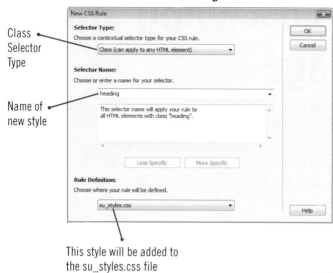

This style will be added to the su_styles.css file

FIGURE D-18: Block Category in the CSS Rule Definition for .heading in su_styles.css dialog box

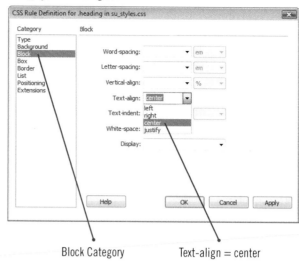

Block Category

Text-align = center

FIGURE D-19: Heading style applied to the Spa Services text

Spa Services text with heading style applied

heading style

Paragraph format

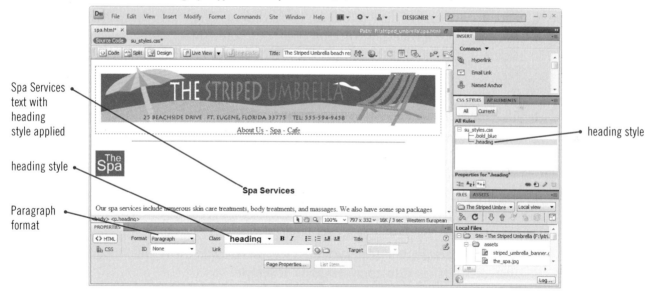

heading style

Design Matters

Choosing fonts

There are two classifications of fonts: sans-serif and serif. **Sans-serif** fonts, such as the font you are reading now, are plain characters without the small strokes at the top and bottom of letters. They are used frequently for headings and subheadings in printed text. Examples of sans-serif fonts are Arial, Verdana, and Helvetica. **Serif** fonts are more ornate, with small extra strokes at the top and bottom of the characters. They are generally easier to read in printed

material because the extra strokes lead your eye from one character to the next. Examples of serif fonts are Times New Roman, Times, and Georgia. Many designers feel that a sans-serif font is preferable when the content of a Web site will be read on the screen. However, if the content is frequently printed and then read from the printed material, a serif font is preferable. When choosing fonts, limit each Web site to not more than three font variations.

Attaching a Cascading Style Sheet to a Page

You see the power of Cascading Style Sheets as you quickly format text using styles. You can also edit rules and see the changes automatically applied to text to which you have applied that style. An even greater advantage of using Cascading Style Sheets is that you can attach an existing style sheet to a different page and use its styles there, either within the same Web site or in a different Web site. ▨▨▨▨ You decide to attach the su_styles.css file to the home page and use it to add another style to format the body text on the home page and the spa page.

STEPS

1. **Open the index.html page**

   You have not created a style sheet for the index page. When you open the index page, you do not see the style sheet in the CSS Styles panel or any styles listed in the HTML Property inspector Class list box or CSS Property inspector Targeted Rule list box. You must attach it to pages other than the original page for which it was created (in this case, the spa page) to use its styles in other locations.

2. **Click the Attach Style Sheet button 📑 on the CSS Styles panel**

   The Attach External Style Sheet dialog box opens.

3. **Click Browse next to the File/URL text box, click su_styles.css in the Select Style Sheet File dialog box if necessary, click OK (Win) or Choose (Mac); compare your screen to Figure D-20, then click OK to close the Attach External Style Sheet dialog box**

   The su_styles.css style sheet file appears in the CSS Styles panel. It is now attached to the index page, in addition to the spa page.

4. **Click the New CSS Rule 📑 button on the CSS Styles panel, verify that Class is the Selector type, type body_text in the Selector Name text box, verify that su_styles.css is the location for the Rule Definition, then click OK**

   The CSS Rule Definition for .body_text in su_styles.css dialog box opens.

5. **Use the settings shown in Figure D-21 to format the new body text style, then click OK**

   The new body_text style appears in the CSS Styles panel as part of the su_styles.css style sheet file. Since we did not designate a color, the default color, black, will be used to format this style.

6. **Select the paragraph of text, click the Class list arrow in the HTML Property inspector, then click body_text to apply the body_text style**

   The Property inspector reflects the settings of the body_text style. Since the only formatting that had been previously applied to this text was the paragraph tag, we did not have to clear prior formatting.

7. **Switch to the spa file by clicking its page tab, then apply the body_text style to the first paragraph of text and the unformatted text under each bullet item's title**

8. **Compare your screen to Figure D-22, then use the File, Save All command to save all open files**

FIGURE D-20: Attach External Style Sheet dialog box

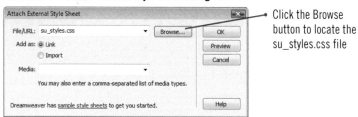

Click the Browse button to locate the su_styles.css file

FIGURE D-21: CSS Rule Definition for .body_text in su_styles.css dialog box

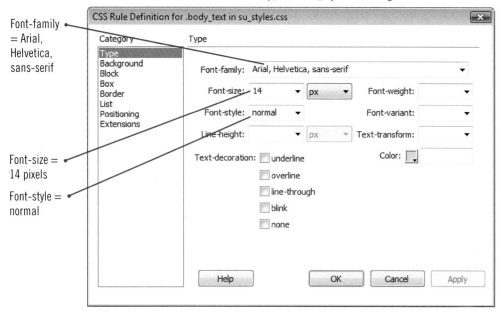

Font-family = Arial, Helvetica, sans-serif

Font-size = 14 pixels

Font-style = normal

FIGURE D-22: CSS Styles panel with four styles listed

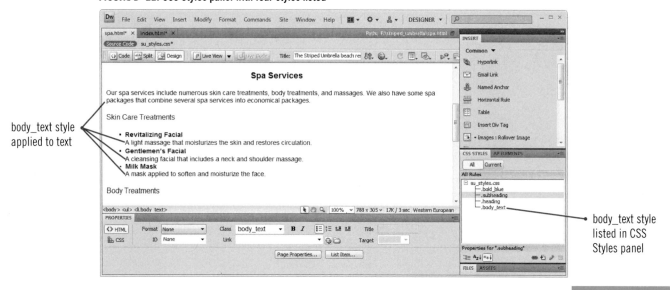

body_text style applied to text

body_text style listed in CSS Styles panel

Checking for Spelling Errors

Dreamweaver has a feature for checking spelling errors that is similar to those you have probably used in word processing programs. It is very important to check for spelling and grammatical errors before publishing a page. A page that is published with errors will cause the viewer to immediately judge the site as unprofessional and carelessly made, and the accuracy of the data presented will be in question. If a file you create in a word processor will be imported into Dreamweaver, run a spell check in the word processor first. Spell check the imported text in Dreamweaver again so you can add words such as proper names to the Dreamweaver dictionary so the program will not flag them again. You check the spelling on the spa page.

STEPS

QUICK TIP
You can also press [Ctrl][Home] to move the insertion point to the top of the document.

1. **Place the insertion point in front of the navigation bar**

   It is a good idea to start a spelling check at the top of the document because Dreamweaver searches from the insertion point down. If your insertion point is in the middle of the document, you will receive a message asking if you want to check the rest of the document. Starting from the beginning just saves time.

2. **Click Commands on the Application bar (Win) or Menu bar (Mac), then click Check Spelling**

   The word "masaged" is highlighted on the page as a misspelled word and suggestions are listed to correct it in the Check Spelling dialog box, as shown in Figure D-23.

3. **Click massaged in the Suggestions list if necessary, then click Change**

   The word is corrected on the page.

4. **Click OK to close the Dreamweaver dialog box stating that the Spelling Check is completed**

5. **Save your work, then preview the spa page in your browser, as shown in Figure D-24**

6. **Close all open pages and exit Dreamweaver**

Using Find and Replace

Another useful editing command is Find and Replace, which is located on the Edit menu. You can use this command to search text in either Design view or in Code view. It is used to make individual or global text edits, such as replacing all instances of "PO Box" with "P.O. Box" for consistency. It is similar to Find and Replace commands in word processing programs. One of the real advantages of this command in Dreamweaver, however, is that you can use it to search through code when you are trying to locate and correct coding errors. For example, you can search for a tag that sets a font to a non-web-safe color. Searching for the code 'src = "file"' can help you to locate links that are not set as relative links.

FIGURE D-23: Check Spelling dialog box

Misspelled word

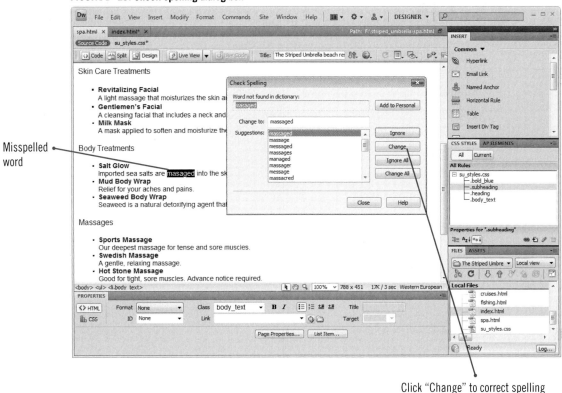

Click "Change" to correct spelling

FIGURE D-24: The finished product

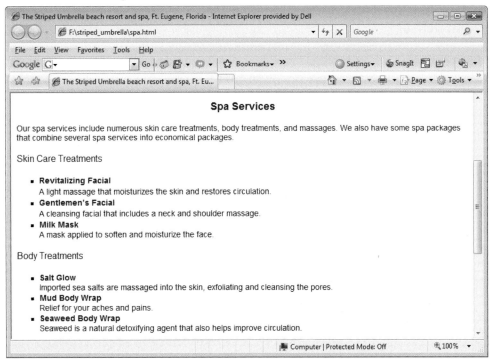

Practice

▼ CONCEPTS REVIEW

Label each element in the document window, as shown in Figure D-25.

FIGURE D-25

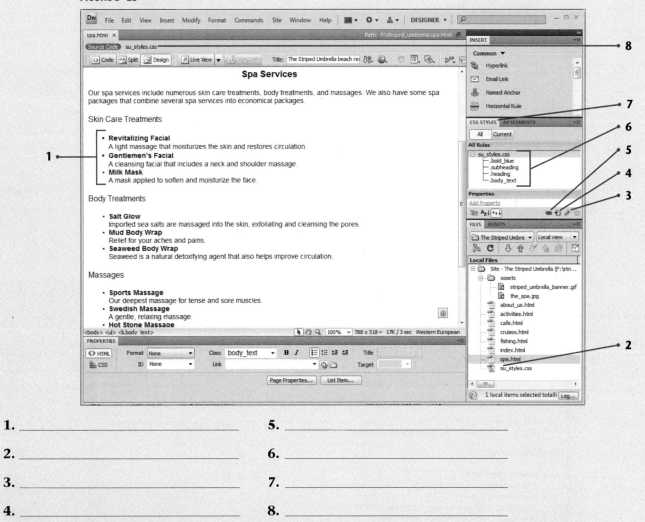

1. _____   5. _____

2. _____   6. _____

3. _____   7. _____

4. _____   8. _____

Match each of the following terms with the statement that best describes its function.

9. **Sans-serif font**   a. Numbered lists

10. **Property inspector**   b. Font without extra strokes at top and bottom

11. **Ordered lists**   c. A set of formatting attributes that creates a CSS style

12. **Unordered lists**   d. A file attached or linked to a Web page to format page elements

13. **CSS styles**   e. A style property and the value

14. **CSS Rule**   f. Bulleted lists

15. **External style sheet**   g. A panel used for formatting page elements

16. **Selector**   h. The name or tag to which style declarations have been assigned

17. **Declaration**   i. Font with extra strokes at the top and bottom

18. **Serif font**   j. Sets of formatting attributes to format page elements

Select the best answer from the following list of choices.

19. The button used to select color is:
- **a.** ▨
- **b.** ▢
- **c.** ✎
- **d.** ⮹

20. External CSS files are saved with the filename extension:
- **a.** .css
- **b.** .cas
- **c.** .stl
- **d.** .csf

21. A CSS Class Style name in the Styles panel is preceded by a:
- **a.** Pound sign.
- **b.** Period.
- **c.** Dash.
- **d.** Number.

22. Styles that are part of the head content of a Web page are called:
- **a.** External styles.
- **b.** Embedded styles.
- **c.** Inline Styles.
- **d.** HTML styles.

23. The type of style used to redefine an HTML tag is called:
- **a.** an advanced style.
- **b.** a class style.
- **c.** a Tag style.
- **d.** a compound style.

▼ SKILLS REVIEW

Important: *If you did not create this Web site in Unit B and maintain it in Unit C, you will need to create a root folder for this Web site and define the Web site using files your instructor will provide. See the "Read This Before You Begin" section for more detailed instructions.*

1. **Import text.**
   - **a.** Start Dreamweaver.
   - **b.** Open the blooms & bulbs Web site.
   - **c.** Open dwd_2.html from the drive and folder where your Unit D Data Files are stored.
   - **d.** Save the file as **tips.html** in the root folder of your blooms & bulbs Web site, overwriting the existing file, and not updating links.
   - **e.** Verify that the path for the blooms banner is linked to the banner in the assets folder of the blooms & bulbs Web site.
   - **f.** Set the path for the garden_tips.jpg to the assets folder of the blooms & bulbs Web site.
   - **g.** With the insertion point below the garden tips graphic text, import (Win) or copy and paste (Mac) the Word document gardening_tips.doc from the drive and folder where your Unit D Data Files are stored.
   - **h.** Save the changes to the tips page, then close the dwd_2.html page.
   - **i.** Use the Clean Up Word HTML command on the tips page (Win).

2. Set text properties.

   a. Select the Seasonal Gardening Checklist heading.

   b. Format the text with the Heading 4 style.

   c. Save your work.

3. Create an unordered list.

   a. Select the items in the Seasonal Gardening Checklist.

   b. Format the list of items as an unordered list. (*Hint*: Be sure not to select the return at the end of the last line or you will accidentally create a fifth item.) Deselect the text.

4. Understand Cascading Style Sheets.

   a. Using a word processor or a piece of paper, list the types of CSS styles classified by their location in a Web site.

   b. Using a word processor or piece of paper, list the types of CSS styles categorized by their function in a Web site.

5. Create a Style in a new Cascading Style Sheet.

   a. Open the CSS Styles panel, if necessary.

   b. Create a new Class style named **seasons** in a new style sheet file.

   c. Save the new style sheet file with the name **blooms_styles.css** in the blooms folder.

   d. Set the Font-family for the seasons style as Arial, Helvetica, sans-serif.

   e. Set the Font-size as 12 pixels, the Font-style as normal, and the Font-weight as bold.

   f. Set the Color as #039.

   g. Save your work. (Use the File, Save All command to include saving the blooms_styles.css file.)

6. Apply and edit a style.

   a. Apply the seasons style to the words Fall, Winter, Spring, and Summer.

   b. Edit the style to increase the text size to 14 pixels.

   c. Save your work. (Use the File, Save All command to include saving the blooms_styles.css file.)

7. Add styles to a Cascading Style Sheet.

   a. Remove all formatting from the text Seasonal Gardening Checklist and delete the colon after the word "Checklist".

   b. Set the format to Paragraph.

   c. Create a new Class style named **headings** in the blooms_styles.css file.

   d. Set the Font-family as Arial, Helvetica, sans-serif.

   e. Set the Font-size as 16 pixels, the Font-style as normal, set the Color as #036, and the Font-weight as bold.

   f. Use the Block category to set the text alignment to center.

   g. Apply the headings style to the text Seasonal Gardening Checklist.

   h. Add a Class style named **body_text** to the style sheet.

   i. Set the Font-family as Arial, Helvetica, sans-serif, the Font-size as 14 pixels, and the Font-style as normal.

   j. Apply the body_text style to the rest of the text on the page.

   k. Save your work. (Use the File, Save All command to include saving the blooms_styles.css file.)

8. Attach a Cascading Style Sheet to a page.

   a. Open the index page in the blooms & bulbs Web site.

   b. Attach the blooms_styles.css file to the index page.

   c. Apply the style body_text to the paragraph and to the contact information on the page.

   d. Save your work. (Use the File, Save All command to include saving the blooms_styles.css file.)

9. Check spelling.

   a. Close the index page and return to the tips page.

   b. Run a spell check on the tips page.

   c. Preview the page in your Web browser and compare your screen to Figure D-26.

   d. Close your browser, then Exit (Win) or Quit (Mac) Dreamweaver.

FIGURE D-26

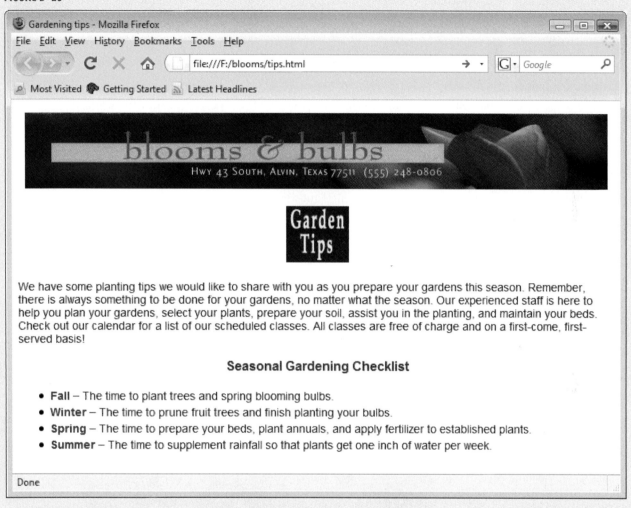

Important: *If you did not create the following Web sites in Unit B and maintain them in Unit C, you will need to create a root folder for the Web sites in the following exercises and define the Web sites using files your instructor will provide. See the "Read This Before You Begin" section for more detailed instructions.*

▼ INDEPENDENT CHALLENGE 1

You have been hired to create a Web site for a river expedition company named Rapids Transit, located on the Buffalo River in Arkansas. In addition to renting canoes, kayaks, and rafts, they have several types of cabin rentals for overnight stays. River guides are available, if requested, to accompany clients on float trips. The clients range from high school and college students to families to vacationing professionals. The owner's name is Mike Andrew. Mike has asked you to add a page to the Web site that will describe the lodge, cabins, and tents that are available for their customers.

a. Start Dreamweaver.

b. Open the Rapids Transit Web site.

c. Open the file dwd_3.html from the drive and folder where your Unit D Data Files are stored and save it as **lodging.html** in the Rapids Transit Web site, replacing the existing file and not updating links.

d. Verify that the rapids banner path is set to the assets folder in the Web site.

e. Create an unordered list from the four types of lodging and their rates.

f. Create a new Class style named **body_text** and save it in a new style sheet file named rapids_transit.css using the following settings: Font-family, Arial, Helvetica, sans-serif; Font-size, 14; Font-style, normal.

g. Apply the body_text style to all text on the page except the navigation bar.

h. Create a new class style in the rapids_transit.css style sheet for the lodging choices named **lodging**.

i. Format the lodging style with the Font-family Arial, Helvetica, sans-serif; Font-size 14; Font-style normal; Font-weight bold; Color #03C.

j. Apply the lodging style to the text The Lodge, Jenny's Cabins, and John's Camp at the beginning of the first three paragraphs.

k. Attach the rapids_transit.css file to the index page, then use the body_text style to format the paragraph of text on the page.

l. Create a new class style in the rapids_transit.css style sheet named **contact_info** using Arial, Helvetica sans-serif; italic style; size 12; then apply it to the contact information on the index page. (*Hint*: Remove the Italic style first.)

m. Close the file dwd_3.html, then save your work using the Save All command on the File menu.

n. Preview the index page in your browser, click the Lodging link, compare your screen to Figure D-27, close your browser, close the files, then exit Dreamweaver.

FIGURE D-27

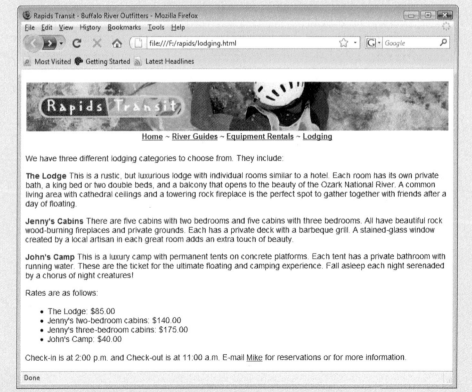

▼ INDEPENDENT CHALLENGE 2

Your company is designing a new Web site for a travel outfitter named TripSmart. TripSmart specializes in travel products and services. In addition to selling travel products, such as luggage and accessories, they sponsor trips and offer travel advice. Their clients range from college students to families to vacationing professionals. You are now ready to work on the newsletter page.

a. Start Dreamweaver and open the TripSmart Web site.

b. Open the file dwd_4.html and save it as **newsletter.html** in the TripSmart Web site, replacing the existing file, but not updating links.

c. Verify that the banner path is set to the assets folder of the Web site, then close dwd_4.html.

d. Create an ordered list from the ten items on the page starting with Expandable clothesline and clothespins.

e. Create a new class style called **body_text** and save it in a new style sheet named **tripsmart_styles.css**.

f. Choose a font, size, style, color, and weight of your choice for the body_text style.

g. Apply the body_text style to all the text on the page.

h. Create another class style in the tripsmart_styles.css style sheet called **heading** with a font, size, style, color, and weight of your choice and apply it to the Ten Packing Essentials heading.

i. Create another class style in the tripsmart_styles.css style sheet named **bold_text** with settings of your choice, then apply it to each ordered list item that begins each ordered list.

j. Type **Travel Tidbits** in the page title text box.

k. Attach the style sheet to the index page and apply the body_text style to the paragraph of text.

l. Create another class style in the tripsmart_styles.css style sheet named **contact_info** with settings of your choice, apply it to the contact information on the page, then save and close the page.

m. Save your work, preview the newsletter page in the browser, then compare it to Figure D-28.

n. Close your browser, close the file, then exit Dreamweaver.

FIGURE D-28

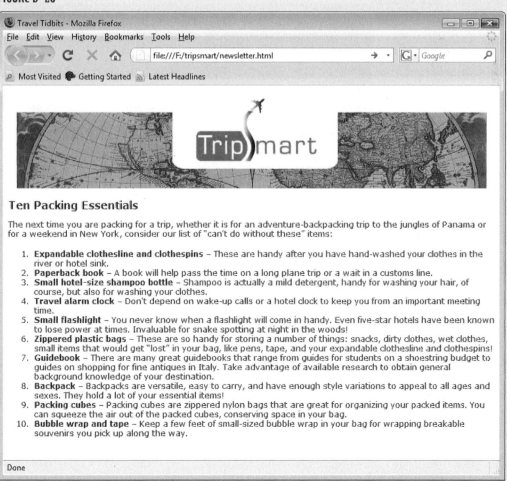

▼ INDEPENDENT CHALLENGE 3

Dr. Chappel is a government historian who is conducting research on the separation of church and state. He has gone to the Library of Congress Web site to look for information he can use. Write your answers to the questions below on paper or in your word processor.

a. Connect to the Internet and go to The Library of Congress Web site at www.loc.gov, shown in Figure D-29.

b. Do you see text that was created and saved as a graphic? If so, on which page or pages? Was the use effective?

c. What font or fonts are used on the pages for the main text? Are the same fonts used consistently on the other pages in the Web site?

d. Do you see an ordered or unordered list on the Web site? If so, how was it used?

e. View the source to see if Cascading Style Sheets were used on the pages in the Web site.

f. Use the search engine of your choice to find another Web site of interest. Compare the use of text on that site with the Library of Congress Web site.

FIGURE D-29

Library of Congress Web site - www.loc.gov

▼ REAL LIFE INDEPENDENT CHALLENGE

This assignment will continue to build on the personal Web site that you created in Unit B and modified in Unit C. You have created and developed your index page. In this lesson, you will work with one of the other pages in your Web site.

   a. Consult your storyboard and decide which page you would like to develop in this lesson.

   b. Create content for this page and format the text attractively on the page using settings for font, size, text color, style, and alignment.

   c. Format some of the text on the page as either an ordered or unordered list.

   d. Create a CSS Style Sheet with a minimum of two styles and apply a style to all text on the page.

   e. Attach the style sheet to any pages you have already developed, and apply styles to all text.

   f. Save the file and preview the pages in the browser.

After you are satisfied with your work, verify the following:

   a. Each completed page has a page title.

   b. All links work correctly.

   c. The completed pages look good using a screen resolution of 800×600 and 1024×768.

   d. All images are properly set showing a path to the assets folder of the Web site.

   e. A Cascading Style Sheet is used to format text.

▼ VISUAL WORKSHOP

Your company has been selected to design a Web site for a catering business named Carolyne's Creations. Open your Carolyne's Creations Web site. Open the file dwd_5.html and save it as **recipes.html** in the Carolyne's Creations Web site, replacing the original file. Close dwd_5.html. Format the page using styles so it looks similar to Figure D-30. (The text may wrap slightly different using browsers other than Internet Explorer.) You will need to save the file cranberry_ice.jpg from the assets folder in the Unit D Data Files folder to your Web site. *Hint*: Use the following styles and settings to match the figure and save them in a CSS file named cc_styles.css:

.heading
Font-family: Verdana, Geneva, sans-serif
Font-size: 14px
Font-weight: bold
Color: #000

.body_text
Font-family: Verdana, Geneva, sans-serif
Font-size: 12px
Font-weight: normal
Color: #000

If you have not maintained this Web site from the previous unit, then contact your instructor for assistance.

FIGURE D-30

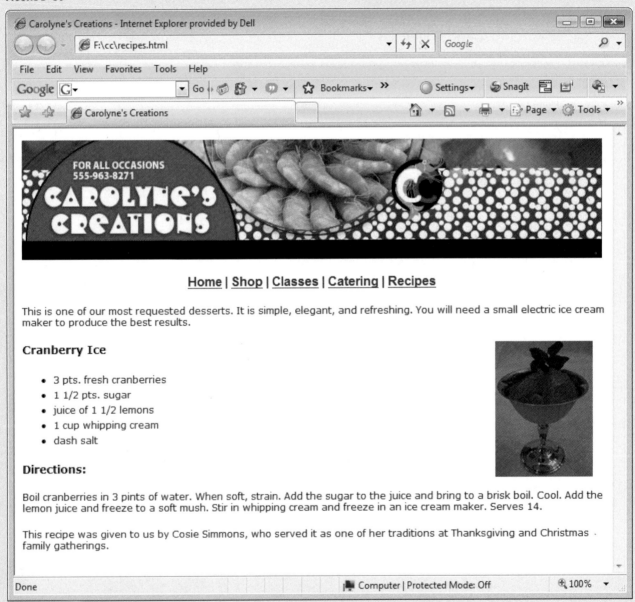

Using and Managing Images

Images make Web pages more exciting than pages with just text. You can position images on your Web pages, then resize them, add borders, and customize the amount of space around them. You can also use images as a Web page, table, or CSS block element background. In this unit you learn how to incorporate images into a Web site and how to manage them effectively using the Assets panel.  You have been asked by The Striped Umbrella to develop the page that describes the resort. You decide to incorporate several photographs taken around the property to illustrate the text.

OBJECTIVES

Insert an image

Align an image

Enhance an image

Use alternate text and set
   Accessibility preferences

View the Assets panel

Insert a background image

Delete image files from a Web site

Create and find images for a
   Web site

Inserting an Image

Images you import into a Web site are automatically added to the Assets panel. The **Assets panel**, located with the other panels on the right side on your screen, lists the assets, such as images and colors, in the Web site. As you add images to a Web page, the page **download time** (the time it takes to transfer the file to a viewer's computer) increases. The Status bar displays the download time for the current Web page. The three primary Web image file formats are GIF, JPEG, and PNG. ▪▪▪▪▪ You selected several photos for the about_us Web page. As you place each image on the page, you check the file size in the Assets panel.

STEPS

1. **Start Dreamweaver, open The Striped Umbrella Web site, open** dwe_1.html **from the drive and folder where your Unit E Data Files are stored, save it as** about_us.html **in the striped_umbrella root folder, overwriting the existing file, and not updating the links, then close** dwe_1.html

   As shown in Figure E-1, the Status bar shows that the page will take two seconds to download at your current connection speed setting.

2. **Click the** Attach Style Sheet button ▪ **in the CSS Styles panel, attach the** su_styles.css **style sheet, then apply the** body_text **style to all of the paragraph text on the page**

   The style sheet for the Web site is attached to the page, and the body_text style is applied to the paragraphs. Using the same style sheet for all pages in a Web site is the fastest way to format text for a consistent look across your site.

3. **Click to place the insertion point in front of** When **in the first paragraph, select the** Common category **on the Insert panel if necessary, click the** Images list arrow **on the Insert panel, click the** Image button **to open the Select Image Source dialog box, navigate to the Unit E Data Files assets folder, double-click** club_house.jpg, **open the Files panel if necessary, then click the** Refresh button ▪ **on the Files panel toolbar if necessary**

   The picture appears at the beginning of the first paragraph, as shown in Figure E-2. The club house image is now located in the Web site assets folder, which is now the location that will be used to load the image in the browser when the page is viewed.

4. **Save the file, click the** Assets panel tab, **click the** Images button ▪ **on the Assets panel if necessary, then click the** Refresh button ▪ **at the bottom of the Assets panel, if necessary**

   After you click the Refresh button, you should see the three images you added to The Striped Umbrella Web site listed: club_house.jpg, striped_umbrella_banner.gif, and the_spa.jpg. The Assets panel, as shown in Figure E-3, is split into two windows. The lower window lists the images in the Web site, and the top window displays a thumbnail of the image selected in the list.

5. **Repeat Steps 3 and 4 to insert the** boardwalk.jpg **image at the beginning of the second paragraph**

   The picture appears on the page at the beginning of the second paragraph, and boardwalk.jpg is added to the list of images in the Assets panel and the Files panel.

6. **Repeat Steps 3 and 4 to add the** pool.jpg, sago_palm.jpg, **and** sports_club.jpg **files at the beginning of each of the next paragraphs, then save your work**

   Your Assets panel should list the seven images shown in Figure E-4.

FIGURE E-1: Status bar displaying page download time

Enjoy our lush landscaping as you explore the grounds. The beautiful sago palms flourish in our Florida weather! We have many native plants that we hope you will enjoy, both within our manicured grounds and along the beach. Remember, the wild vegetation are all protected species.

`<body>`   100% | 788 x 514 | 15K / 2 sec | Western European

Your screen size may differ

Page download time (yours may differ, depending on connection speed)

FIGURE E-2: About_us page with image inserted

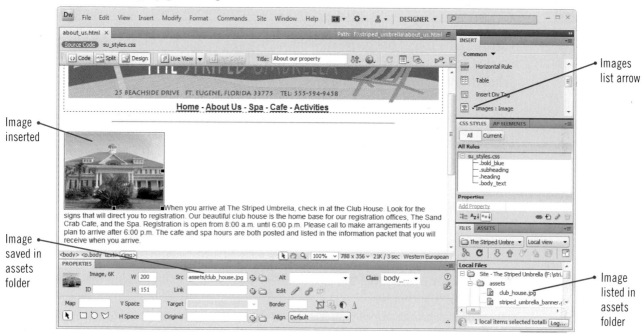

Images list arrow

Image inserted

Image saved in assets folder

Image listed in assets folder

FIGURE E-3: Assets panel listing for the The Striped Umbrella Web site

FIGURE E-4: Assets panel with seven images

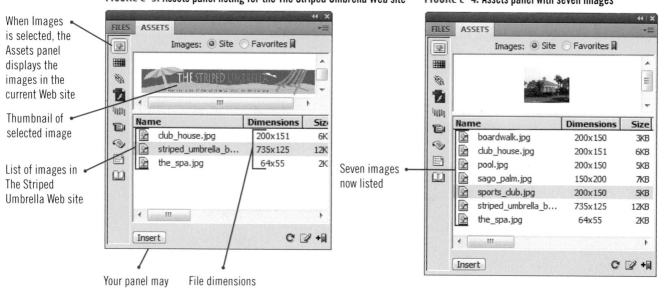

When Images is selected, the Assets panel displays the images in the current Web site

Thumbnail of selected image

List of images in The Striped Umbrella Web site

Name	Dimensions	Size
club_house.jpg	200x151	6K
striped_umbrella_b...	735x125	12K
the_spa.jpg	64x55	2K

Your panel may be larger

File dimensions

Seven images now listed

Name	Dimensions	Size
boardwalk.jpg	200x150	3KB
club_house.jpg	200x151	6KB
pool.jpg	200x150	5KB
sago_palm.jpg	150x200	7KB
sports_club.jpg	200x150	5KB
striped_umbrella_b...	735x125	12KB
the_spa.jpg	64x55	2KB

Aligning an Image

Like text, images can be positioned on the page in relation to other page elements in the same line or paragraph. Positioning an image is called **aligning** the image. When an image is selected, the Property inspector displays options for aligning images, instead of for aligning text. You can align an image on the same line as text by using one of the alignment options in the Property inspector. See Table E-1 for a description of each alignment option. You should experiment with the options to find the best alignment for your image. When you first place an image on a page, it has the **Default** alignment which aligns the bottom of the image with the text **baseline**, the bottom of the line of text, not including descending characters such as "y" or "g." After experimenting with several alignment options, you decide to stagger the alignment of the images on the page to make the page appear to be more balanced.

STEPS

QUICK TIP

You can double-click the right side of the Property inspector to return it to its original size.

1. **Scroll to the top of the page, click the club house image to select it, double-click the empty space in the right side of the Property inspector to expand it if necessary, then click the Align list arrow in the Property inspector**

   The expanded Property inspector displays additional settings, including those for the image map, horizontal and vertical spacing, border size, and alignment settings. Notice the ten alignment options in the list, as shown in Figure E-6.

2. **Click Left**

   The club house photo is aligned to the left side of the paragraph. The text is repositioned to align with the top and right sides of the photo.

3. **Scroll down the page if necessary, click the boardwalk image to select it, click the Align list arrow in the Property inspector, then click Right**

   The boardwalk photo is aligned to the right of the paragraph. The text is repositioned to align with the top and left of the photo.

TROUBLE

Your text may wrap differently on your screen depending on how wide your window is sized on your monitor.

4. **Repeat Steps 1 through 3 to align the next three images, alternating the alignment between left and right**

   The photos are now all aligned in staggered positions on the page, as shown in Figure E-7.

5. **Save your work**

   The file is saved with the alignment settings.

6. **Click the Preview/Debug in browser button ⊙ on the Document toolbar, then click Preview in [your browser name]**

   The about_us page appears in the browser window.

7. **Close the browser**

   The about_us page reappears in Design view.

Design Matters

Using dynamic images

To make a page even more interesting, you can place images on the page that change frequently, called **dynamic images**. To insert dynamic images, you must first create a **recordset**, or database stored on a server. The recordset will contain the image files. You then insert the images on the page using the Data sources option, rather than the File System option, in the Select Image Source dialog box, as shown in Figure E-5. You can also use dynamic images to display multiple items with a similar layout. For example, a Web site for a retail store might display images of current sale items in one window on a Web page, one item at a time.

FIGURE E-5: Using the Data sources option

Select this option

FIGURE E-6: Alignment options for images

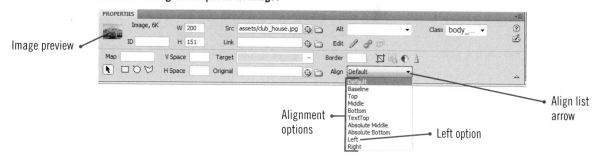

Image preview

Alignment options

Align list arrow

Left option

FIGURE E-7: Aligned images on the about_us page

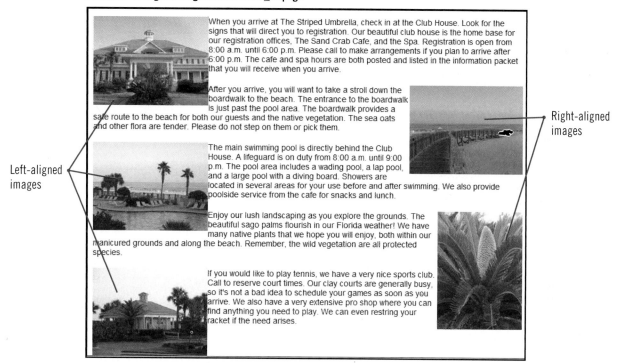

Left-aligned images

Right-aligned images

TABLE E-1: Aligning elements to text

alignment option	description
Default	This is the default setting. The element is aligned with the text baseline. The default can vary by browser.
Baseline	The element is aligned with the baseline of the text.
Top	The element is aligned with the top of the tallest item, whether that item is text or another object.
Middle	The element is aligned with the text baseline or another object at the vertical middle of the image.
Bottom	The bottom of the item is aligned with the bottom of the text.
TextTop	The element is aligned with the top of the tallest character in a line of text.
Absolute Middle	The element is aligned with the absolute middle of the current line.
Absolute Bottom	The element is aligned with the bottom of a text line or another object. This applies to letters that fall below the baseline, such as the letter y.
Left	The element is placed on the left margin with text wrapping to the right.
Right	The element is placed on the right margin with text wrapping to the left.

Enhancing an Image

After you select, place, and align an image on a Web page, you can enhance it to improve its appearance. You'll need to use an image editor, such as Adobe Illustrator or Adobe Photoshop to change the image itself, for example, to remove scratches from it or significantly resize it. However, you can enhance an image in Dreamweaver using borders, cropping or resizing, adjusting its brightness, and adjusting the horizontal and vertical space around an image. **Borders** are like frames that surround an image to make it stand out on the page. **Cropping** an image removes part of the image, both visually (on the page) and physically (the file size). A cropped image is smaller and takes less time to download. **Horizontal** and **vertical space** refers to blank space above, below, or on the sides of an image that separates the image from other elements on the page. You decide to enhance the images on the about_us page by adding borders around the images, and adjusting the horizontal and vertical space around each image.

After you apply the border, your images might move to different positions than those shown in the figure, depending on the size of your Dreamweaver window. This is not a problem; you can continue with the steps.

You can also use the Brightness and Contrast ◑ and Sharpen buttons △ to slightly adjust images. It is wise to perform major edits in an image editing program such as Adobe Photoshop. Clicking the Edit button [Ps] will open the image in Photoshop if it is installed on your computer.

1. **Click the** club house image **to select it**

2. **Type** 1 **in the Border text box, then press** [Tab] **to apply the border size, as shown in Figure E-8**
   A black border with a thickness of 1 pixel will appear around the image in the browser, replacing the default size of zero.

3. **Repeat Steps 1 and 2 for the other four images**
   All images will now have black borders. The borders are not visible in Dreamweaver, but you will be able to see them when you preview the document in your browser later. You notice that the surrounding text wraps closer to the sides of the images than to the bottoms of the images.

4. **Click the** club house image **to select it, type** 10 **in the V Space text box in the Property inspector, press** [Tab], **type** 10 **in the H Space text box, press** [Tab], **then deselect the image**
   V Space refers to vertical space above and below the image. H Space refers to horizontal space on the sides of the image. You like the way the text is more evenly wrapped around the image, so you decide to apply the same option to the other images.

5. **Repeat Step 4 for the rest of the images**
   The five images reflect the horizontal and vertical space settings.

6. **Click the** sago palm image **to select it, note the W and H settings in the Property inspector, click the** Crop button ⬚ **in the Property inspector, then click** OK **to close the warning message that says you are about to permanently alter the image**

7. **Position the pointer over the bottom-center resizing handle, as shown in Figure E-9, slowly move the handle up toward the center of the image to remove part of the lower leaves, then double-click the image to crop it**
   The image appears smaller, and the Property inspector shows that the file dimensions have changed.

8. **Click** Edit **on the Application bar (Win) or Menu bar (Mac), click** Undo Crop **(Win) or click** Undo **(Mac) to restore the image to the original size, then save the file**
   The image returns its original size.

Resizing an image using the Property inspector

When you crop an image, you remove part of it. If you want to resize the whole image rather than crop it, you can select the image, then drag a selection handle toward the center of the image. Dragging a selection handle can distort the image; to resize an image while retaining its original proportions, press and hold [Shift], then drag a corner selection handle. (You can also enlarge an image using these methods.) After you drag an image handle to resize it, the image dimensions in the Property inspector appear in bold and a black Refresh icon appears to the right of the dimensions. If you click the Refresh icon, the image reverts to its original size.

FIGURE E-8: Changing the border size

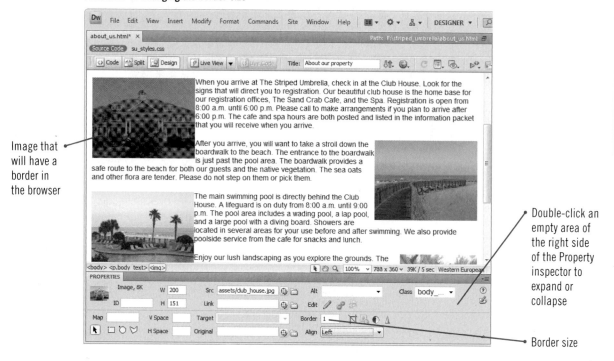

Image that will have a border in the browser

Double-click an empty area of the right side of the Property inspector to expand or collapse

Border size

FIGURE E-9: Cropping an image

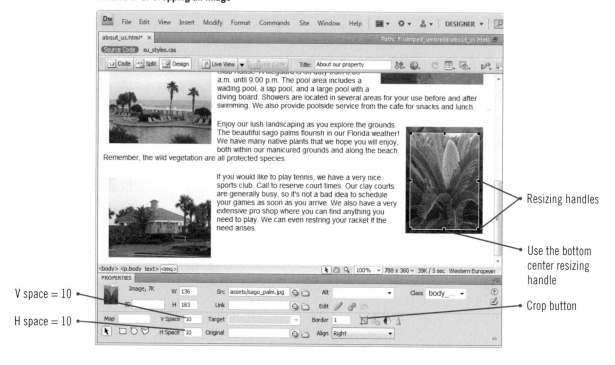

V space = 10

H space = 10

Resizing handles

Use the bottom center resizing handle

Crop button

Design Matters

Resizing graphics using an external editor

Each image on a Web page takes a specific number of seconds to download, depending on the size of the file. Larger files (in kilobytes, not width and height) take longer to download than smaller files. You should determine the smallest acceptable size that an image can be for your Web page, and then, if you need to resize the image, use an external image editor, instead of resizing it in Dreamweaver. You can use the H Size (height) and W Size (width) settings in the Property inspector to resize the image on the screen, but these settings do not affect the file size. If you decrease the size of an image using the Property inspector settings, you are not reducing the time it will take to download the file unless you use the crop tool. The ultimate goal is to use graphics that have the smallest file size and the highest quality possible. Many designers feel that an ideal page will download in less than five or six seconds.

Using Alternate Text and Setting Accessibility Preferences

One of the easiest ways to make your Web page viewer-friendly and handicapped-accessible is through the use of alternate text. **Alternate text** is descriptive text that can be set to appear in place of an image while the image is downloading or when users place the mouse pointer over an image. Some browsers can be set to display only text and to download images manually. In such instances, alternate text is used in place of images. Alternate text can be read by a **screen reader**, a device used by the visually impaired to convert written text on a computer monitor to spoken words. Using a screen reader and alternate text, visually-impaired viewers can have an image described to them in detail. In a new installation, Adobe has turned all accessibility preferences on by default. In this lesson you will check that your computer has the correct accessibility settings. ▰▰▰▱▱ You add alternate text that describes each of the images on the about_us page. You also verify that the Images option in the Accessibility preferences is set so Dreamweaver will prompt you to enter alternate text each time you add an image to the Web site.

STEPS

1. **Click the** club house image **to select it, type** The Striped Umbrella Club House **in the Alt text box in the Property inspector, press** [Tab], **then save the file**

   The alternate text is entered for the image, as shown in Figure E-10.

2. **Preview the page in your browser, then place the pointer over the club house image**

   When the pointer is over the image, a small text box containing the alternate text appears on the screen, as shown in Figure E-11. The borders and the horizontal and vertical spacing you entered in the previous lesson are also visible.

TROUBLE

If you are using a Macintosh and do not see the alternate text, contact your instructor or technical support person. If you are using a Windows computer with Mozilla Firefox, you may not see the alternate text.

3. **Close your browser window**

4. **Click the** boardwalk image **to select it, type** Boardwalk to the beach **in the Alt text box in the Property inspector, then press** [Tab]

5. **Click the** pool image **to select it, type** The pool area **in the Alt text box in the Property inspector, then press** [Tab]

6. **Click the** sago palm image **to select it, enter** Sago palm **in the Alt text box in the Property inspector, then press** [Tab]

7. **Click the** sports club image **to select it, enter** The Sports Club **in the Alt text box in the Property inspector, then press** [Tab]

   You decide to verify that Dreamweaver will prompt you to enter alternate text each time you add a new image.

QUICK TIP

Once you set the Accessibility preferences, they will be in effect for all of your Web sites. You will not have to set each Web site separately.

8. **Click** Edit (Win) **or** Dreamweaver (Mac) **on the Application bar (Win) or Menu bar (Mac), click** Preferences, **click** Accessibility **in the Category list if necessary, click the** four options shown **to select them if necessary, as shown in Figure E-12, then click** OK

   With these options selected, Dreamweaver will prompt you to enter alternate text for new objects you add to the Web site, including images.

9. **Save your work, preview the page in your browser, then place your pointer over each image on the page**

   Each image now displays alternate text.

10. **Close your browser to return to the Dreamweaver window**

FIGURE E-10: Alternate text setting in the Property inspector

Alternate text for the
club house image

FIGURE E-11: Alternate text appears in browser

Black borders
frame images

Alternate text

Red circles
show where
white space
was added

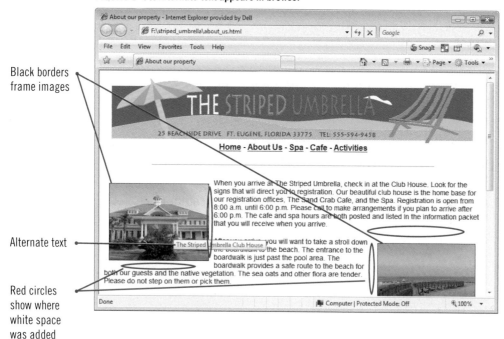

FIGURE E-12: Accessibility preferences

Accessibility preferences

Macintosh users may not
see these options

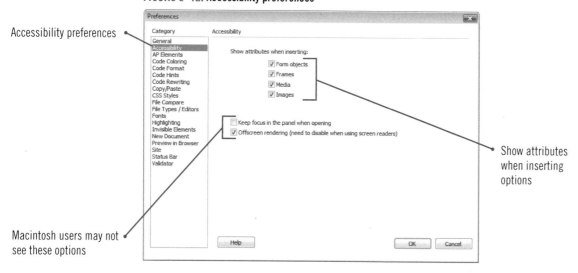

Show attributes
when inserting
options

Setting alternate text limits

The alternate text for an image stays on the user's screen for a limited time, so you should consider the text length. A general rule is to avoid using over 50 characters. If you need to enter more than 50 characters, create a separate file with the information you want to convey. Enter the location of the file in the Long Description text box that appears under the Alternate Text text box in the Image Tag Accessibility Attributes dialog box that opens when you insert a new image. This information will appear in the browser when the viewer clicks the image.

Viewing the Assets Panel

The **Assets panel** displays all of the assets in a Web site. There are nine categories of assets represented by buttons on the Assets panel. These include Images, Colors, URLs, SWF, Shockwave, Movies, Scripts, Templates, and Library. There are two options for viewing the assets in each category. You can click the Site option button to view all the assets in a Web site, or the Favorites option button to view those assets that you have designated as **favorites**—assets that you expect to use repeatedly while you work on the site. So far, your Web site includes several images and several colors. You explore the Assets panel to understand how Dreamweaver organizes your assets.

STEPS

TROUBLE
Make sure that the page you have open is in the current Web site. If you open a page outside the current Web site, the Assets panel will not display the assets associated with the open page.

1. **Click the Assets tab in the Files Tab group, if necessary**

   The first time you use the Assets panel, it displays the Images category; after that, it displays the category that was selected in the last Dreamweaver working session.

2. **Click each category button on the Assets panel**

   Each time you click a button, the contents in the Assets panel window change. Figure E-13 displays the Images category, and lists the seven images in the Web site.

3. **Click the Colors button ⊞ to display the Colors category**

   Two colors are listed in the Web site, and both colors are Websafe, as shown in Figure E-14. If you see another color listed, click the Refresh button 🗘 to remove it.

Using the terms "graphics" versus "images"

In discussing Web pages, people often use the terms "graphics" and "images." This text uses the term **graphics** to refer to most non-text items on a Web page, such as photographs, logos, navigation bars, Flash animations, graphs, background images, and illustrations. Any of these can be called a graphic or a **graphic file**. **Images** is a narrower term, referring to pictures or photographs. Image files are referred to by their file type, or graphic file format, such as **JPEG**

(Joint Photographic Experts Group), **GIF** (Graphics Interchange Format), or **PNG** (Portable Network Graphics). See Table E-2 on page 116 for descriptions for each of these formats. This text refers to the pictures that you see on the pages as images. But don't worry too much about which term to use; many people use one term or the other according to habit, region, or type of business, or use them interchangeably.

FIGURE E-13: Assets panel

Images button selected

Favorites option

Site option

Assets categories

Seven images in Web site

Click the column headings to sort the items by Name, Dimensions, Size, Type, or Full Path

Scroll to view other columns

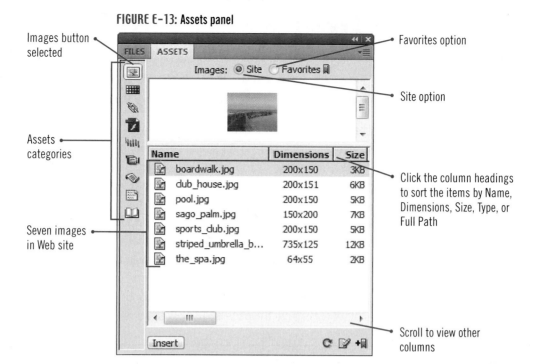

Name	Dimensions	Size
boardwalk.jpg	200x150	3KB
club_house.jpg	200x151	6KB
pool.jpg	200x150	5KB
sago_palm.jpg	150x200	7KB
sports_club.jpg	200x150	5KB
striped_umbrella_b...	735x125	12KB
the_spa.jpg	64x55	2KB

FIGURE E-14: Assets panel showing Colors category

Colors button

Both colors are Websafe

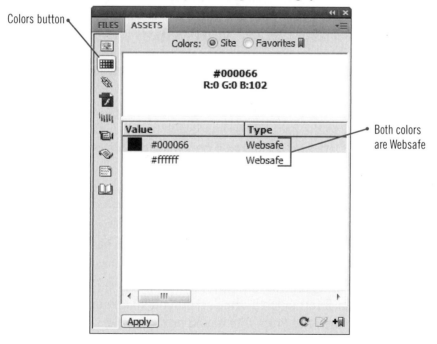

#000066
R:0 G:0 B:102

Value	Type
#000066	Websafe
#ffffff	Websafe

Using Favorites in the Assets panel

For assets such as graphics that you plan to use repeatedly, you can place them in the Favorites list in the Assets panel to make them readily available. There are a few ways to add favorites to the Favorites list in the Assets panel. You can right-click (Win) or [ctrl]-click (Mac) an image in Design view, then click Add to Image Favorites. When you click the Favorites option in the Assets panel, you will see the image in the list. You can also right-click (Win) or [ctrl]-click (Mac) the name of an image in the Site list (when the Site option is selected in the Assets panel), then click Add to Favorites. In addition, you can create a folder for storing assets by category by clicking the Favorites option in the Assets panel, clicking the Files panel options list arrow on the Files panel group, then clicking New Favorites Folder. You can give the folder a descriptive name, then drag assets in the Favorites list on top of the folder to place them in the folder. You can create nicknames for assets in the Favorites list by right-clicking (Win) or [ctrl]-clicking (Mac) the asset in the Favorites list, then clicking Edit Nickname.

Inserting a Background Image

Some Web pages have a background image in order to provide depth and visual interest to the page. **Background images** are image files used in place of background colors. Background images may create a dramatic effect; however, they may be too distracting on Web pages that have lots of text and other elements. Although some may consider them too plain, standard white backgrounds are usually the best choice for Web pages. If you choose to use a background image on a Web page, it should be small in file size. A **tiled image** is a small image that repeats across and down a Web page, appearing as individual squares or rectangles. A **seamless image** is a tiled image that is either blurred at the edges so that it appears to be all one image, or made from a pattern that, when tiled, appears to be one image, such as vertical stripes. You can convert a tiled image into a seamless image by using an image editor to blend the edges. ▄▄▄▄ You experiment with the background of the about_us page by choosing two tiled images: one with a stripe that repeats across the page and one with an umbrella image.

STEPS

1. **Click Modify on the Application bar (Win) or Menu bar (Mac), then click Page Properties**

QUICK TIP
You should use either a background color or a background image, but not both on the same page, unless you need the background color to appear while the background image finishes downloading.

2. **Click Browse next to the Background image text box, navigate to the drive and folder where your Unit E Data Files are stored if necessary, double-click the assets folder, double-click umbrella_back.gif, then click OK**

   The file is copied to the assets folder for the The Striped Umbrella Web site. Small umbrella images replace the white background on the about_us page. The background is made up of individual umbrellas, as shown in Figure E-15. You realize that the text is hard to read against this busy background.

3. **Click Modify on the Application bar (Win) or Menu bar (Mac), click Page Properties, click Browse next to the Background image text box, navigate to the drive and folder where your Unit E Data Files are stored if necessary, double-click the assets folder, double-click stripes_back.gif, then click OK**

   The file is copied to the assets folder for The Striped Umbrella Web site. The umbrellas have been replaced with multi-colored stripes. Notice that, because of the pattern, it is now harder to tell where one square stops and the other begins. See Figure E-16. The page is still too busy.

4. **Click Modify on the Application bar (Win) or Menu bar (Mac), then click Page Properties**

   You can remove a background image from a Web page by removing the background image filename in the Page Properties dialog box.

QUICK TIP
Even when you remove an image from a Web page, it remains in the assets folder in the local root folder of the Web site.

5. **Highlight the information in the Background image text box, press [Delete], then click OK to close the Page Properties dialog box**

   Much better! The background returns to white.

6. **Save your work**

Inserting Files with Adobe Bridge

You can manage project files, including video and Camera Raw files, with a file management tool called Adobe Bridge that is included with Dreamweaver. Bridge is an easy way to view files outside the Web site before bringing them into the Web site. It is an integrated application, working with other Adobe programs such as Photoshop and Illustrator. You can also use Bridge to add meta tags and search text in your files. To open Bridge, click the Browse in Bridge command on the File menu or click the Browse in Bridge button 📷 on the Standard toolbar. For more information on Adobe Bridge, see the Appendix.

FIGURE E-15: about_us page with a tiled background

Individual squares make a tiled background

FIGURE E-16: about_us page with a seamless background

Stripes make a seamless background

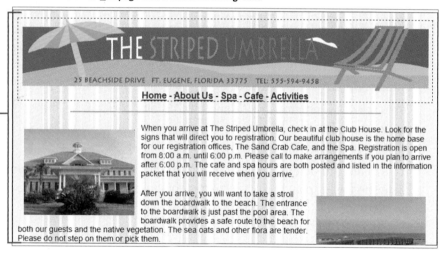

Integrating Photoshop CS4 with Dreamweaver

Dreamweaver has many functions integrated with Photoshop CS4. This partnership includes the ability to copy and paste a Photoshop PSD file directly from Photoshop into Dreamweaver. After you use the Paste command, Dreamweaver will prompt you to optimize the image by choosing a file format and settings for the Web. After optimization, Dreamweaver will then paste the image on the page. If you want to edit the image later, double-click the image in Dreamweaver and it will open in Photoshop.

Photoshop users can set Photoshop as the default image editor in Dreamweaver. Click Edit on the Application bar (Win), or click Dreamweaver on the Menu bar (Mac), click Preferences, click File Types/Editors, click the Editors plus sign button if necessary, then click Adobe Photoshop CS4 to add Photoshop (if you don't see it listed already), and then click Make Primary. You can view a tutorial for Photoshop and Dreamweaver integration on the Adobe Web site at www.adobe.com.

Deleting Image Files from a Web Site

As you work on a Web site, it is very common to accumulate files that are never used on any page in the site. One way to avoid this is to look at an image first, before you copy it to the default images folder. If the file has already been copied to the default images folder, however, you should delete it or at least move it to another location to ensure that the Assets panel only lists the assets actually used in the Web site. This practice is considered good Web site management. ▰▰▰▰▰ You delete the two background images from the assets folder since you decided not to use them on the about_us page.

STEPS

QUICK TIP
The Refresh button does not appear when the Favorites option is selected.

1. **Display the Assets panel if necessary; click the Images button 🖼 on the Assets panel, verify that the Site option is selected, then click the Refresh button ⟳ to refresh the list of images**

   The two background files are listed in the Images list, even though you have deleted them from the page. You navigate to the location of the images in the Web site folder structure.

QUICK TIP
You could skip this step and just use the Files panel to delete the file. However, the Locate in Site command is a handy tool to know when you have a large number of images to search.

2. **Right-click (Win) or [ctrl]-click (Mac) stripes_back.gif in the Assets panel, then click Locate in Site, as shown in Figure E-17**

   The Files panel appears, and the stripes_back.gif file is highlighted. If the file is not listed, click ⟳.

3. **Press [Delete] to delete the file, click Yes in the dialog box asking if you really want to delete the file, display the Assets panel, then click ⟳ on the Assets panel to refresh the list of images if necessary**

   The file is no longer listed in the Assets panel because it has been deleted from the Web site.

4. **Right-click (Win) or [ctrl]-click (Mac) the umbrella_back.gif file in the Assets panel, then click Locate in Site**

   The Files panel appears, and the umbrella_back.gif is highlighted.

5. **Press [Delete] to delete the file, click Yes in the dialog box asking if you really want to delete the file, display the Assets panel, then click ⟳ to refresh the list of images**

   Because you deleted the file from the Web site, it no longer appears in the site. You have cleaned up the list of images in the Assets panel and in the Web site.

6. **Save your work, then preview your file in your browser**

   Your about_us page is finished for now and should resemble Figure E-18.

7. **Close the page, then Exit (Win) or Quit (Mac) Dreamweaver**

Design Matters

Image file management

It is a good idea to have an additional storage space for your Web site image files, besides the assets folder in the Web site. Keep all original image files outside the Web site and save them once with their original settings. As you edit them, save them using a different name. This way, you will always be able to find the original file before it is resized or edited. You may also have files you don't want to use now but may need later. Store them outside your Web site to keep from cluttering up the assets folder.

FIGURE E-17: Locate in Site command in Assets panel

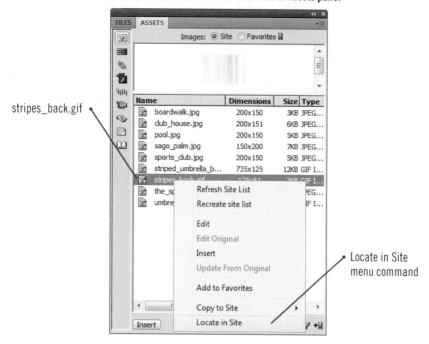

stripes_back.gif

FIGURE E-18: The finished page

Creating and Finding Images for a Web Site

There are several resources for locating high-quality images for a Web site. You can create images "from scratch" using an image-editing or drawing program, such as Adobe Fireworks, Adobe Illustrator, or Adobe Photoshop. Original photography is another option for colorful, rich images. You can also purchase images as clip art collections. **Clip art collections** are groups of image files collected on CDs and sold with an **index**, or directory of the files. The Internet, of course, is another source for finding images. Table E-2 describes three image types frequently used on Web pages.  Now that you understand how to incorporate images into The Striped Umbrella Web site, you explore the advantages and disadvantages of the different ways to accumulate images.

DETAILS

- **Original images**

  Programs such as Adobe Fireworks, Adobe Illustrator, and Adobe Photoshop, give you the ability to create and modify original artwork. These image editing programs have numerous features for manipulating images. For example, you can adjust the color, brightness, or size of an image. You can also set a transparent background for an image. **Transparent backgrounds** have transparent pixels, rather than pixels of another color, resulting in images that blend easily on a Web page background. Figure E-19 shows an example of an image with a colored background, while Figure E-20 has a transparent background.

- **Original photography**

  High-quality photographs can greatly enhance a Web site. Fortunately, digital cameras and scanners have made this venture much easier than in the past. Once you scan a photograph or shoot it with a digital camera, you can further enhance it using an image editing software program. Photographs taken with digital cameras are very large images. Resize them using an image editing program before placing them on Web pages. Many digital cameras come with software programs that you can use to resize and enhance digital photographs.

- **Clip art collections**

  Clip art collections are available in computer software stores, office supply stores, and over the Internet. When using clip art collections, you should read the terms of the copyright statement in the user's manual. The publisher may have placed limitations on the use of the clip art. Not all clip art is **royalty-free**, that is, free for the purchaser to copy and publish without having to pay a royalty to the company that published the clip art.

- **The Internet**

  There are many Web sites that allow you to copy their graphics, but, again, look carefully for copyright statements regarding the use of the graphics. There are many collections of clip art online that are free for you to use, but some sites ask that you give them credit on your Web site with either a simple statement or a link to their Web site. The Web site in Figure E-21 is an example of a source for public domain images. Images that are labeled as **public domain** are free to use without restrictions. *If you copy and paste images you find while accessing other Web sites and use them for your own purposes, you may be violating copyright laws.*

TABLE E-2: Common graphic file formats for Web page images

format (file extension)	stands for	details
.jpg	Joint Photographic Experts Group	Pixel-based; a Web standard. Can set image quality in dots per inch (dpi), which affects file size. Supports millions of colors. Use for full-color images, such as photographs or those with lifelike artwork.
.png	Portable Network Graphics	Can be compressed for storage and quicker download, without loss of picture quality. Supports variable levels of transparency and control of image brightness on different computers. Used for small graphics, such as bullets and banners, as well as for complex photographic images.
.gif	Graphics Interchange Format	Most popular Web graphics format, but limited to 256 colors. Low color quality and limited detail makes GIFs unsuited for printing. Small file size means faster transmission. Use for images with only a few colors, such as cartoons, simple illustrations, icons, buttons, and horizontal rules. This format is used for transparent images.

FIGURE E-19: Graphic with colored background

FIGURE E-20: Graphic with transparent background

Alternating squares indicate transparent areas

FIGURE E-21: Example of a Web site with public domain images

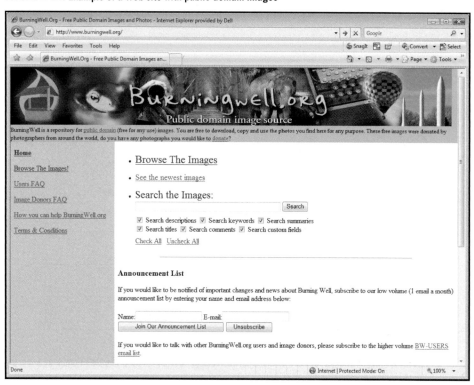

The BurningWell.org Web site used with permission by Jay Summett—www.burningwell.org

Managing image files

It is a good idea to store original, unedited copies of your Web site image files in a separate folder outside your Web site assets folder. If you edit the original files, save them in that folder again using different names. That way you will always be able to find an image in its original, unaltered state and you will always have backup copies in case you accidentally delete a file from the Web site. You might also have image files on your computer that you are not currently using in your site at all, but that you might need to use in the future. Store these in a folder outside your site as well, to keep your assets folder free of clutter.

Practice

▼ CONCEPTS REVIEW

Label each element shown in Figure E-22.

FIGURE E-22

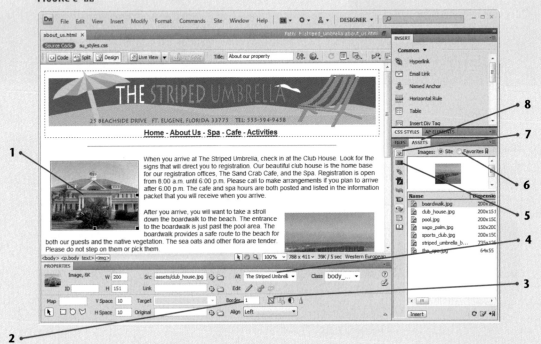

1. _____   5. _____

2. _____   6. _____

3. _____   7. _____

4. _____   8. _____

Match each of the following terms with the statement that best describes its function.

9. **Assets panel**   a. Positioning an image on a page

10. **JPEG**   b. Updates the current list of assets in the Assets panel

11. **Aligning an image**   c. Includes only those assets designated as Favorites

12. **Background image**   d. Small image that repeats across and down a Web page

13. **Favorites list**   e. Used in place of a background color

14. **Refresh button**   f. Describes an image on a Web page

15. **Tiled image**   g. A frame placed around an image

16. **Seamless image**   h. An image file format

17. **Alternate text**   i. Small background image that is tiled, but appears to be one image

18. **Border**   j. Lists all the assets of the Web site, including favorites

Select the best answer from the list of choices.

19. The following category is not found on the Assets panel:

   a. URLs.

   b. Colors.

   c. Tables.

   d. Movies.

20. When you no longer need files in a Web site, you should:

   a. Leave them in the Assets panel.

   b. Drag them off the Web page to the Recycle Bin (Win) or the Trash icon (Mac).

   c. Place them in the Site list.

   d. Delete them from the Web site.

21. Background images:

   a. Are never appropriate.

   b. Are always appropriate.

   c. Cannot be tiled.

   d. Can be seamless.

22. Tiled background images generally:

   a. Appear as one image on a Web page.

   b. Appear as many small squares on a Web page.

   c. Appear as many rows across a Web page.

   d. Appear as many columns down a Web page.

▼ SKILLS REVIEW

Important: *If you did not create this Web site in Unit B and maintain it during the preceding units, you will need to create a root folder for this Web site and define the Web site using files your instructor will provide. See the "Read This Before You Begin" section for more detailed instructions.*

1. Insert an image.

   a. Start Dreamweaver.

   b. Open the blooms & bulbs Web site.

   c. Open dwe_2.html from the drive and folder where your Unit E Data Files are stored, then save it as **plants.html** in the blooms & bulbs Web site, overwriting the existing plants.html file but not updating the links.

   d. Close dwe_2.html.

   e. Insert the petunias.jpg file from the assets folder in the drive and folder where your Unit E Data Files are stored, in front of the words "Pretty petunias...". (Enter alternate text, if prompted.)

   f. Insert the verbena.jpg file in front of the words "Verbena is one...". (Enter alternate text, if prompted.)

   g. Insert the lantana.jpg file in front of the words "Dramatic masses...". (Enter alternate text, if prompted.)

   h. Attach the blooms_styles.css file to the plants page.

   i. Apply the body_text style to all of the paragraph text on the page.

   j. Apply the headings style to the text "Drop by to see our Spring Plants."

   k. Save your work.

2. Align an image.

   a. Select petunias.jpg and use the Property inspector to left-align the image.

   b. Right-align the verbena.jpg and left-align the lantana.jpg images.

   c. Save your work.

3. Enhance an image.

   a. Select petunias.jpg and apply a 2-point border to it.

   b. Add a 2-point border to the verbena.jpg and lantana.jpg images.

   c. Add vertical spacing of 5 pixels and horizontal spacing of 20 pixels around each image.

   d. Save your work.

4. Use alternate text.

   a. If you did not add alternate text in Step 1 above, select petunias.jpg, then use the Property inspector to enter **Petunias** as alternate text.

   b. If necessary, add the alternate text **Verbena** for verbena.jpg, and **Lantana** for lantana.jpg.

   c. If necessary, edit the Web site preferences to set the Accessibility prompt for graphics.

   d. Save your work.

5. **View the Assets panel.**

   a. Display the Assets panel, if necessary.

   b. View the Images list to verify that there are five images in the list. Refresh the Images list, if necessary.

   c. View the Colors list to verify that there are four Websafe colors.

6. **Insert a background image.**

   a. Use Page Properties to insert the daisies.jpg file as a background image and refresh the Assets panel. (This file is in the assets folder in the drive and folder where your Unit E Data Files are stored.)

   b. Save the page, then view it in your browser.

   c. Close the browser window.

   d. Remove the daisies.jpg image from the background, then save the file.

7. **Delete image files from a Web site.**

   a. Delete the daisies.jpg file from the Files panel.

   b. Refresh the Files panel and verify that the daisies.jpg file has been removed from the Web site. (You may have to refresh the Site list first.)

   c. Preview the page in the browser, compare your screen with Figure E-23, and close the browser. (*Note*: Depending on your screen settings, your text wrapping may differ.)

   d. Close the page, Exit (Win) or Quit (Mac) Dreamweaver.

FIGURE E-23

Drop by to see our Spring Plants

Pretty petunias blanket your beds with lush green leaves and bright blooms in assorted colors. Shown is the Moonlight White Petunia (Mini-Spreading). This variety is fast-growing and produces spectacular blooms. Cut them back in July for blooms that will last into the fall. Full sun to partial shade. Great for border plants or hanging baskets.

Verbena is one of our all-time favorites. The variety shown is Blue Silver. Verbena grows rapidly and is a good choice for butterfly gardens. The plants can spread up to two feet wide, so it makes excellent ground cover. Plant in full sun. Heat resistant. Beautiful also in rock gardens. We have several other varieties equally as beautiful.

Dramatic masses of Lantana display summer color for your beds or containers. The variety shown is Golden Dream. Blooms late spring through early fall. This variety produces outstanding color. Plant in full sun with well-drained soil. We carry tall, dwarf, and trailing varieties. You can also overwinter with cuttings.

Stop by to see us soon. We will be happy to help you with your selections.

Important: *If you did not create the following Web sites in Unit B and maintain them during the preceding units, you will need to create a root folder for the Web sites in the following exercises and define the Web sites using files your instructor will provide. See the "Read This Before You Begin" section for more detailed instructions.*

▼ INDEPENDENT CHALLENGE 1

You have been hired to create a Web site for a river expedition company named Rapids Transit, located on the Buffalo River in Arkansas. In addition to renting canoes, kayaks, and rafts, they have lodging for overnight stays. River guides are available, if requested, to accompany clients on float trips. The clients range from high school and college students to families to vacationing professionals. The owner's name is Mike Andrew. Mike has asked you to develop the page that introduces the Rapids Transit guides available for float trips. Refer to Figure E-24 as you work on this page.

  a. Start Dreamweaver and open the Rapids Transit Web site.

  b. Open dwe_3.html from the drive and folder where your Unit E Data Files are stored and save it in the Rapids Transit Web site as **guides.html**, overwriting the existing guides file but not updating links.

  c. Close dw3_3.html.

  d. Check the path for the Rapids Transit banner and reset the path to the assets folder for the Web site, if necessary.

  e. Verify that the Rapids Transit banner has alternate text. If it doesn't, add it.

  f. Insert the image buster_tricks.jpg at an appropriate place on the page. (This file is in the assets folder in the drive and folder where your Unit E Data Files are stored.)

  g. Create alternate text for the buster_tricks.jpg image, add a border to the image, then left-align it.

  h. Crop the image as shown in Figure E-24 and add some horizontal and vertical space around the image.

  i. Format the text on the page appropriately by attaching the rapids_transit.css style sheet and applying the body_text style to the paragraph text. Apply the lodging style to the navigation bar.

  j. Save your work, preview the page in the browser, then compare your screen to Figure E-24 (Your image location, border size, and vertical and horizontal space settings may differ.).

  k. Close the browser and Exit (Win) or Quit (Mac) Dreamweaver.

FIGURE E-24

Home ~ **River Guides** ~ **Equipment Rentals** ~ **Lodging**

We have four of the best river guides you will ever find — Buster, Tucker, Max, and Scarlett. Buster has been with us for fourteen years and was born and raised here on the river. Tucker joined us two years ago "from off" (somewhere up north), but we've managed to make a country boy out of him! Max and Scarlett are actually distant cousins and joined us after they graduated from college last year. They're never happier than when they're out on the water floating and fishing. Each of our guides will show you a great time on the river.

Our guides will pack your supplies, shuttle you to the put-in point, maneuver the raging rapids for you, and then make sure someone is waiting at the take-out point to shuttle you back to the store. They haven't lost a customer yet! Give us a call and we'll set up a date with any of these good people. Here's a photo of Buster showing off his stuff. The river is always faster and higher in the spring. If you want to take it a little slower, come visit us in the summer or fall. Leave your good camera at home, though, no matter what the time of the year. You may get wet! Life jackets are provided and we require that you wear them while on the water. Safety is always our prime concern.

Your company is designing a new Web site for TripSmart, a travel outfitter. TripSmart specializes in travel products and services. In addition to selling travel products, such as luggage and accessories, they sponsor trips and offer travel advice. Their clients range from college students to families to vacationing professionals. You are now ready to work on the destinations page. Refer to Figure E-25 as you work through the following steps.

a. Start Dreamweaver and open the TripSmart Web site.

b. Open dwe_4.html from the drive and folder where your Unit E Data Files are stored and save it in the TripSmart Web site as **destinations.html**, overwriting the existing destinations file but not updating links.

c. Close the file dwe_4.html.

d. Check the path for the TripSmart banner and reset the path to the assets folder for the Web site, if necessary.

e. Apply the heading style to the Destination: Kenya heading and the body_text style to the rest of the text on the page. (*Hint*: You probably formatted your styles differently from the example, so your text may look different than Figure E-25.)

f. Change the Web site preferences to prompt you to add alternate text as you add new images to the Web site, if necessary.

g. Insert the images zebra_mothers.jpg and lion.jpg at the appropriate places on the page, adding alternate text for each image. (These files are in the assets folder in the drive and folder where your Unit E Data Files are stored.)

h. Add a border to each image, then choose an alignment setting for each one.

i. Add the page title **Destination: Kenya**, then add appropriate horizonal and vertical spacing around both graphcs.

j. Save your work, preview the page in the browser, then compare your page to Figure E-25 for one possible design solution.

k. Close the browser and Exit (Win) or Quit (Mac) Dreamweaver.

FIGURE E-25

Destination: Kenya

Our next Photo Safari to Kenya has now been scheduled with a departure date of May 5 and a return date of May 23. Come join us and take some beautiful pictures like these two Grevy's zebras nursing their young at Samburu National Reserve. Our flight will leave New York for London, where you will have dayrooms reserved before flying all night to Nairobi, Kenya. To provide the finest in personal attention, this tour will be limited to no more than sixteen persons. Game drives will take place early each morning and late afternoon to provide maximum opportunity for game viewing, as the animals are most active at these times. We will visit five game reserves to allow for a variety of animal populations and scenery.

This lion is relaxing in the late afternoon sun. Notice the scar under his right ear. He might have received that when he was booted out of his pride as a young lion. We will be spending most nights in tented camps listening to the night sounds of hunters such as this magnificent animal. Enjoy visiting native villages and trading with the local businesspeople. Birding enthusiasts will enjoy adding to their bird lists with Kenya's over 300 species of birds. View the beginning of the annual migration of millions of wildebeest, a spectacular sight. The wildebeest are traveling from the Serengeti Plain to the Mara in search of water and grass. Optional excursions include ballooning over the Masai Mara, fishing on Lake Victoria, camel rides at Amboseli Serena Lodge, and golfing at the Aberdare Country Club. Lake Victoria is the largest freshwater lake in the world.

The price schedule is as follows: Land Tour and Supplemental Group Air, $4,500.00; International Air, $1,350.00; and Single Supplement, $1,000.00. Entrance fees, hotel taxes, and services are included in the Land Tour price. A deposit of $500.00 is required at the time the booking is made. Trip Insurance and Luggage Insurance are optional and are also offered at extra charge. A passport and visa will be required for entry into Kenya. Call us at *(555) 848-0807* for further information from 8:00 a.m. to 6:00 p.m. (Central Standard Time).

DESIGN QUEST

▼ INDEPENDENT CHALLENGE 3

Donna Wasson raises and shows horses professionally. She is learning how to use Dreamweaver to be able to create a Web site to showcase her horses. She would like to look at some other Web sites about horses to get a feel for the types of images she may want to use in her site. Use a word processor or paper to answer the questions below.

a. Connect to the Internet and go to USHorse.biz at www.ushorse.biz, as shown in Figure E-26.

b. How are background colors used? Would you have selected different ones? Why, or why not?

c. Evaluate the graphics used in the Web site. Do they add interest to the pages, or are they distracting? Was alternate text used for any or all of the images?

d. How long did the home page take to download on your computer? In your opinion, was it too slow?

e. Are there too few graphics, too many, or just enough to add interest?

f. Go to Google at www.google.com or Yahoo! at www.yahoo.com to find another horse Web site.

g. Compare the site you found to the USHorse.biz site by answering questions b through e above.

FIGURE E-26

The USHorse.biz Web site used with permission from www.USHorse.biz

YOUR SITE

▼ INDEPENDENT CHALLENGE 4

This assignment will continue to build on the personal Web site that you created in Unit B. You have created and developed your index page. You have also added a page with either an ordered or an unordered list, and a CSS Style Sheet with a minimum of two styles. In this lesson, you work with one of the other pages in your Web site.

a. Consult your storyboard and decide which page you would like to develop in this lesson.

b. Create content for this page and format the text attractively on the page using styles for all formatting.

c. Set the Accessibility option to prompt you for alternate text for new images added to the Web site, if necessary.

d. Add at least two images with appropriate alternate text. Resize the images in an image-editing program if they are too large to place on the Web page.

e. Align and enhance the images to place them attractively on the page.

f. Document the source for the images and print proof that they are royalty free. Use your own photographs or drawings if you have difficulty obtaining royalty-free images.

g. Document the estimated download time for the page and the setting you used to estimate download time.

h. Save the file and preview the page in the browser.

After you are satisfied with your work, verify the following:

a. Each completed page has a page title.

b. All links work correctly.

c. The completed pages show well using a screen resolution of 1024 × 768.

d. All images are properly set showing a path to the assets folder of the Web site.

e. All images have alternate text and are legal to use.

▼ VISUAL WORKSHOP

Your company has been selected to design a Web site for Carolyne's Creations, a small catering business. Open your Carolyne's Creations Web site. Chef Carolyne has asked you to create a page that displays featured items in the kitchen shop. Open dwe_5.html from the drive and folder where your Unit E Data Files are stored. Save the file as **shop.html** in the Carolyne's Creations Web site, then add the pot_knives.jpg image from the Unit E assets folder to create the page shown in Figure E-27. (*Hint*: You will need to attach the cc_styles.css style sheet to the page and create a new rule to use for formatting the text "January Specials: Multifunctional Pot and Cutlery Set." Create a rule named sub_head in your cc_styles.css file with the following settings: Font-family: Verdana, Geneva, sans-serif; Font-size: 16px; Color: #333; Font-weight: bold.) Apply the headings style to the navigation bar.

FIGURE E-27

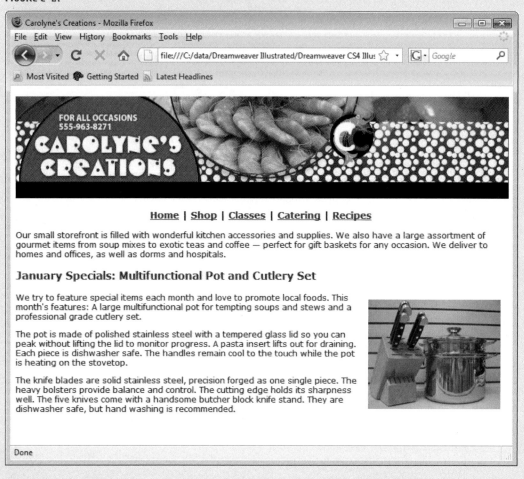

Creating Links and Navigation Bars

As you learned in Unit C, links are the real strength of a Web site because they give viewers the freedom to open various Web pages as they choose. You created a navigation bar using a group of text links that helps viewers navigate between pages of a Web site. In this unit, you will learn how to create links using button images with text and how to create another type of link called an image map. An **image map** is an image that has clickable areas defined on it that, when clicked, serve as links to take the viewer to another location. 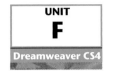 You decide to start working on the link structure for The Striped Umbrella Web site. You also add links to the activities page and create a navigation bar and image map.

OBJECTIVES

Understand links and paths

Create an external link

Create an internal link

Insert a named anchor

Create internal links to named anchors

Create a navigation bar with images

Modify a navigation bar

Copy a navigation bar to other pages in a Web site

Create an image map

Manage Web site links

Understanding Links and Paths

You can use two types of links on Web pages. **Internal links** are links to Web pages within the same Web site, and **external links** are links that connect to pages in other Web sites or to e-mail addresses. Internal and external links both have two important parts that work together. The first part of a link is what the viewer actually sees and clicks, such as a word, an image, or an animated button. When the viewer places the mouse pointer over a link, the pointer's appearance changes to a pointing finger icon 👆. The second part of a link is the **path**, which is the name and physical location of the Web page file that opens when the link is clicked. The information in a path depends on whether a link is internal or external. A link that returns an error message, or a **broken link**, occurs when files are renamed or deleted from a Web site, the filename is misspelled, or the Web site is experiencing technical problems. You spend some time studying the various types of paths used for internal and external links.

DETAILS

- **Absolute paths**

    Absolute paths are used with external links. They reference links on Web pages outside the current Web site, and include **"http"** (hypertext transfer protocol) and the **URL** (Uniform Resource Locator), or address, of the Web page. When necessary, the Web page filename and the folder hierarchy are also part of an absolute path. Figure F-1 shows an example of an absolute path.

- **Relative paths**

    Relative paths are used with internal links. They reference Web pages and graphic files within one Web site and include the filename and the folder hierarchy where the file resides. Figure F-1 also shows an example of a relative path. Relative paths are further classified as root-relative (relative to the root folder) and document-relative (relative to the current document).

    - **Root-relative paths**

        Root-relative paths are referenced from a Web site's root folder. As shown in Figure F-2, a root-relative path begins with a forward slash, which represents the Web site's root folder. This method is used when several Web sites are published to one server, or when a Web site is so large that it uses more than one server.

    - **Document-relative paths**

        Document-relative paths reference the path in relation to the Web page that appears. A document-relative path includes only a filename if the referenced file resides in the same folder as the current Web page. For example, index.html and spa.html both reside in the root folder for The Striped Umbrella. So you would simply type spa.html to link to the spa page from the index page. However, when an image is referenced in the assets folder, since the assets folder is a subfolder of the root folder, you must include the word assets/ (with the slash) in front of the filename, for example, assets/the_spa.jpg. See Figure F-2 for an example of a document-relative path.

    In the exercises in this book, you will use document-relative paths because it is assumed that you will not use more than one server to publish your Web sites. For this reason, it is very important to make sure that the Relative to text box in the Select File dialog box is set to Document, rather than Site Root, when creating links. This option can also be set in the Site Definition dialog box.

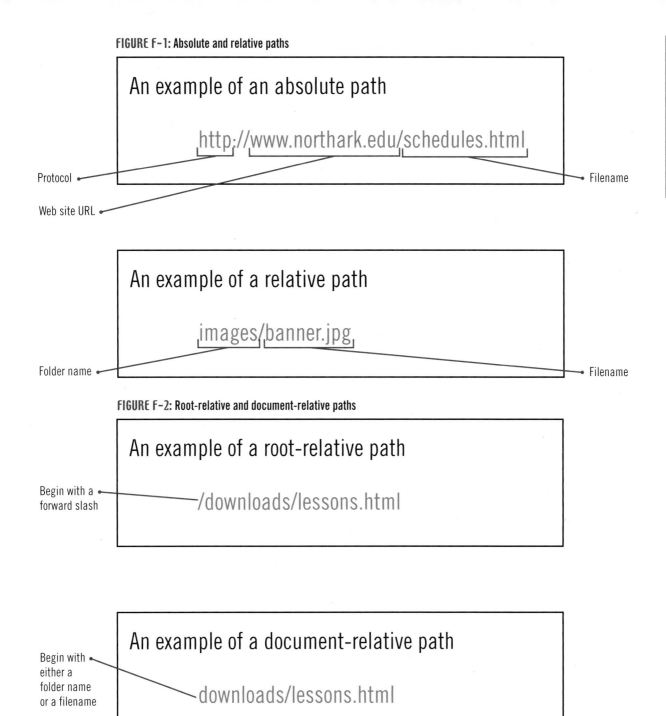

FIGURE F-1: Absolute and relative paths

An example of an absolute path

http://www.northark.edu/schedules.html

Protocol

Web site URL

Filename

An example of a relative path

images/banner.jpg

Folder name

Filename

FIGURE F-2: Root-relative and document-relative paths

An example of a root-relative path

/downloads/lessons.html

Begin with a
forward slash

An example of a document-relative path

downloads/lessons.html

Begin with
either a
folder name
or a filename

Creating an effective navigation structure

When you create a Web site, it's important to consider how your viewers will navigate from page to page within the site. A navigation bar is a critical tool for moving around a site, so it's important that all text, buttons, and icons you use in a navigation bar have a consistent look across all pages. If you use a complex navigation bar, such as one that incorporates JavaScript or Flash, it's a good idea to include plain text links in another location on the page for accessibility. Otherwise, viewers might become confused or lost within the site.

A navigation structure can include more links than those included in a navigation bar, however. For instance, it can contain other sets of links that relate to the content of a specific page and which are placed at the bottom or sides of a page in a different format. No matter which navigation structure you use, make sure that every page includes a link back to the home page. Don't make viewers rely on the Back button on the browser toolbar to find their way back to the home page. It's possible that the viewer's current page might have opened as a result of a search and clicking the Back button will take the viewer out of the Web site.

Creating an External Link

As you have learned, external links use absolute paths. Absolute paths must include the complete name and path of the Web address to link to the destination Web page successfully. Because the World Wide Web is a constantly changing environment, you should check external links frequently. Web sites may be up one day and down the next. If a Web site changes server locations or shuts down because of technical difficulties or a power failure, the links to it become broken. An external link can also become broken when an Internet connection is not working properly. Broken links, like misspelled words on a Web page, indicate that the Web site is not being maintained diligently. You create external links on the activities page.

STEPS

1. **Open** The Striped Umbrella Web site, **open** dwf_1.html **from the drive and folder where your Unit F Data Files are stored, then save it as** activities.html **in the striped_umbrella root folder, overwriting the existing file but not updating links**

   The new activities page opens in Design view. The activities page lists two Web sites of possible interest to visitors to the resort. There are two broken image placeholders that represent images that must be copied to the Web site.

2. **Close** dwf_1.html

   TROUBLE

   Remember to browse in the Data Files assets folder, not the site assets folder, to locate the heron_waiting.jpg image.

3. **Select the leftmost broken image, click the** Browse for File icon ▢ **next to the Src text box in the Property inspector, select** heron_waiting.jpg **in the Data Files assets folder to save the image in your assets folder, then click to the right of the placeholder**

   The image is copied to the Web site and now appears on the page.

4. **Repeat Step 3 for the second image,** two_dolphins.jpg

   The second image appears.

5. **Attach the** su_styles.css **file, then apply the** body_text **style to the paragraphs of text on the page (not to the navigation bar)**

6. **Scroll to the bottom of the page if necessary, then select the text** Blue Angels

   You are ready to make the Blue Angels text into an external link that will lead viewers to the Blue Angels Web site.

7. **Click the** Link text box **in the HTML Property inspector, type** http://www.blueangels.navy.mil, **compare your screen to Figure F-3, then press [Tab]**

   The link information is complete. You want to make sure the link works correctly.

   TROUBLE

   If your link does not work correctly, check for errors in the link path you typed. Be sure you type the letters exactly. If you have typed the link correctly and it still doesn't work, the site may be down.

8. **Click** File **on the Application bar (Win) or Menu bar (Mac), click** Save, **click the** Preview/Debug in browser button ⊙, **click** Preview in [your browser], **click** Blue Angels **on the Web page, verify that the link works, then close your browser**

   You are ready to add the last external link on the activities page.

9. **Repeat Steps 6 and 7 to create the link for the** USS Alabama **text in the last paragraph, using this URL:** http://www.ussalabama.com

10. **Save your work**

11. **Preview the page in the browser to test the USS Alabama link**

12. **Close the browser**

FIGURE F-3: Creating an external link to the Blue Angels Web site

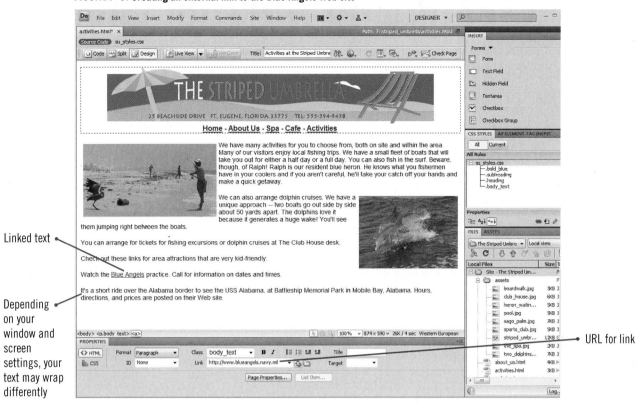

Linked text

Depending
on your
window and
screen
settings, your
text may wrap
differently

URL for link

Creating an Internal Link

As you know, internal links are used to link Web pages within the same Web site. A Web site usually contains individual pages for each category or major topic covered in the site. Within those pages, viewers may be able to link to other pages that relate to the particular topic. The home page should provide intuitive navigation to each category or major topic in a Web site. A good rule of thumb is to design your Web site so that viewers are never more than three clicks away from the page they are seeking. Refer to your storyboard frequently as you create pages to help manage your site's navigation structure. ▆▆▆▆ You create internal links on the activities page that will link to other pages in The Striped Umbrella Web site.

STEPS

1. **Using Figure F-4 as a reference, select** fishing excursions **in the third paragraph**
   The fishing excursions text will become an internal link to the fishing page.

QUICK TIP
You can also select the file to which you want to link in the Files panel and drag it to the Link text box or use the Point to File icon ⊕ in the Property inspector to create an internal link.

2. **Click the** Browse for File icon 🗁 **next to the Link text box in the HTML Property inspector, make sure the Relative to box is set to Document, then double-click** fishing.html **in The Striped Umbrella root folder in the Select File dialog box**
   Figure F-4 shows fishing.html in the Link text box in the HTML Property inspector. When viewers click the fishing excursions link, the fishing page will open.

3. **Select** dolphin cruises **in the same sentence**
   The dolphin cruises text will be an internal link to the cruises page.

4. **Click** 🗁 **in the Property inspector, then double-click** cruises.html **in the Select File dialog box**
   The words dolphin cruises are now a link to the cruises page in The Striped Umbrella Web site.

5. **Save your work**
   There are now nine links on the activities page: seven internal links (five on the navigation bar and two in the paragraph text linking to the fishing and cruises pages), and two external links (the Blue Angels and USS Alabama Web sites), as shown in Figure F-5.

6. **Close the activities page**

Design Matters

Linking to the home page

It is important to provide your viewers with instant access to the home page. Every page on your Web site should include a link to the home page so a viewer who has become "lost" in your Web site can quickly go back to the starting point without relying on the Back button. Also, and more important, if the page was opened as the result of a search, the Back button will take the viewer away from your Web site.

FIGURE F-4: Creating internal links on the activities page

Selected text to be used for a link

Selected text links to this file   Browse for File icon

FIGURE F-5: Viewing the internal and external links on the activities page

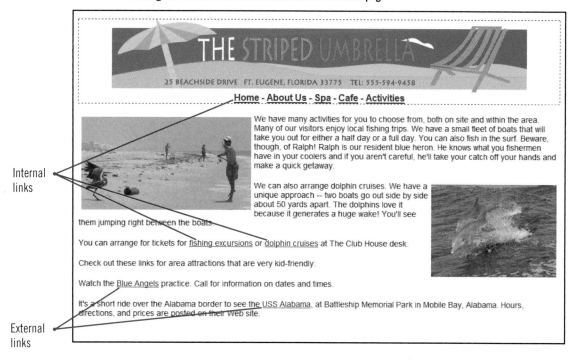

Internal links

External links

Inserting a Named Anchor

While the links you have learned so far are good for linking to other site pages or to other Web sites, they are not useful to link to another location on the same page. Some Web pages have so much content that viewers must scroll repeatedly to get to the bottom of the page and then back to the top. To make it easier for viewers to navigate to specific areas of a page without scrolling, you can use a combination of internal links and named anchors. **Named anchors** are specific locations on a Web page that are represented by a special icon and are given descriptive names. You then create internal links on the page that the user clicks to jump to the named anchor location. For example, you can insert a named anchor called "top" at the top of a Web page, then create a link at the bottom of the page that, when clicked, will display the anchor location, the top of the Web page, in the browser window. You can also insert named anchors at strategic spots on a Web page, such as paragraph headings. You should create a named anchor before you create a link to it to avoid possible errors. You insert five named anchors on the spa page: one for the top of the page and four more that will help viewers quickly access the Spa Services headings on the page.

STEPS

1. **Open the** spa.html **page, click** The Striped Umbrella banner, **then press the** left arrow key **on your keyboard to place the insertion point directly before the banner**
    The insertion point is now at the top of the page. This will be the location for the first named anchor.

2. **Click** View **on the Application bar (Win) or Menu bar (Mac), point to** Visual Aids, **then click** Invisible Elements **to select it if necessary**
    Named anchors are an example of Invisible Elements. Invisible Elements must be "on" to reveal where named anchors are located on the page. A check mark to the left of the Invisible Elements menu item indicates that the feature is turned on.

3. **Click the** Common category **on the Insert panel if necessary**
    The Named Anchor button is in the Common category on the Insert panel.

4. **Click the** Named Anchor button **on the Insert panel, type** top **in the Anchor name text box of the Named Anchor dialog box, as shown in Figure F-6, then click** OK
    The named anchor icon appears before The Striped Umbrella banner.

QUICK TIP
You should use only lowercase characters for named anchor names; do not use spaces or special characters, or begin an anchor name with a number. The name used for a named anchor should be short and should reflect its page location.

5. **Click to place the insertion point to the left of the Skin Care Treatments heading, click the** Named Anchor button, **type** skin_care **in the Anchor name text box, then click** OK
    The second named anchor appears before the Skin Care Treatments heading.

6. **Insert named anchors in front of the** Body Treatments, Massages, **and** Spa Packages **headings, using the following names:** body_treatments, massages, **and** packages
    Your screen should resemble Figure F-7. The Property inspector shows the name of the selected anchor.

7. **Save your work**
    You are now ready to create internal links for the five named anchors.

FIGURE F-6: Named Anchor dialog box

Named Anchor button

Anchor name text box

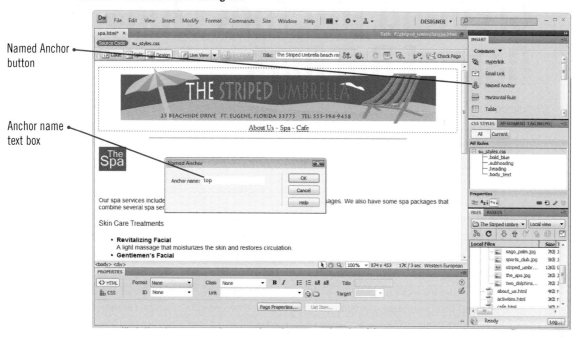

FIGURE F-7: Named anchor icons

Named anchors appear blue when selected, yellow when not selected

Name of selected anchor

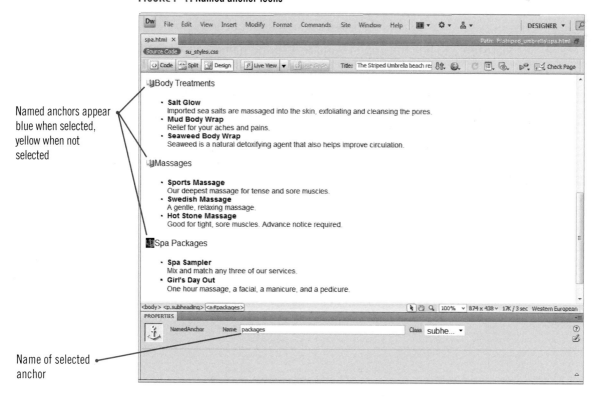

Creating Internal Links to Named Anchors

Named anchors act as targets for internal links. A **target** is the location on a Web page that the browser will display when a link is clicked. You use the Point to File icon in the Property inspector to connect an internal link to a named anchor. ░░░░░ You create internal links and link them to each named anchor on the spa page. You also create a link at the bottom of the page that viewers can use to return to the top of the page.

STEPS

1. **Using Figure F-8 as a guide, select** skin care treatments **in the first paragraph, then click and drag the** Point to File icon ⊙ **in the HTML Property inspector on top of the anchor named** skin_care **in front of the Skin Care Treatments heading, as shown in Figure F-8**
   The words "skin care treatments" are now a link that, when clicked, will display the Skin Care Treatments heading at the top of the browser window because the skin_care named anchor is the target for the skin care treatments link. The name of a named anchor is always preceded by a pound (#) sign in the Link text box in the HTML Property inspector, as shown in Figure F-8.

QUICK TIP
After you select the text you are going to use for a link, you can scroll the text off the screen and still be able to use ⊙ to create a link.

2. **Create internal links for the headings** Body Treatments, Massages, **and** Spa Packages **by first selecting each item in the first paragraph, then clicking and dragging** ⊙ **on top of the** body_treatments, massages, **and** packages **named anchors**
   Body treatments, massages, and packages are now links that link to the Body Treatments, Massages, and Spa Packages headings. You are ready to type text at the bottom of the spa page that, when clicked, will bring viewers to the top of the page.

3. **Click at the end of the last line on the page, press [Enter] (Win) or [return] (Mac), then type** Top of Page
   This text will be used to link to the named anchor at the top of the page.

4. **Repeat step 2 to link the Top of Page text to the named anchor at the top of the page.**

5. **Click anywhere in the text Top of Page, wait for a few seconds until the** Click indicator to bring up the Code Navigator icon ▦ **appears, then click the** Click indicator to bring up the Code Navigator icon ▦
   The Code Navigator, as shown in Figure F-9, tells you that the Top of Page text has the body_text CSS style applied to it. When you placed the insertion point at the end of the paragraph and entered a paragraph break, the formatting was retained.

6. **Save your work, preview the page in your browser and test each link, then close your browser**

FIGURE F-8: Using the Point to File icon

Your named anchor icon may appear above the banner rather than beside it

Selected text

Drag Point to File icon to skin_care named anchor

sign in anchor name

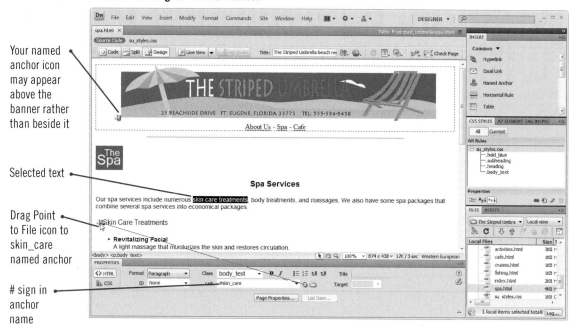

FIGURE F-9: Code Navigator displaying rule properties

Text linking to the top of the page

Code Navigator shows rule name and location

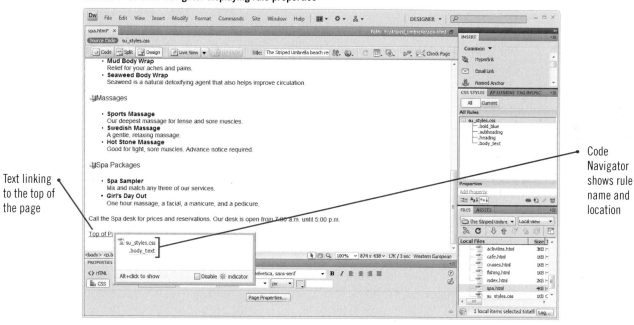

Using the Code Navigator

When you click on a page element in either Code view or Design view, wait a second or two; the Click indicator to bring up the Code Navigator icon ⊞ will appear. You can also [Alt]-click (Win) to display ⊞ instantly. Clicking this icon will open a pop-up window called the Code Navigator. The **Code Navigator** lists the CSS rule name linked to the page element, along with the name of the style sheet that contains the rule. Pointing to the rule name will display the properties and values of the rule, as shown in Figure F-10. This is a quick way to view the rule definition. If you click the rule name,

the code for the rule will open in Code and Design views, where you can then edit it.

FIGURE F-10: Code Navigator displaying rule properties

Pointing to rule displays its properties and values

su_styles.css
.body_text
font-family: Arial, Helvetica, sans-serif;
font-size: 14px;
font-style: normal;

Alt+click to show ☐ Disable ⊞ indicator

Creating a Navigation Bar with Images

Recall from Unit C that a **navigation bar** is a set of text or image links that viewers can use to navigate between pages of a Web site. When you create a navigation bar with images rather than text, you use images created in a graphics program. All image links created for a navigation bar must be exactly the same size to be displayed correctly in a browser. The Insert Navigation Bar dialog box refers to each link as an **element**. Each element can have four possible **states**, or appearances, based on the location of the mouse pointer. These states include **Up image** (when the mouse pointer is not on the element), **Over image** (when the mouse pointer is over the element), **Down image** (when you click the element with the mouse pointer), and **Over while down image** (when you click the element and continue holding with the mouse pointer). You can create a rollover by using different images to represent each button state. When the mouse rolls over the button or link, the button's appearance changes.  You begin creating a navigation bar that will have five navigation elements: home, about us, cafe, spa, and activities.

STEPS

QUICK TIP

You can also insert a navigation bar by clicking Insert on the Application bar (Win) or Menu bar (Mac), pointing to Image Objects, then clicking Navigation Bar.

1. **Make sure the spa page is open in Design view, click** View **on the Application bar (Win) or Menu bar (Mac), point to** Visual Aids, **click** Invisible Elements **to uncheck Invisible Elements, then change to the** Common category **on the Insert panel if necessary**
   You want to replace the current navigation bar right below The Striped Umbrella banner.

2. **Select the navigation bar (About Us - Spa - Cafe), delete it, click the** Images list arrow **on the Insert panel, then click** Navigation Bar
   The Insert Navigation Bar dialog box opens. You use this dialog box to name each element and assign graphics for each element's four states.

3. **Type** home **in the Element name text box, click the** Insert list arrow **at the bottom of the dialog box, then click** Horizontally, **if necessary, to place the navigation bar horizontally**
   The Element Name is the name that you choose for the image that will appear on the navigation bar. The home link will have two appearances: one for the Up image state, and a different one for the Over image, Down image, and Over while down image states.

TROUBLE

Click Yes when you are asked if you want to replace the existing Down image files in the Adobe Dreamweaver CS4 dialog box. You can also copy the first instance of the down image and paste it into the next two text boxes to prevent this dialog box from opening.

4. **Using Figure F-11 as a reference, click each** Browse button **next to the Up image, Over image, Down image, and Over while down image text boxes, click the drive and folder where your Unit F Data Files are stored, double-click the** assets **folder, then double-click the filenames shown in Figure F-11**
   These images were created in Adobe Photoshop. To insert a navigation bar in Dreamweaver, you must create your own images before you can begin. Next, you need to link the home element to The Striped Umbrella home page, which is named index.html.

5. **Type** Link to home page **as the alternate text, as shown in Figure F-11**

6. **Type** index.html **in the When clicked, Go to URL text box, as shown in Figure F-11, make sure the Use tables option is checked**
   You can also use the Browse button to link to the index.html file in the root folder.

TROUBLE

Mac users may not see the Add or Remove item buttons in the Modify Navigation Bar dialog box. If this happens, use Code view to edit the navigation bar by copying the code for an existing button, then pasting and modifying it to add an additional button.

7. **Click the** Add item button ⊞, **then repeat Steps 3 through 6 to add another element to the navigation bar that will link to the about_us page, using the settings shown in Figure F-12**
   You use the Add item button ⊞ to add a new navigation element to the navigation bar, and the Remove item button ⊟ to delete a selected navigation element from the navigation bar.

8. **Click** OK, **then save your work**
   The first two elements of your navigation bar appear on the spa page.

FIGURE F-11: Insert Navigation Bar dialog box

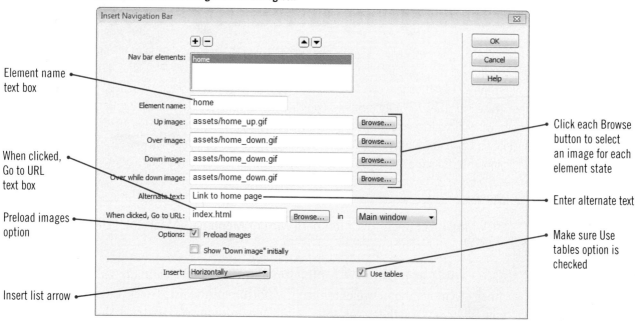

Element name text box

When clicked, Go to URL text box

Preload images option

Insert list arrow

Click each Browse button to select an image for each element state

Enter alternate text

Make sure Use tables option is checked

FIGURE F-12: Add elements to a navigation bar

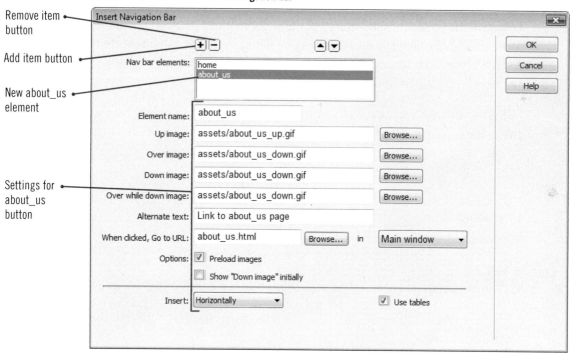

Remove item button

Add item button

New about_us element

Settings for about_us button

Creating buttons for navigation bars

If you design a navigation bar that uses images, you will either have to locate or create buttons to use for each state. Some buttons are made from images, but most buttons incorporate text that has been converted to an image. To design a text-based button, use a program such as Adobe Photoshop to create a file that is the size of the button you need. Determine the width by deciding how wide you want the navigation bar, then divide by the number of buttons that

will be next to it. Next, determine the height of each button. (In The Striped Umbrella Web site, the buttons are 120 pixels wide and 24 pixels tall.) Next, type the text for each button and set the button background color. Be very careful to place the text exactly the same way in each button, so the buttons will be uniform. Modify the first button to create the other buttons. You can save your button files as .gifs, .jpegs, or .pngs.

Modifying a Navigation Bar

After you create a navigation bar, you can modify it using the Modify Navigation Bar dialog box. Modifying a navigation bar allows you to customize its appearance on various Web pages. For example, if you are editing the spa Web page, you can change the image for the services' element's Up image state to the image used for the Down image state (which is a different color). This method acts as a visual clue to remind viewers which page or section of a Web site they are viewing. It also allows you to place the same navigation bar on all pages in a Web site and customize it for each page. **▓▓▓▓** You finish creating the navigation bar, then modify the spa element by changing the Up image state to the Down image state.

STEPS

QUICK TIP

You don't have to select the navigation bar to modify it.

1. **Click** Modify **on the Application bar (Win) or Menu bar (Mac), then click** Navigation Bar

   The Modify Navigation Bar dialog box opens.

QUICK TIP

To rearrange the order of the elements while the Modify Navigation Bar dialog box is open, select the element you want to move, then click the up ▲ or down ▼ arrow in the Modify Navigation Bar dialog box to move the element backward or forward. If the dialog box is closed, you can drag any of the navigation bar images in Design view to rearrange them.

2. **Click the** Add item button ⊞ **at the top of the Modify Navigation Bar dialog box, click the** ▼ **to move the new element to the bottom of the list, select the default element name if necessary, then type** cafe **in the Element name text box, as shown in the Cafe section of Figure F-13**

   A new element is inserted below the last element in the list. If a dialog box asks if you want to overwrite a selected file, click Yes. Macintosh users refer to page 136, step 7 if you don't see the Add item and Remove item buttons.

3. **Using the three sections in Figure F-13 as a guide, finish the cafe element and create two more elements called** spa **and** activities **by filling in the four image state text boxes, the alternate text boxes, and the When clicked, Go to URL text boxes**

   You are now ready to modify the spa element.

4. **With the Modify Navigation Bar dialog box open, click** spa **in the Nav bar elements text box, then click the** Show "Down image" initially check box **to select it, as shown in Figure F-14**

   An asterisk appears next to spa in the Nav Bar Elements text box, indicating that this element will initially appear in the Down image state.

TROUBLE

If you see spaces between each navigation bar element when you preview the page in your browser, return to Dreamweaver, select the home button, press the right arrow key, then press delete. Repeat these steps for each of the next three buttons.

5. **Click** OK **to close the dialog box, click anywhere on the page to deselect the text, then save the file**

   The Up image state of the spa element displays the pink graphic normally used for the Down image state of the navigation bar elements. This "trick" reminds viewers which page of a Web site they are currently viewing.

6. **Preview the page in your browser, allowing blocked content to be displayed if necessary**

7. **Click each button in the navigation bar, click the** Back button **to return to the spa page, then close the browser**

   The cafe page is still blank. You will add content to this page in Unit G. You will copy the navigation bar to the rest of the pages in the site that have content in the next lesson. When you return to the spa page, it loads with the spa element in the Down image state. As you place your mouse over each of the other elements, they go to their Down state.

Design Matters

Creating navigation bars

Using the Dreamweaver Insert Navigation Bar program feature is only one way to create a navigation bar. Other ways include creating image maps, which you will learn about later in this unit; creating interactive navigation bars using the Adobe Flash program; creating simple tables with either text, images, or a combination of the two placed in the table cells; or by using a Cascading Style Sheet.

FIGURE F-13: Creating three navigation elements

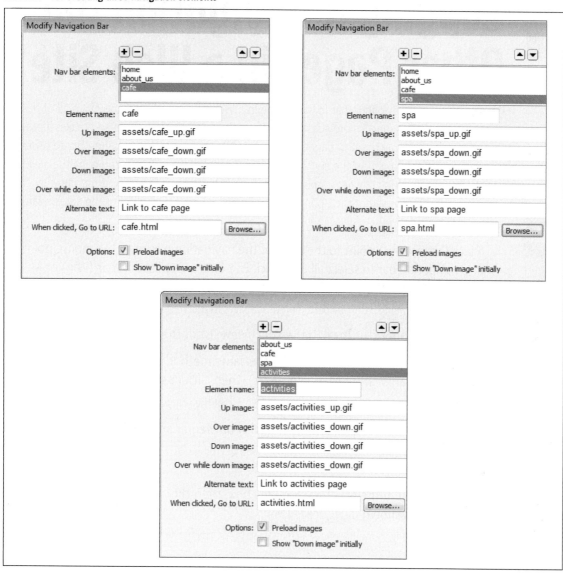

FIGURE F-14: The Modify Navigation Bar dialog box

Asterisk indicates element is shown in "Down image" initially

Show "Down image" initially selected

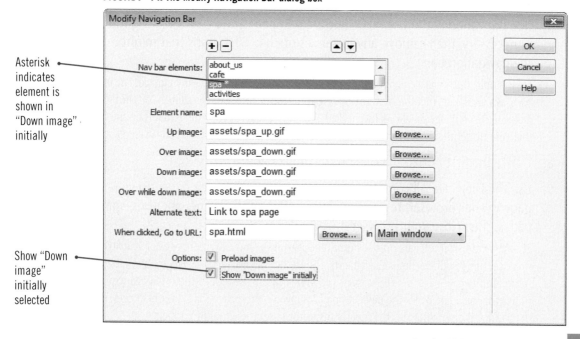

Copying a Navigation Bar to Other Pages in a Web Site

When you create a navigation bar for one page in a Web site, you should copy it to all of the other main pages in the site. This practice provides continuity in the navigation structure and makes it easy for viewers to navigate comfortably through pages in your site. After copying the navigation bar to other pages, you can modify it further to reflect the content of the individual pages. ■■■■■ You copy the navigation bar to the about_us, cafe, and activities pages in The Striped Umbrella Web site, and modify it by changing the navigation bar elements from the Up image state to the Down image state for the appropriate pages.

STEPS

QUICK TIP

You can also use the [Shift]-click method to select the navigation bar, but be careful to select only the navigation bar.

1. **Place the insertion point to the right of the navigation bar, drag the mouse pointer over the navigation bar to select all of it, click Edit on the Application bar (Win) or Menu bar (Mac), then click Copy**

   The navigation bar can now be pasted on other pages in the Web site.

2. **Double-click about_us.html in the Local View list of the Files panel**

TROUBLE

If you have trouble with the alignment and spacing between the banner and the navigation bar, click beside the banner and set the Format to None in the Property inspector or try copying both and pasting the banner and navigation bar together.

3. **Select the current navigation bar by the same method used in Step 1, click Edit on the Application bar (Win) or Menu bar (Mac), then click Paste**

   The new navigation bar appears on the page in place of the previous one.

4. **Click Modify on the Application bar (Win) or Menu bar (Mac), then click Navigation Bar**

   The Modify Navigation Bar dialog box opens. You need to set the Down image state to show initially when the about_us page opens.

5. **Click about_us in the Nav bar elements box, then click the Show "Down image" initially check box, as shown in Figure F-15**

   Now you are ready to modify the spa element so it appears in the Up image state.

6. **Click spa in the Nav bar elements box, click the Show "Down image" initially check box to remove the check mark, as shown in Figure F-16, then click OK**

QUICK TIP

When you work on multiple open pages, use the filename tabs at the top of the Document toolbar to move quickly between pages.

7. **Paste the navigation bar on the activities and index pages, replacing the existing navigation bars, modify the Up image and Down image states for the navigation bar elements, as necessary, then remove any instances of <h4></h4> tags that might remain around the navigation bars**

   For example, the home element on the navigation bar should show the Down image state initially on the index page, as a visual clue that the viewer is looking at the index page. The spa element on the index page should not have the Down image state initially checked. A copy of the navigation bar remains on the Clipboard, meaning that you can continue pasting it without copying it each time you want to paste it onto a new page.

8. **Delete the first horizontal rule on the index page**

QUICK TIP

If possible, view the page at a high resolution to make sure that the navigation bar does not start at the right side of the banner, rather than under it. If it does, enter a line break to force it under the banner.

9. **Use the File, Save All command to save your work on each page, preview the current page in your browser, test the navigation bar on the home, about us, spa, and activities pages, then close your browser**

   The navigation bar appears on the home, about us, spa, and activities pages of The Striped Umbrella Web site. Feel free to adjust the page elements as necessary so no page appears to "jump" when you link to it. Although the cafe page is not designed yet, you see that the link to the cafe page works correctly. (If you notice that on some pages the navigation bar is lower on the page than on other pages, click to the right of the banner, then use the HTML Property inspector to set the Format to none.)

FIGURE F-15: Changing settings for the about_us element

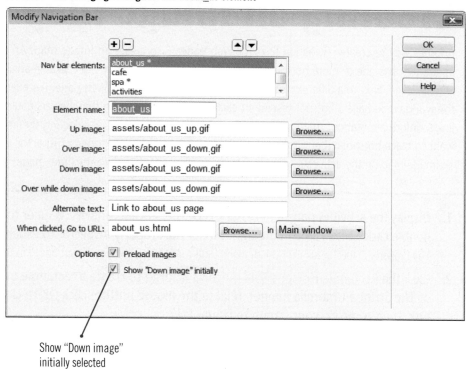

Show "Down image"
initially selected

FIGURE F-16: Changing settings for the spa element

Only one element
should have the
Show "Down
image" initially
check box
selected

Show "Down
image" initially
check box
deselected

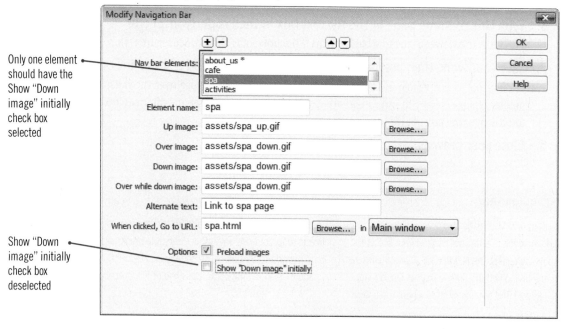

Creating an Image Map

Another way to create navigation links for Web pages is to create an image map. An **image map** is an image that has one or more hotspots placed on top of it. A **hotspot** is a clickable area on an image that, when clicked, links to a different location on the page or to another Web page. For example, a map of the the world could have a hotspot placed on each individual country so that viewers could click a country to link to information about that country. You can create hotspots by first selecting the image on which you want to place hotspots, then using one of the hotspot tools in the Property inspector. ![tools] You create an image map on the activities page to provide another way to link to the index page.

STEPS

1. **Display the activities page if necessary, click** The Striped Umbrella banner **to select it, then double-click a blank area in the right side of the Property inspector to expand it, if necessary**

   The Property inspector displays the drawing tools for creating hotspots on an image in the lower-left corner.

> **TROUBLE**
> If you don't see the blue box, click View, point to Visual Aids, then click Image Maps to select it.

2. **Click the** Rectangle Hotspot Tool button ▢**, drag to create a rectangle over the left side of The Striped Umbrella banner, release the mouse button, click** OK **to close the dialog box, then compare your screen to Figure F-17**

   A shaded blue box appears over the area that you outlined. This blue box is the hotspot. The dialog box reminds you to add alternate text to the hotspot.

3. **Drag the** Point to File icon ⊕ **in the Property inspector to** index.html **in the Files panel**

   This links the hotspot to the index.html file. When the hotspot is clicked, the index file opens.

> **TROUBLE**
> If you don't see the Map text box in the Property inspector, click the image map object to select it.

4. **Select** Map **in the Map text box, then type** home **in the Map text box in the Property inspector**

   Each image map should have a unique name, especially if a page contains more than one image map.

5. **Click the** Target list arrow **in the Property inspector, then click** _self

   When the hotspot is clicked, the home page opens in the same window.

6. **Type** Link to home page **in the Alt text box in the Property inspector**

   This gives the viewer a clue to what happens if the hotspot is clicked. See Figure F-18.

> **TROUBLE**
> Macintosh users may not see alternate text.

7. **Save your work, then preview the page in your browser and test the link on the image map**

   The hotspot is not visible in the browser, but if you place the mouse over the hotspot, you will see the pointer change to 🖑, to indicate a link is present, and you will see the alternate text. You need to click directly over the hotspot for the alternate text to appear.

8. **Close your browser**

Troubleshooting image maps

If you create an image map on a Web page and notice white space around the image map when you preview the page in your browser, you can remove the space by editing the HTML code. Place the insertion point right before the image with the image map in Design view. Next, switch to Code view and find the line of code where the image

map code begins, with the code for the image associated with the image map. Remove any unnecessary line breaks at the end of the lines of code so that all of the code associated with the image and the image map share one continuous line (it will probably be wrapped).

For instance, if you see code that looks like this:

```
<img src="assets/striped_umbrella_banner.gif" alt="The Striped Umbrella banner" width="735" height="125" border="0" usemap="#home" />
<map name="home" id="home"><area shape="rect" coords="8,25,237,109" href="index.html" target="_self" alt="Link to home page" />
</map>
```

Remove all line breaks so it looks like this:

```
<img src="assets/striped_umbrella_banner.gif" alt="The Striped Umbrella banner" width="735" height="125" border="0" usemap="#home" />
<map name="home" id="home"><area shape="rect" coords="8,25,237,109" href="index.html" target="_self" alt="Link to home page" /></map>
```

FIGURE F-17: Drawing a Rectangle hotspot on The Striped Umbrella banner

Outline of hotspot

Rectangle Hotspot tool

Pointer Hotspot tool

Circle Hotspot tool

Polygon Hotspot tool

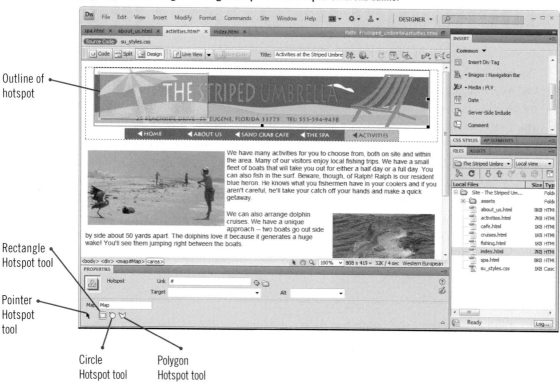

FIGURE F-18: Adding a link, a target, and alternate text to a hotspot

Rectangle Hotspot tool

Target text box

Link text box

Alt text box

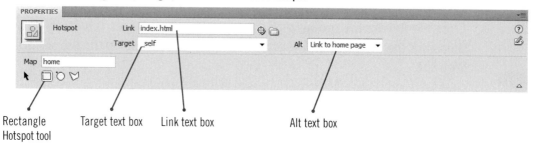

Design Matters

Creating and modifying hotspots

The hotspot tools in Dreamweaver make creating image maps a snap. In addition to the Rectangle Hotspot tool, there is a circle tool and a polygon tool. These tools can be used to create any shape hotspot that you need. For instance, on a map of the United States, you can draw an outline around each state with the polygon tool. You can then make each state "clickable." Hotspots can be easily changed and rearranged on the image. Use the Pointer Hotspot tool to select the hotspot you would like to edit. You can drag one of the hotspot selector handles to change the size or shape of a

hotspot. You can also move the hotspot by dragging it to a new position on the image. It is a good idea to limit the number of complex or irregularly shaped hotspots in an image because the code can become too lengthy for the page to download in a reasonable amount of time. You should also make the hotspot boundaries a little larger than they need to be to cover the area you want to set as a link. This allows a little leeway for viewers when they place their mouse over the hotspot by creating a larger target area for them.

Managing Web Site Links

As your Web site grows, so will the number of links in it. Checking links to make sure they work is a crucial and ongoing task that you should perform regularly. The Check Links Sitewide feature is a helpful tool for managing your links. It checks your entire Web site for the total number of links and for the number of links that are OK, external, or broken, and then displays the information in the Link Checker panel. The Link Checker panel also provides a list of all the files used in a Web site, including those that are **orphaned files**, files that are not linked to any pages in the Web site. **Broken links** are links that cannot find their destination. When you find broken internal links (linking to files within the Web site), you should carefully check the code entered in the Link text box for errors. You can either use the Browse for File icon in the Link Checker panel to correct the link, or type the correction in the Link text box in the Property inspector. You check broken external links (links to files outside the Web site) by testing the links in your browser. Due to the volatility of the Web, it is important to check external links routinely as Web sites go up, go down, and change addresses. ▓▓▓▓ You check The Striped Umbrella Web site for any broken links or orphaned files.

STEPS

TROUBLE

If you show broken links, click Site, point to Advanced, then click Recreate Site Cache.

1. **Click Site on the Application bar (Win) or Menu bar (Mac), then click Check Links Sitewide**

   The Link Checker panel in the Results Tab group opens. By default, the Link Checker panel initially displays any broken internal links found in the Web site. The Striped Umbrella Web site has no broken links, as shown in Figure F-19.

2. **Click the Show list arrow in the Link Checker panel, then click External Links**

   See Figure F-20. There are three external links: two to external Web sites and one email link. You may have to float the Results Tab group to be able to see all of the links without scrolling.

QUICK TIP

If you show orphaned files, click the Site menu, point to Advanced, click Recreate Site Cache, then run the report again.

3. **Click the Show list arrow, then click Orphaned Files**

   The Link Checker shows no orphaned files for the Web site. See Figure F-21.

4. **Close the Results Tab group, click the Assets tab on the Files Tab group if necessary, then click the URLs button ▨ on the Assets panel to display the list of links in the Web site**

   The Assets panel displays the external links used in the Web site. See Figure F-22.

QUICK TIP

If you don't see the links, click the Refresh button ⟳.

5. **Close any open files and Exit (Win) or Quit (Mac) Dreamweaver**

   You now see how easy it is to manage your Web site links in Dreamweaver.

Design Matters

Designing for easy navigation

As you work on the navigation structure for a Web site, you should try to limit the number of internal links on each page. Too many links may confuse visitors to your Web site. Another thought is to design links so that viewers can reach the information they seek within three clicks. Otherwise viewers may become discouraged or lost in the site.

You should also provide visual clues on each page to let viewers know where they are, much like a "You are here" marker on a store directory at the mall, or a bread crumbs trail. A **bread crumbs trail** is a list of links that provides a path from the initial page you opened in a Web site to the page that you are currently viewing.

FIGURE F-19: Link Checker displaying no broken internal links

Show list arrow

No broken links listed

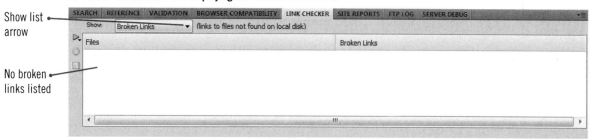

FIGURE F-20: Link Checker displaying external links

External links listed

FIGURE F-21: Link Checker displaying no orphaned files

No orphaned files listed

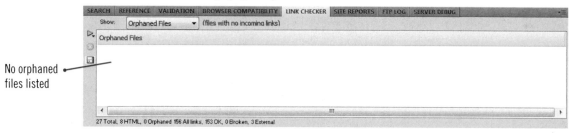

FIGURE F-22 Assets panel displaying links

List of Web site links

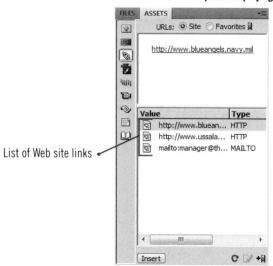

Practice

▼ CONCEPTS REVIEW

Label each element in the Dreamweaver window shown in Figure F-23.

FIGURE F-23

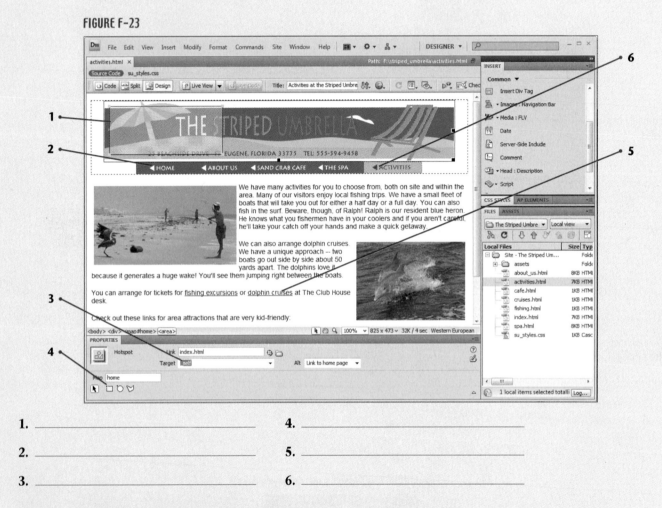

1. _____   4. _____

2. _____   5. _____

3. _____   6. _____

Match each of the following terms with the statement that best describes its function.

7. **Internal links**
8. **External links**
9. **Broken links**
10. **Named anchor**
11. **Navigation bar**
12. **Rollover**
13. **Image map**
14. **Hotspot**
15. **Orphaned file**

a. Links that do not work correctly

b. A set of text or image links used to navigate between pages of a Web site

c. An image with hotspots on it

d. Links to pages within the Web site

e. Clickable area on an image that serves as a link

f. The effect of an image changing its appearance when the mouse pointer is positioned over it

g. A specific location on a Web page, represented by a special icon, that will fully display in the browser window when a user clicks the link tagged to it

h. A file that is not linked to any pages in a Web site

i. Links to pages outside the Web site

Select the best answer from the following list of choices.

16. Which type of path begins with a forward slash?

a. Document-relative   c. Absolute

b. Root-relative   d. Image-relative

17. Which icon in the Property inspector do you use to connect an internal link to a named anchor?

a. Point to File   c. Anchor to File

b. Point to Anchor   d. Point to Named Anchor

18. The four possible states of an element in a navigation bar are:

a. Up image, Over image, Down image, Under image.

b. Up image, Over image, Down image, Over while down image.

c. Up image, Over image, Down image, Up while down image.

d. Up image, Over image, Down image, Up while under image.

19. To see all links in a Web site, you click which icon on the Assets panel?

a. Links   c. URLs

b. Paths   d. Anchors

20. Which dialog box shows you a list of orphaned files?

a. Orphaned Files   c. Check Links Sitewide

b. Link Checker   d. Assets

▼ SKILLS REVIEW

Important: *If you did not create this Web site in Unit B and maintain it during the preceding units, you will need to create a root folder for this Web site and define the Web site using files your instructor will provide. See the "Read This Before You Begin" section for more detailed instructions.*

1. Create an external link.

a. Start Dreamweaver and open the blooms & bulbs Web site.

b. Open dwf_2.html from the drive and folder where your Unit F Data Files are stored, save it as **newsletter.html** in the blooms root folder, replacing the existing file and not updating links, then close dwf_2.html.

c. Apply the headings style to the heading "Gardening Matters," the seasons style to the five subheadings on the page, and the body_text style to the rest of the text on the page.

d. Scroll to the bottom of the page and link the National Gardening Association text to **http://www.garden.org**.

e. Link the Better Homes and Gardens Gardening Home Page text to **http://bhg.com/gardening**.

f. Link the Southern Living Home Page text to **http://www.southernliving.com/southern**.

g. Save the file and preview it in your browser.

h. Test the links to make sure they all work correctly, then close the browser.

2. Create an internal link.

a. Select the text "gardening tips" in the last sentence in the Gardening Issues paragraph.

b. Use the Point to File icon to link the text to the tips.html page.

c. Save the file and test the link in your browser, then close the browser.

3. Insert a named anchor.

a. Show Invisible Elements if necessary.

b. Insert a named anchor in front of the Grass subheading, then name it **grass**.

c. Insert a named anchor in front of the Plants subheading, then name it **plants**.

d. Insert a named anchor in front of the Trees subheading, then name it **trees**.

e. Save the file.

4. Create an internal link to a named anchor.

   a. Using the Point to File icon on the Property inspector, create a link from the word grass in the Gardening Issues paragraph to the grass named anchor.

   b. Create a link from the word trees in the Gardening Issues paragraph to the trees named anchor.

   c. Create a link from the word plants in the Gardening Issues paragraph to the plants named anchor.

   d. Save the file and test the links in your browser.

5. Create a navigation bar with images.

   a. Using the Insert bar, create a navigation bar at the top of the newsletter page under the banner.

   b. Type **home** as the first element name, and use the b_home_up.jpg file for the Up image state and the b_home_down.jpg file for the three remaining states. These files are in the drive and folder where your Unit F Data Files are stored.

   c. Add the alternate text **Link to home page**.

   d. Set the index.html file as the link for the home element.

   e. Create a new element named **plants**, and use the b_plants_up.jpg file for the Up image state and the b_plants_down.jpg file for the remaining three states from your Unit F Data Files folder.

   f. Add the alternate text **Link to plants page**.

   g. Set the plants.html file as the link for the plants element.

6. Modify a navigation bar.

   a. Create a new element named **tips**, and use the b_tips_up.jpg file for the Up image state and the b_tips_down.jpg file from your Unit F Data Files folder for the remaining three states.

   b. Add the alternate text **Link to tips page**.

   c. Set the tips.html file as the link for the tips element.

   d. Create a new element named **classes** and use the b_classes_up.jpg file for the Up image state and the b_classes_down.jpg file from your Unit F Data Files folder for the remaining three states.

   e. Add the alternate text **Link to classes page**.

   f. Set the classes.html file as the link for the classes element.

   g. Create a new element named **newsletter**, and use the b_newsletter_up.jpg file for the Up image state and the b_newsletter_down.jpg file (both from your Unit F Data files folder) for the remaining three states.

   h. Add the alternate text **Link to newsletter page**.

   i. Set the newsletter.html file as the link for the newsletter element, then close the Insert Navigation Bar dialog box.

   j. Modify the navigation bar to Show "Down image" initially for the newsletter element in the Modify Navigation Bar dialog box.

   k. Save the page and test the links in your browser, then close the browser. (The classes page will be a blank page.)

7. Copy a navigation bar to other pages in a Web site.

   a. Select and copy the navigation bar.

   b. Open the home page, place the insertion point to the left of the banner, then use the HTML Property inspector to set the Format to None.

   c. Delete the current navigation bar and paste the new navigation bar on the home page under the banner. (*Hint*: There should only be a line break between the banner and the navigation bar.)

   d. Modify the newsletter element on the navigation bar so it does not show the Down image state initially.

   e. Modify the home element on the navigation bar so that it shows the Down image state initially.

   f. Save the page and test the links in your browser, then close the browser.

   g. Copy the navigation bar to the plants page and the tips page, making the necessary modifications.

8. Create an image map.

   a. On the newsletter page, create a rectangle hotspot over the words "blooms & bulbs" on the the blooms & bulbs banner. (If you want to remove space between the banner and the navigation bar, remove unnecessary line breaks in the image map code.)

   b. Name the image map **home** and link it to the home page.

   c. Set the target as _top.

   d. Enter the alternate text **Link to home page**.

   e. Save all pages, then preview the newsletter page in the browser, testing all links. Refer to Figure F-24 to check your work.

9. Manage Web site links.

   a. Use the Check Links Sitewide command to view broken links, external links, and orphaned files.

   b. Refresh the Site list in the Files panel if you see broken links or orphaned files. If you see any, locate them and analyze the problem.

   c. View the external links in the Assets panel. Exit (Win) or Quit (Mac) Dreamweaver.

FIGURE F-24

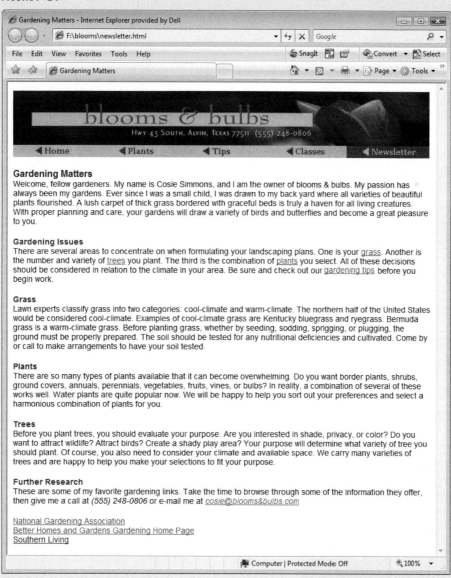

Important: *If you did not create the following Web sites in Unit B and maintain them during the preceding units, you must create a root folder for the Web sites in the following exercises and define the Web sites using files your instructor will provide. See the "Read This Before You Begin" section for more detailed instructions.*

▼ INDEPENDENT CHALLENGE 1

You have been hired to create a Web site for a river expedition company named Rapids Transit, located on the Buffalo River in Gilbert, Arkansas. In addition to renting canoes, kayaks, and rafts, they have lodging available for overnight stays. River guides are available to accompany clients on float trips. The clients range from high school and college students to families to vacationing professionals. The owner's name is Mike Andrew. Mike has asked you to create a new Web page that lists helpful links for his customers. Refer to Figure F-25 as you work on this page.

a. Start Dreamweaver and open the Rapids Transit Web site.

b. Open dwf_3.html in the drive and folder where your Unit F Data Files are stored, then save it as **before.html**, replacing the existing file and without updating the links. You need to save the buffalo_fall.gif file (the photo) in the assets folder of the Rapids Transit Web site and correct the path for the banner if necessary.

c. Close the file dwf_3.html.

d. Create the following links:

Buffalo National River	http://www.nps.gov/buff/
Arkansas, the Natural State	http://www.arkansas.com/
Buffalo River Floater's Guide	http://www.ozarkmtns.com/buffalo/index.asp

e. Attach the style sheet for the Web site and apply a style to all text on the page.

f. Design a navigation bar on the before.html page, using either text or images. The navigation bar should include the following text: Home, Our Guides, Rentals, Lodging, and Before You Go. Link the text to the appropriate files in your Rapids Transit site. Create a new rule to apply to the navigation bar links. If you decide to use images for the navigation bar, you must create your own files.

g. Copy the completed navigation bar to the guides, index, and lodging pages. Preview each page to make sure the navigation bar doesn't appear to "jump," or shift position, when you move from page to page. (*Hint*: It will probably be easier to copy the navigation bar and banner, then paste them together onto each of the other pages. Delete the original navigation bars and banners before you paste the new ones. Also remember to remove any remaining <p></p> and <h4></h4> tags around the banner by setting the Format to None.)

h. Save your work and test all links in your browser.

i. Exit your browser, then close all files and Dreamweaver.

FIGURE F-25

▼ INDEPENDENT CHALLENGE 2

Your company is designing a new Web site for TripSmart, a travel outfitter. TripSmart specializes in travel products and services. In addition to selling travel products, such as luggage and accessories, they sponsor trips and offer travel advice. Their clients range from college students to families to vacationing professionals. You are now ready to work on the services page. The services will include several helpful links for their clients to use in planning trips.

a. Start Dreamweaver and open the TripSmart site.

b. Open the file dwf_4.html from the drive and folder where your Unit F Data Files are stored and save it as **services.html** in the tripsmart root folder, replacing the existing file but not updating the links, then close dwf_4.html.

c. Apply the heading style from the attached style sheet to the four paragraph headings and apply the body_text style to the rest of the text on the page. (*Hint:* the Helpful Hints in Travel Planning is the fourth paragraph heading, but is not shown in the figure.)

d. Create the following links:
CNN Travel Channel:
http://www.cnn.com/TRAVEL
US Department of State:
http://travel.state.gov
MapQuest: http://www.mapquest.com
Rand McNally:
http://www.randmcnally.com
AccuWeather:
http://www.accuweather.com
The Weather Channel:
http://www.weather.com

e. Create named anchors called **reservations**, **outfitters**, **tours**, and **links** in front of the respective headings on the page, then link each named anchor to "Reservations", "Travel Outfitters", "Escorted Tours", and "Helpful Links in Travel Planning" in the first paragraph.

f. Create a navigation bar with either text or images that links to the home, destinations, newsletter, services, and catalog pages, replacing any existing navigation bars. If you decide to use image links you must create the supporting files. If you use text links, create a new style and apply it to the navigation bar.

FIGURE F-26

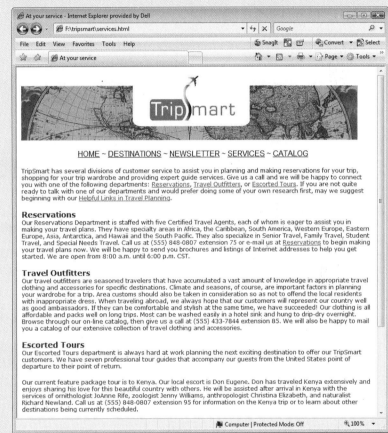

g. Indent the navigation bar using three text indents.

h. Copy the navigation bar to the other completed pages in the Web site: index, newsletter, and destinations pages, replacing any existing navigation bars. (*Hint*: It will probably be easier to copy the navigation bar and banner, then paste them together onto each of the other pages. Delete the original navigation bars and banners before you paste the new ones.)

i. Save any unsaved changes, then preview the services page in the browser, as shown in Figure F-26, and test all links.

j. Use the Link Checker to check for broken links and orphaned files.

k. Exit your browser, then close all files and exit Dreamweaver.

▼ INDEPENDENT CHALLENGE 3

Dr. Joan Sullivent's patients often ask her questions about the current treatment protocol for Parkinson's disease, a debilitating neurological disease. She would like to post some helpful links in her clinic Web site to provide information for her patients. She begins her research at the National Institutes of Health Web site.

a. Connect to the Internet and go to the National Institutes of Health Web site at www.nih.gov.

b. What do you like or dislike about the navigation links?

c. Note the placement and appearance of the navigation bar. Does it use text, images, or a combination of the two to form the links?

d. Using your favorite search engine, locate at least five helpful links that Dr. Sullivent should consider for her site, including the National Institutes of Health pictured in Figure F-27. Use paper or your word processor to record your links.

FIGURE F-27

National Institutes of Health—www.nih.gov

▼ INDEPENDENT CHALLENGE 4

This assignment will continue to build on the personal Web site that you created in Unit B. In Unit C you created and developed your index page. In Unit D you added a page with either an ordered or an unordered list, and a CSS Style Sheet with a minimum of two styles. In Unit E you added a page that included at least two graphics. In this lesson, you work with one of the other pages in your Web site.

   a. Consult your storyboard and decide which page you would like to develop in this lesson.

   b. Create content for this page and format the text attractively on the page using styles.

   c. Add at least three external links to this page.

   d. Think about a creative use for an image map, and add it to the page.

   e. Add at least one named anchor and link to it.

   f. Design a navigation bar linking to the main pages of your Web site and copy it to all of the main pages.

   g. Save the file and preview the page in the browser.

After you are satisfied with your work, verify the following:

   a. Each completed page has a page title.

   b. All links work correctly.

   c. The completed pages show well using a screen resolution of 1024×768.

   d. All images are properly set showing a path to the Web site assets folder.

   e. All images have alternate text and are legal for you to use.

   f. The Link Checker shows no broken links or orphaned files. If there are orphaned files, note your plan to link them.

▼ VISUAL WORKSHOP

You are continuing your work on the Carolyne's Creations Web site that you started in Unit B and developed in subsequent units. Chef Carolyne has asked you to create pages describing her cooking classes offered every month. Use the files dwf_5.html to replace the classes.html page, dwf_6.html to create a new children.html page, and dwf_7.html to create a new adults.html page. (Remember not to update the links when prompted.) Copy all new images, including the new banner, to the assets folder in the Web site. Last, create an image map at the bottom of the banner on the classes page with hotspots for each link and copy it to all pages in the Web site, replacing all existing navigation bars. Create an e-mail link on the classes page using the text "Sign me up!" and carolyne@carolynescreations.com for the link. Create links in the last sentence to the adults and childrens' pages, as shown in Figure F-28. Refer to Figures F-28, F-29, and F-30 as you complete this project. Check that each completed page uses styles from the cc_styles.css file and attach and apply these styles if you find pages without styles. (*Hint*: Remember to remove any formatting from the banners to prevent any pages from appearing to "jump.")

FIGURE F-28

Cooking Classes are fun!

Chef Carolyne loves to offer a fun and relaxing cooking school each month in her newly refurbished kitchen. She teaches an adult class on the fourth Saturday of each month from 6:00 to 8:00 pm. Each class will learn to cook a complete dinner and then enjoy the meal at the end of the class with a wonderful wine pairing. This is a great chance to get together with friends for a fun evening.

Chef Caroline also teaches a children's class on the second Tuesday of each month from 4:00 to 5:30 pm. Our young chefs will learn to cook two dishes that will accompany a full meal served at 5:30 pm. Kids aged 5–8 years accompanied by an adult are welcome. We also host small birthday parties where we put the guests to work baking and decorating the cake! Call for times and prices.

We offer several special adult classes throughout the year. The Valentine Chocolate Extravaganza is a particular favorite. You will learn to dip strawberries, make truffles, and bake a sinful Triple Chocolate Dare You Torte. We also host the Not So Traditional Thanksgiving class and the Super Bowl Snacks class each year with rave reviews. Watch the Web site for details!

Prices are $40.00 for each adult class and $15.00 for each children's class. Sign up for classes by calling 555-963-8271 or by emailing us: Sign me up!

See what's cooking this month for the adults' class and children's class.

FIGURE F-29

Adult Cooking Class for March: Chinese Cuisine

The class in March will be cooking several traditional Chinese dishes: Peking dumplings, wonton soup, fried rice, Chinese vegetables, and shrimp with lobster sauce. For dessert: banana spring rolls.

This looks easier than it is! Chef Carolyne is demonstrating the first steps in making Chinese dumplings, known as *jiaozi* (pronounced geeow dz). Notice that she is using a traditional wooden rolling pin to roll out the dough. These dumplings were stuffed with pork and then steamed, although other popular fillings are made with chicken and leeks or vegetables with spiced tofu and cellophane noodles. Dumplings can be steamed, boiled, or fried, and have unique names depending on the preparation method.

FIGURE F-30

Children's Cooking Class for March: Oven Chicken Fingers, Chocolate Chip Cookies

This month we will be baking oven chicken fingers that are dipped in a milk and egg mixture, then coated with breadcrumbs. The chocolate chip cookies are based on a famous recipe that includes chocolate chips, candy pieces, oatmeal, and pecans. Yummy! We will be learning some of the basics like how to cream butter and crack eggs without dropping shells into the batter.

We will provide French fries, green beans, fruit salad, and a beverage to accompany the chicken fingers.

Using CSS to Lay Out Pages

You have learned how to position elements on a Web page using alignment and paragraph settings. These settings let you create simple Web pages, but they limit your page layout choices. The best way to position page elements is to use Cascading Style Sheets, or CSS page layouts. You have already learned to use CSS to format individual page elements. Now you will learn to use CSS to lay out pages. This method has become the preferred method of page layout. With CSS page layouts, you use blocks of content formatted with CSS styles to place information on Web pages. In this unit, you will use a predefined CSS page layout with div tags to redesign the index page for The Striped Umbrella Web site.

OBJECTIVES

Understand CSS layouts

Create a page using CSS layouts

Add content to CSS layout blocks

Edit content in CSS layout blocks

Edit CSS layout properties

Insert an AP div

Position and size an AP element

Add content to an AP element

Use the AP Elements panel

Understanding CSS Layouts

Web pages built with Cascading Style Sheets use HTML div tags to place and format page content. **HTML div tags** are pieces of code that set the appearance and position of blocks of Web page content. Think of div tags as building blocks. To build a Web page with a layout based on CSS, you begin by placing div tags on the page. The div tags set up the framework for "containers" to hold information. Next, you add content to each of the containers created by the div tags. Last, you format the div tags and position them on the page. For beginning designers, the predesigned CSS page layouts that are available with Dreamweaver make creating pages based on CSS easy. You simply choose a predesigned CSS layout, and Dreamweaver places the div tags in the page code. ▓▓▓▓ You spend some time researching how Cascading Style Sheets are used for page layout.

DETAILS

Before using CSS layouts for page layout, you review the following concepts:

- **Using Cascading Style Sheets vs. tables for page layout**

    An alternative to using CSS layouts is to use tables for page layouts. You will learn about using tables to position objects in Unit H. Tables allow you to place content in rows and columns across and down a page. You alter the position of elements inside the table cells by modifying cell dimensions or by merging and splitting cells. Like tables, div tags let you organize and control element placement by creating containers for blocks of information. Unlike tables, however, div tags let you place the content anywhere on the page, giving you more layout flexibility.

- **Using Dreamweaver CSS page layouts**

    Dreamweaver offers 32 predesigned layouts in the New Document dialog box, some of which are shown in Figure G-1. These layouts are a great way to begin learning about how to create page layouts based on CSS. As you select each option, a preview of the layout appears on the right side of the dialog box with a description below it. Once you select a layout, you can modify it to fit your needs. After you are comfortable with using the predesigned layouts, you can move on to using div tags to build your pages from scratch. One of the great advantages of using the predesigned CSS page layouts is that each of these layouts has been tested using different browsers. Some hand-coded CSS layouts do not display correctly with all browsers.

- **Using div tags for other purposes**

    Div tags are used in many ways other than in CSS layouts. For example, when you center an image on a page or inside a table cell, Dreamweaver automatically inserts a div tag in the HTML code, such as <div align="center">. Div tags are also used to designate different colors for blocks of content, text that uses a CSS style, and other properties. Div tags used for page layout are identified by an ID, or name. You can see the ID in the HTML code for the div tag, in the Property inspector when the div tag is selected, and in the CSS Styles panel. In Code view, the code for a div tag named header would be <div id="header">.

- **Using AP div tags**

    One type of div tag is an AP div tag. AP stands for absolutely positioned, so an **AP div tag** has a specified position that doesn't change even in different-sized windows. An AP div tag creates a container called an **AP element**. You create an AP div tag by drawing the container with the Draw AP Div button, as shown in Figure G-2. You can stack AP div tag containers on top of each other to create interesting effects, such as animations. You can also use them to show or hide content on the page by using them with JavaScript behaviors. **JavaScript behaviors** are action scripts that allow you to add dynamic content to your Web pages. **Dynamic content** is content that the user can change by interacting with content on the screen. For example the user might enter a zip code to display a local weather forecast. The code in the JavaScript behavior would direct the AP element with the correct forecast to appear after the user enters the corresponding zip code in a text box.

FIGURE G-1: New Document dialog box

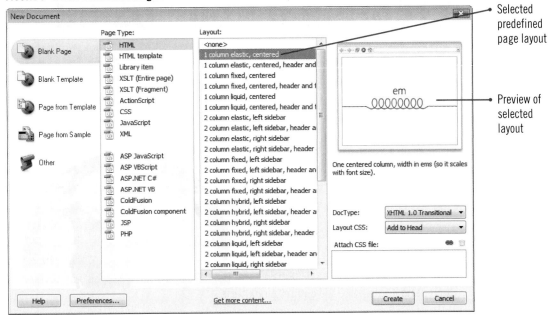

- Selected predefined page layout
- Preview of selected layout

FIGURE G-2: Inserting an AP Div Tag using the Draw AP Div button

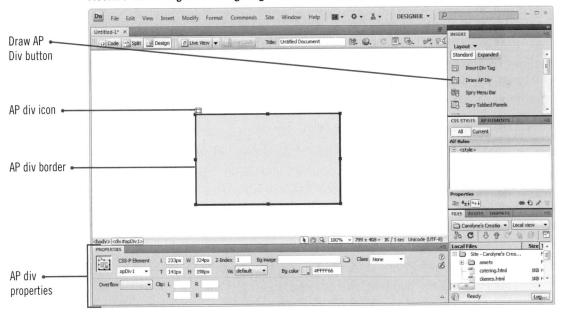

Draw AP Div button

AP div icon

AP div border

AP div properties

Using Dreamweaver sample pages

You can use either the Welcome Screen or the New Document dialog box, shown in Figure G-1, to create several different types of pages. The predesigned CSS page layouts make it easy to design accessible Web pages based on Cascading Style Sheets without expertise in writing HTML code. In the Page from Sample category, CSS Style Sheet and Frameset are options that create pages you can use as starting points to develop framesets and style sheets. **Framesets** are documents that contain the instructions that tell a browser how to lay out a set of frames showing multiple individual documents on a page. It is worth the time to explore each category to understand what is available to you as a designer. Once you have selected a sample page, you can customize it to fit your client's needs and the site design. You can also find a variety of sample pages on the Internet. Some sites offer sample pages free of charge and some offer them for sale. Do a quick search on the Internet and you will find many attractive page options available for download.

Creating a Page Using CSS Layouts

With the predesigned CSS layouts available in Dreamweaver, it is easy to create a page based on Cascading Style Sheets. After you choose a layout for a new page, the page opens with placeholder text displayed in the div tag blocks until you replace it with your own content. Some blocks not only have placeholder text, but also instructional text on how to use or modify that block. Each block has preset styles applied. Some of the font properties may be applied from the attributes in the CSS body style, and some may be from HTML heading styles that have been applied directly to the placeholder text. The properties and values of these styles are displayed in the CSS Styles panel, where you can modify them to fit your needs. The CSS layouts are based on one-, two-, or three-column layouts. Some have sidebars and some have headers or footers. Some are designed to stretch across a browser window, and some have a fixed width. ⬛️🔲 You have decided to redesign the existing Striped Umbrella index page by creating a new page based on a predefined CSS layout, then using it to replace the current index page.

STEPS

1. **Open The Striped Umbrella Web site**

2. **Click File on the Application bar (Win) or Menu bar (Mac), click New, verify that Blank Page is highlighted in the left section, click HTML in the Page Type category if necessary, then click 1 column, fixed, centered, header and footer in the Layout category, as shown in Figure G-3**
    The layout description confirms that this is a fixed layout, measured in pixels.

3. **Click the Attach Style Sheet button ⬛️ in the lower-right corner of the dialog box, then click Browse in the Attach External Style Sheet dialog box**
    The Select Style Sheet File dialog box opens.

4. **Click the su_styles.css file in the Select Style Sheet File dialog box, click OK (Win) or click Choose (Mac), then click OK to close the information box about the document-relative path**
    The links will not be document-relative until you save the page in the Web site.

5. **Verify that the Add as: Link option button is selected in the Attach External Style Sheet dialog box, then click OK**
    The su_styles.css file is attached to the new page, as shown in Figure G-4.

6. **Click Create in the New Document dialog box, open the CSS Styles panel if necessary, then expand the two style sheets: <style> and su_styles.css**
    A new page opens based on the predefined CSS layout with placeholder text, as shown in Figure G-5. It contains one column of centered text, as well as a header and footer. Heading styles have been applied to the placeholder headings. You will replace the placeholder text with content for The Striped Umbrella Web site. There are two style sheets in the CSS Styles panel: the su_styles.css file you imported and the embedded style sheet file that is part of the predefined page layout.

FIGURE G-3: Predefined layout selected for new page

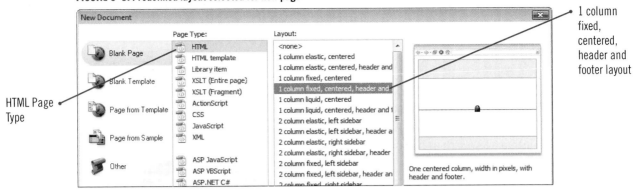

HTML Page Type

1 column fixed, centered, header and footer layout

FIGURE G-4: The su_styles.css file is attached to the new page

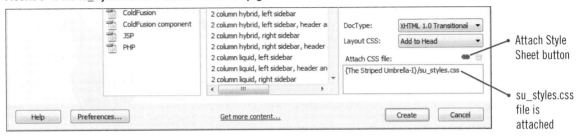

Attach Style Sheet button

su_styles.css file is attached

FIGURE G-5: New page based on CSS layout

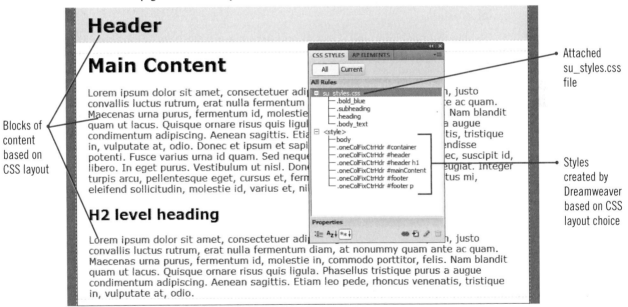

Blocks of content based on CSS layout

Attached su_styles.css file

Styles created by Dreamweaver based on CSS layout choice

Understanding column width options

The predefined CSS layouts are classified in several ways to give you a maximum number of choices for your pages. First, you can choose a layout with one, two, or three columns. Next, you can choose a header at the top of the page, a footer at the bottom of the page, or both. Last, you can choose how the column widths are calculated. An **elastic layout** has columns expressed in ems (a unit of measure in typography). It will scale according to the font sizes used. A **fixed** layout has columns expressed in pixels and will not change sizes when viewed in different window sizes. A **liquid layout** has columns expressed as percents based on the browser window width, so it will change sizes according to the window size. A **hybrid layout** means that the main column is expressed as liquid and the side columns as elastic.

Adding Content to CSS Layout Blocks

A page composed of div tag content containers makes it easy to apply formatting to blocks of information on a Web page. These formats can include colors, container widths, font settings, and alignment settings, to name a few, such as background colors, images, links, tables, and text. The div tags that control CSS blocks also determine the content's position on the page. You may well have developed your page content previously, so you can easily copy it and paste it into the placeholders, replacing existing placeholder text and instructions. You are ready to copy the content from the existing Striped Umbrella index page and place it on the new page, replacing the placeholder content.

STEPS

1. **Open The Striped Umbrella index page and select the paragraph that begins with "Welcome"**

QUICK TIP
Press [Ctrl][Tab] to switch between two open pages.

2. **Copy the selected text, then switch to the new, unsaved page**

3. **Select the content between the Header and Footer in the main section of the page, as shown in Figure G-6, then paste the copied text in its place**

   The paragraph from the index page appears in the center container of the new page, replacing the placeholder text.

4. **Display the index page, then select and copy the contact, copyright, and last updated information**

5. **Display the new, unsaved page, then paste the contact, copyright, and last updated information in the footer section, replacing the placeholder text, as shown in Figure G-7**

6. **Display the index page and copy both the banner and navigation bar**

QUICK TIP
Your banner and navigation bar may retain their alignment settings when you copy them, depending on how you selected them.

7. **Display the new, unsaved page and paste the banner and navigation bar into the header section, replacing the placeholder text**

   The banner and navigation bar display as broken images, as shown in Figure G-8, but after you save the page in the Web site root folder, the paths to the images will be fixed.

8. **Display the index page and close it**

9. **Place the insertion point to the left side of the banner on the new, untitled page, click the Format list arrow on the HTML Property inspector, then click None**

   This removes the H1 tag from the CSS block, removing the extra space between the navigation bar and the banner.

10. **Save the new, untitled page as index.html in The Striped Umbrella root folder, overwriting the original index page**

    The banner and navigation bar image paths are no longer broken links, as shown in Figure G-9.

FIGURE G-6: Text selected in mainContent block of new, unsaved page

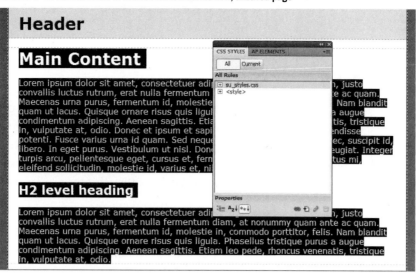

FIGURE G-7: Text copied into footer block of new, unsaved page

Select the Footer placeholder text, then paste the text

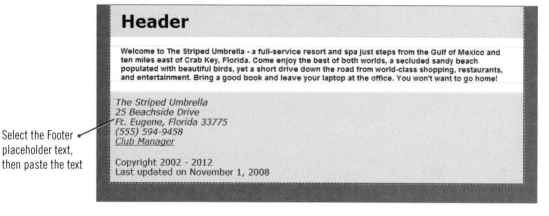

FIGURE G-8: Images appear broken until page is saved

Broken images

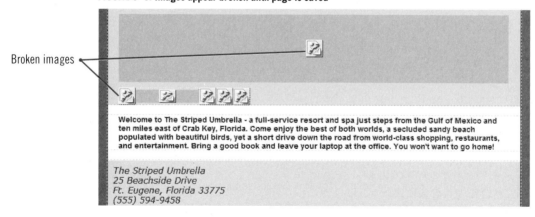

FIGURE G-9: Images not broken after page is saved

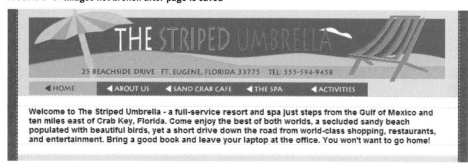

Editing Content in CSS Layout Blocks

After you replace placeholder content in CSS layout blocks with your Web site content, you will probably need to adjust some formatting elements. Styles that you have previously applied might conflict with styles from the CSS layout blocks, so you might want to remove selected style properties, such as font and alignment settings. ▓▓▓▓▓ You continue working on the new index page by changing the navigation bar alignment to match the other pages, and by removing formatting that the new layout styles have automatically applied.

STEPS

1. **Place the insertion point in front of the navigation bar, press and hold [Shift], then click immediately after the navigation bar to select it**

QUICK TIP

You can also triple-click a paragraph to select it.

2. **Click the Align list arrow in the Property inspector, then click Center**
    The navigation bar is now centered, which matches the alignment setting for the banner.

3. **Place the insertion point in front of the word "Welcome" in the first line, press and hold [Shift], then click at the end of the paragraph**

TROUBLE

If you don't see the div tag borders, click the Visual Aids button 🔲 on the Document toolbar, then click CSS Layout Outlines to select it. If you don't see the floating window, click the CSS Layout Box Model in the Visual Aids menu to select it.

4. **Click the Format list arrow in the Property inspector, click None, then deselect the text**
    The preformatted text automatically applied the Heading 1 tag to the main_content block, as shown in Figure G-10. By removing the Heading 1 tag, you are leaving the existing body_text style to format the paragraph.

5. **Move the mouse pointer over the bottom of the header block, click the yellow border to select the block, then move the pointer along the block border until the floating window shown in Figure G-11 appears**
    The properties of the div tag appear in a floating window, indicating that the ID for the div tag is header and the Tag is div. The Property inspector displays the Div ID, which is header.

6. **Save your work**

TABLE G-1: Div tag properties

div tag	property
ID	Displays the name used to identify the div tag in the code
Class	Displays the class style currently applied to the div tag
Tag	Identifies the HTML tag (div)
Float	Sets the float, or position, of the div tag in relation to adjacent elements as left, right, none, or inherit
Position	Sets the position of the div tag as absolute, fixed, relative, static, or inherit
Top	Sets the div tag position in relation to the top of the page or parent element
Right	Sets the right position of the div tag as either auto or inherit
Bottom	Sets the bottom position of the div tag as either auto or inherit
Left	Sets the div tag position in relation to the left side of the page or parent element
Width	Sets the width of the div tag in pixels (px) by default
Height	Sets the height of the div tag in pixels (px) by default
Overflow	Controls how the div tag will appear in the browser if the content is larger than the div tag

FIGURE G-10: Centering the navigation bar in the header layout block

Text appears in the body_text style, because it is no longer overwritten by the Heading 1 style

Navigation bar is centered in header

FIGURE G-11: Viewing the div tag properties

Border for div block

Properties of div tag

Div ID = header

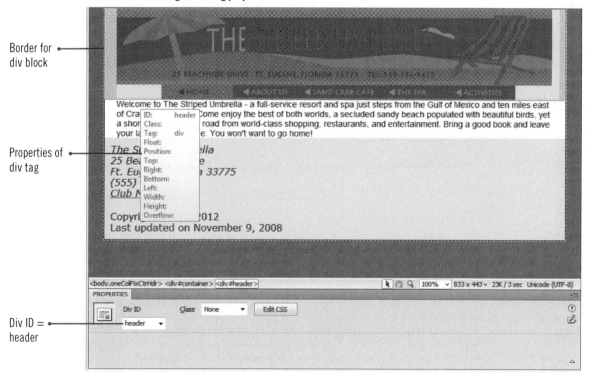

Using Visual Aids as design tools

There are several options for viewing your layout blocks in Design view. You can choose to show or hide outlines, temporarily assign different background colors to each individual layout block, or view the **CSS Layout Box Model** (padding and margins) of a selected layout. To change these options, use the View, Visual Aids menu, and then select or deselect the CSS Layout Backgrounds, CSS Layout Box Model, or CSS Layout Outlines menu choice. You can also use the Visual Aids button on the Document toolbar.

Editing CSS Layout Properties

It is unlikely that you will find a preformatted CSS page layout that is exactly what you have in mind for your Web site. However, once you have created a page with a predefined CSS layout, it is easy to modify the properties for individual rules to change text placement or formatting on the page to better fit your needs. If you have attached a style sheet to a page using CSS for page layout, you will see two sets of rules in the CSS Styles panel: those from the attached external style sheet and those from the style sheet created with the page that contains properties for the layout blocks. Ideally, every page element should be formatted using rules rather than by applying individual formatting properties in the Property inspector. Use the rules in attached external style sheets to format individual page elements with styles, such as text or horizontal rules. The styles generated by the CSS page layout format the CSS blocks, such as the block width or background color, but they can also include formatting for the page elements within the blocks. You continue working on the new index page by changing the container formatting and the page properties.

STEPS

1. **Click the oneColFixCtrHdr #header style in the CSS Styles panel to select it**

   This style contains the formatting for the header block. The current formatting includes a gray background and top, right, bottom, and left padding settings.

   > **QUICK TIP**
   > You can enter either #FFFFFF or #FFF (the shorthand version).

2. **Click to select the background color #DDDDDD in the CSS Styles palette properties section, type #FFF as shown in Figure G-12, then press [Enter] (Win) or [return] (Mac)**

   Rather than using the Edit Rule button in the CSS Styles panel to edit rules, you can change, add, or delete property values in the bottom pane, or Properties pane, of the CSS Styles panel. The background color of the header is now white, to match the background color in the main_content block.

   > **TROUBLE**
   > You may need to resize panels to be able to see the page background behind the blocks.

3. **Repeat Steps 1 and 2 to change the #footer style to white**

   Now all the layout blocks have a white background. The page background is still gray, but you can change it by editing the body tag.

4. **Select the body tag in the CSS Styles panel**

5. **Click to select the background color #666666, type #FFF, then press [Enter] (Win) or [return] (Mac)**

   The body tag for the page is now set to display a white background.

6. **Add the page title The Striped Umbrella Beach Resort and Spa, Ft. Eugene, Florida in the title text box on the Document toolbar**

7. **Select the contact information in the footer, then remove the italic setting in the HTML Property inspector**

   > **QUICK TIP**
   > You can also open the CSS Rule definition dialog box by double-clicking a rule name on the CSS Styles palette.

8. **Select the oneColFixCtrHdr #footer style, click the Edit Rule button 🖉 at the bottom of the CSS Styles palette, select the Type category, change the Font-family to Arial, Helvetica, sans-serif, the Font-size to x-small, and the Font-style to italic, as shown in Figure G-13, then click OK**

9. **Save your work, preview the page in the browser, compare your screen to Figure G-14, then close the browser**

FIGURE G-12: Editing the properties of the oneColFixCtrHdr #header style

Select the oneColFixCtrHdr #header style

Change the background color value to #FFF

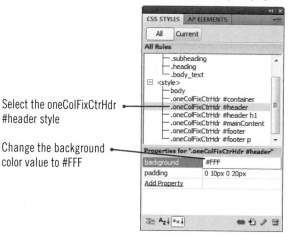

FIGURE G-13: Editing the properties of the oneColFixCtrHdr #footer style

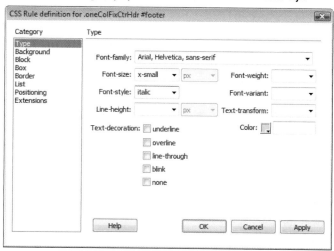

FIGURE G-14: Viewing the new index page in the browser

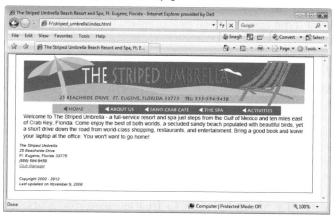

Design Matters

Using the Adobe CSS Advisor for cross-browser rendering issues

You can use the **Browser Compatibility Check (BCC)** feature to check for problematic CSS features that may render differently in multiple browsers. It flags and rates code on three levels: an error that could cause a serious display problem; an error that probably won't cause a serious display problem; or a warning that it has found code that is unsupported, but won't cause a serious display problem. Each bug is linked to the **CSS Advisor**, a part of the Adobe Web site that offers solutions for that particular bug and other helpful information for resolving any issues with your pages. To use the Browser Compatibility Check feature, use the File, Check Page, Browser Compatibility command.

Inserting an AP Div

An **AP element** (an **absolutely positioned** element) is a div tag you use to place content on a Web page in a fixed position. You can specify a selected AP element's exact position using the Left and Top settings on the Property inspector or in the CSS Styles panel. (By contrast, **relative positioning** places div tags in relation to other page elements.) Using AP div tags, you can stack AP elements on top of each other as if they were transparency sheets and specify that only certain elements be visible at certain times or in specified conditions. To insert an AP element, you can click the Draw AP Div button in the Layout category on the Insert panel, then drag a rectangular shape anywhere on a page. You have been asked to place a temporary advertisement for a children's sand castle contest on the index page. An AP element would be a good way to display the ad because it is time-sensitive information that you can easily add and then remove after the contest is over, without disturbing the rest of the page content. You begin by inserting an AP div at the bottom of the page.

STEPS

1. **Click** View **on the Application bar (Win) or Menu bar (Mac), point to** Rulers**, click** Show **(if necessary), place the mouse pointer over the horizontal ruler, then drag a** horizontal guide **from the top ruler near the** 250 pixel mark **on the vertical ruler**

   Guides are lines you can drag onto your pages to help you place objects more precisely. On this page, the guide will help you position the AP element. Guides are not visible in the browser. When you hold your pointer over the guide, a yellow box with the exact location of the guide will appear in it.

2. **Click the** Layout category **on the Insert panel, then click the** Draw AP Div button

> **QUICK TIP**
> You can also insert an AP element using the Insert, Layout Objects, AP Div command.

3. **Using Figure G-15 as a guide, drag a** rectangle **in the middle of the home page, under the guide, that is approximately 315 pixels wide and 130 pixels tall**

   A new AP element appears on the page, but it is not selected. An AP Div icon ▦ appears in the upper-left corner of the element.

> **QUICK TIP**
> You can also select an AP div by clicking one of its borders.

4. **Click the** AP Div icon ▦ **above the AP element to select it**

   The AP div element now has sizing handles around it, indicating that it is selected.

5. **With the AP div selected, select** apDiv1 **in the CSS-P Element text box in the Property inspector, type** contest**, then press** [Enter] **(Win) or** [return] **(Mac)**

   Giving an AP div a unique name helps you to identify the element quickly as you view the code.

6. **Verify that** <div#contest> **is selected in the Tag selector, click the** Overflow list arrow **in the Property inspector, then click** auto

   The Overflow property controls how the content in an AP div will appear in a browser when there is more content than will fit in the AP element. The Auto setting will allow extra content to display, but will only add scroll bars if they are needed.

7. **Click the** Vis list arrow**, then click** visible

   The Vis property specifies whether the AP element is visible or not when the page loads in the browser.

8. **Compare your screen to Figure G-16, then save your work**

Understanding AP element code

As you examine the HTML code for div tags and AP elements, you will see that the code is actually split between the head section and the body section of the code. The head section contains the code that sets the position, size, overflow, and formatting. Comments are also included with the styles to provide explanation for each style. The body section contains the code for the div tag ID and for the div tag content. This is similar to the way CSS styles are written: the code for the CSS style, properties, and values resides in the head section for internal style sheets. For external style sheets, the code linking the style sheet to the page resides in the head section. The code where each CSS style is applied to a page element resides in the body section.

FIGURE G-15: New AP element added to the home page

Drag guide from horizontal ruler

Horizontal guide

250 pixel mark on vertical ruler

AP div icon

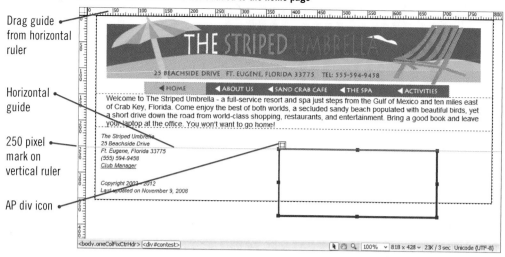

FIGURE G-16: Property inspector showing properties of selected AP element

Selected AP element

CSS-P Element text box

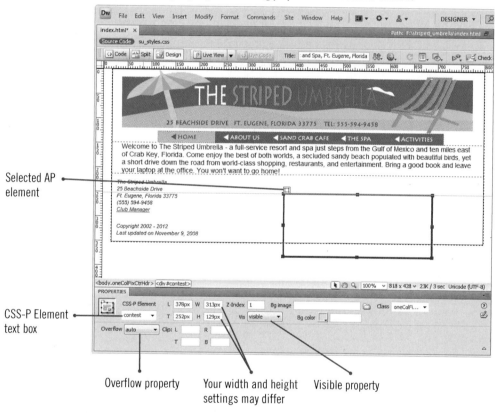

Overflow property

Your width and height settings may differ

Visible property

Positioning and Sizing an AP Element

To use AP elements, you must understand absolute positioning. An AP element is positioned absolutely by specifying the distance between the upper-left corner of the AP element and the upper-left corner of the page or parent AP element in which it is contained. You control the placement of AP elements by setting attributes in the Property inspector. The **Left property (L)** specifies the distance between the left edge of an AP element and the left edge of the page or parent AP element that contains it. The **Top property (T)** specifies the distance between the top edge of the AP element and the top edge of the page or AP element that contains it. The **Width (W)** and **Height (H) properties** specify the dimensions of the AP element in either pixels or as a percentage of the page. After drawing the AP element on the index page, you are ready to set the dimensions that will determine the size and position of the content on the page.

STEPS

1. **Click the AP div border to select the AP div element if necessary**

   First you'll set the position of the upper-left corner on the element by specifying the Left and Top properties.

2. **Type 420px in the L text box in the CSS-P Element section of the Property inspector, then press [Enter] (Win) or [return] (Mac)**

   The left side of the AP element automatically aligns with the 420px location on the horizontal ruler.

3. **Type 260px in the T text box, then press [Enter] (Win) or [return] (Mac)**

   The top of the AP element aligns with the 260 location on the vertical ruler. Save your work, then compare your screen to Figure G-17. Next you want to set the AP element's width and height.

4. **Type 200px in the W text box, then press [Tab]**

5. **Type 175px in the H text box, then press [Tab]**

   The AP element automatically adjusts to the width and height you specified. Notice that the upper-left corner stays in the same position you specified earlier.

6. **Save your work, then compare your screen to Figure G-18**

Design Matters

Placing the most important information first

People on the Internet are notoriously hurried and will often read only information that is located on the first screen that they see on a Web page, rather than scroll though the entire length of the page. Therefore, it is a good idea to put the most important information at the top of the page. In other words, the most important information should be on the part of the page that is visible before you have to scroll to see the rest. You can use guides to emulate a newspaper **fold line**, which represents the place where a newspaper is folded. The most important stories are usually printed "above the fold" line.

FIGURE G-17: AP element moved down and to the right on the page

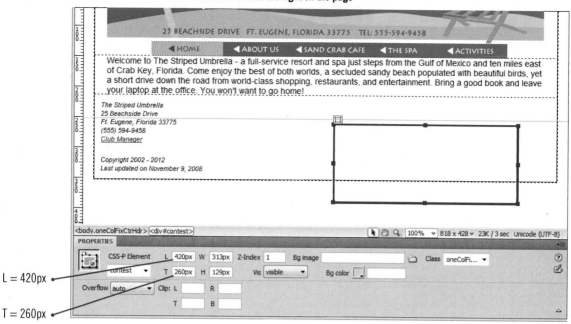

L = 420px

T = 260px

FIGURE G-18: Resized AP Element

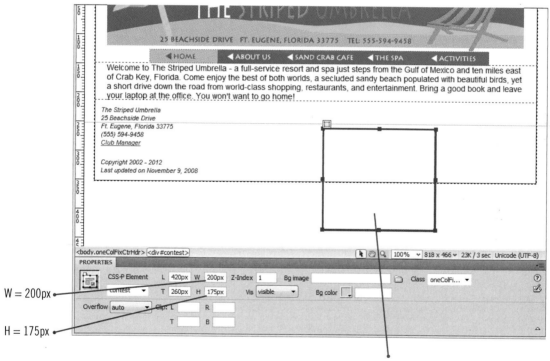

W = 200px

H = 175px

AP element is resized, but stays in
the same position on the page

Understanding the z-index property

The **z-index property** in the Property inspector is used to specify the vertical stacking order of multiple AP elements on a page. If you think of the page as being AP element 0, then any number higher than that will appear on top of the page. For instance, if you have three AP elements with z-index values of 1, 2, and 3, then 1 will appear underneath 2 and 3, while 3 will always appear on top of 1 and 2. AP elements are assigned default z-index values as they are created beginning with the number 1, but you can easily change the stacking order by reassigning the z-index values.

Adding Content to an AP Element

Because an AP element is like a separate document within a Web page, it can contain the same types of elements that a page contains, such as background colors, images, links, tables, and text. If you add more content than will fit in the present size, the AP element will enlarge to display the content on your page in Dreamweaver. However, when you preview the page in a browser, the amount displayed will depend on how you set your Overflow settings. As with formatting text on Web pages, you should use CSS styles to format text on AP elements. You are ready to add text to advertise the date of a sand castle contest that will be held on the Fourth of July. You want to use a picture of some children on the beach as a background image to add interest to the AP element.

STEPS

1. **Select the** AP div **if necessary, then click the** Browse for File icon ☐ **next to the Bg image text box in the Property inspector**

   The Select Image Source dialog box opens.

2. **Navigate to the drive and folder where your Unit G Data Files are stored, open the** assets **folder, then double-click** contestants_bak.jpg

3. **Compare your screen to Figure G-19**

   The photograph fills the background of the AP element.

4. **Refresh the Files panel to verify that contestants_bak.jpg was copied to the assets folder of the Web site**

TROUBLE

If you are having trouble setting the insertion point, click or double-click directly in the middle of the AP element.

5. **Click inside the AP element to set the insertion point, then press** [Shift][Enter] **(Win) or** [Shift][return] **(Mac) to enter a line break**

6. **Type** Sand Castle Contest July 4, **press** [Shift][Enter] **(Win) or** [Shift][return] **(Mac), then type** Bring your buddies!

7. **Select the** contest style **in the CSS Styles panel, then click the** Edit Rule button ✎

   You created the contest style when you created the AP div tag. It had a default name until you changed the default AP div name to contest.

QUICK TIP

When you type text on an AP element, you should always format the text using styles in the CSS Styles panel, rather than using manual formatting.

8. **Click the** Type category, **as shown in Figure G-20, change the Font-family to** Arial, Helvetica, sans-serif, **the Font-size to** small, **the Font-weight to** bold, **the Color to** #006 **then click the** Apply button

9. **Click the** Block category, **change the Text-align setting to** center, **then click** OK

   The text changes to reflect the properties you have added to the contest style. It is blue and centered on the AP element.

10. **Save your work, preview the page in your browser, compare your screen with Figure G-21, close your browser, then** Exit **(Win) or** Quit **(Mac) the Dreamweaver program**

    Your page may look slightly different from Figure G-21, depending on the browser you are using.

FIGURE G-19: AP element with a background image

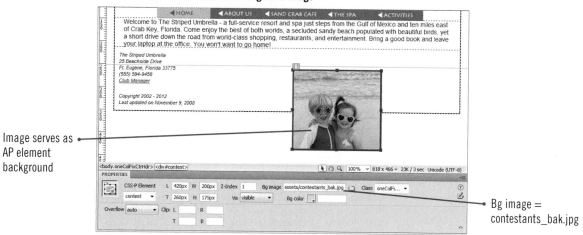

Image serves as
AP element
background

Bg image =
contestants_bak.jpg

FIGURE G-20: Editing the contest style

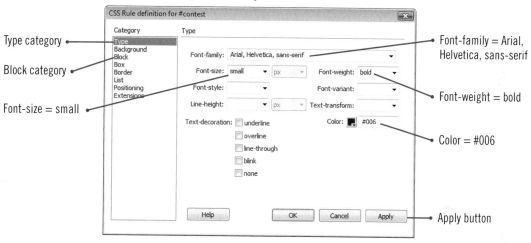

Type category

Block category

Font-size = small

Font-family = Arial,
Helvetica, sans-serif

Font-weight = bold

Color = #006

Apply button

FIGURE G-21: Index page with the formatted AP element

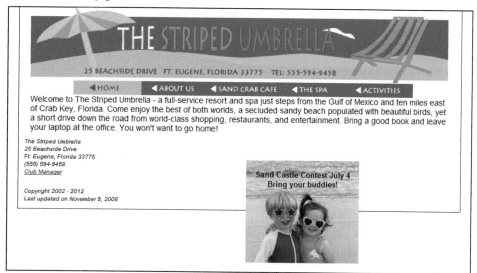

Understanding the Overflow property

Sometimes there is more content than will fit in the dimensions of an AP element. To allow for this possibility, you can set the Overflow property to direct the browser to display the extra content or to hide it. The visible value means that the AP element will stretch to display any extra content. The hidden value means that extra content will not be displayed. The scroll value means that the browser will display scroll bars in the AP element whether they are needed or not. The auto value means that extra content will be displayed, and scroll bars will be added if needed.

Using the AP Elements Panel

UNIT
G
Dreamweaver CS4

The easiest way to manage AP elements is with the AP Elements panel, which is in the CSS tab group next to the CSS Styles panel. You use the **AP Elements panel** to control the properties of all AP elements on a Web page, and you open it as you do other panels, through the Window menu. The AP Elements panel provides a quick way to scan the number of AP elements on a page, their names, their z-indexes, and to control their visibility settings. You study the uses of the AP Elements panel to better understand how manage them.

DETAILS

- **Change AP element order and names**

  The AP Elements panel lists all AP elements on the open page in order of their z-index. The first AP element you create appears by default at the bottom of the stack, with the most recent at the top. You can reorder them by changing the z-index settings. Assigning an AP element a logical name that represents its content helps you quickly identify each page element. To rename an AP element, double-click its default name in the Property inspector, then enter a new name.

- **Select AP elements**

  When you select the AP element name from the list in the AP Elements panel, the AP element will be selected on the page. This is an especially handy feature when you are trying to select an AP element at the bottom of a stack.

> **QUICK TIP**
> If you want to show or hide all AP elements on the page, click the header eye icon at the top of the column to toggle between all visible or all hidden.

- **Control visibility**

  The first column in the AP Elements panel contains icons that show the visibility setting for each AP element, with eye icons representing the visibility settings. An open eye icon means that the AP element is visible on the page. A closed eye icon means the AP element is not visible on the page. If neither icon appears in the column, the AP element will inherit the visibility status of its parent object. See Figure G-22. If an AP element is not part of a group, the parent object is the Web page. Clicking in this column next to an element will toggle between the icons, thus changing the visibility settings for that element.

> **QUICK TIP**
> You can also change the z-index by entering a new value in the Z-Index text box on the Property inspector.

- **Control the visible stacking order and overlaps**

  You can change the stacking order of an AP element by dragging the AP element name up or down in the AP Elements panel. As you drag past other names in the list, you will see a placement line appear to let you know where the AP element would move if you released the mouse button. After you drag an element in the list, its z-index changes automatically to reflect its new position in the stacking order. See Figures G-23 and G-24.

- **Change the nesting status of nested AP elements**

  Besides stacking, another option for placing AP elements is nesting. **Nested AP elements** are AP elements whose HTML code resides inside other AP div tags. In the AP Elements panel, nested AP elements are indented under the parent AP element. See Figure G-25. Nesting AP elements ties them together for such purposes as visibility. Nested AP elements move with their parent AP elements. If you want to nest AP elements, be sure that the Prevent overlaps check box is deselected in the AP Elements panel, as shown in Figure G-25. You must also select the "Nest when created within an AP div" check box in the Dreamweaver Preferences dialog box, as shown in Figure G-26. If you have existing AP elements that are not nested that you would like to nest, simply Ctrl-drag (Win) or ⌘-drag (Mac) the AP element you want to nest on top of the AP element that will be the parent in the AP Elements panel.

Using CSS to Lay Out Pages

FIGURE G-22: The AP Elements panel visiblity settings

Click header
eye icon to
toggle visibility
settings for all
AP elements

Closed
eye icon

No eye icon
displayed

Open eye icon

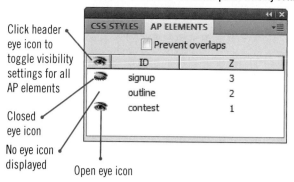

FIGURE G-23: The outline AP div with a z-index of 2

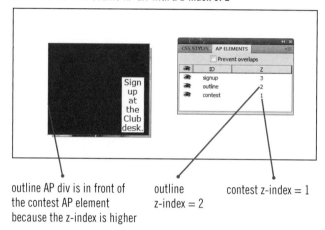

outline AP div is in front of
the contest AP element
because the z-index is higher

outline
z-index = 2

contest z-index = 1

FIGURE G-24: The outline AP div with a z-index of 1

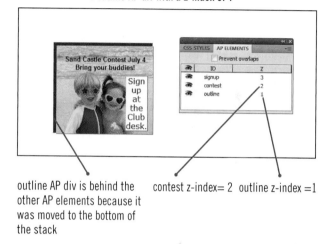

outline AP div is behind the
other AP elements because it
was moved to the bottom of
the stack

contest z-index= 2   outline z-index =1

FIGURE G-25: Viewing a nested AP Div in the AP Elements panel

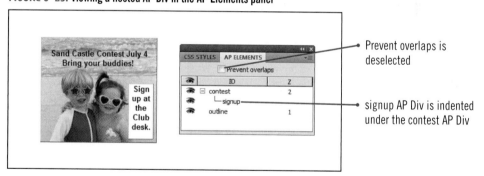

Prevent overlaps is
deselected

signup AP Div is indented
under the contest AP Div

FIGURE G-26: Viewing the AP Elements preferences

Nest when
created
within an
AP div option
is checked

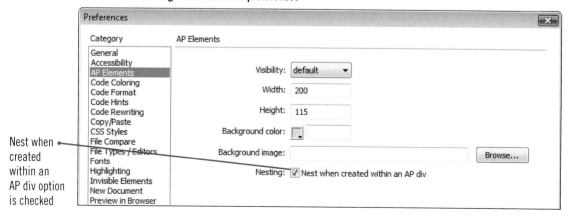

Practice

▼ CONCEPTS REVIEW

Label each element shown in Figure G-27.

FIGURE G-27

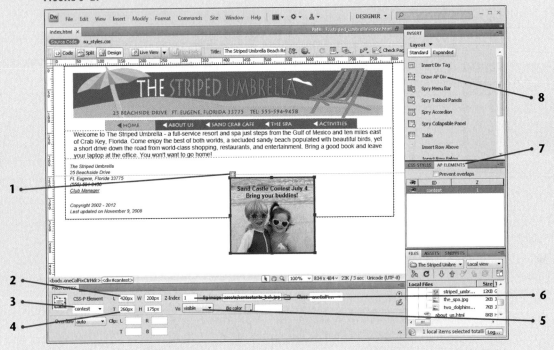

1._____   5._____

2._____   6._____

3._____   7._____

4._____   8._____

Match each of the following terms with the statement that best describes its function.

9. **AP Elements panel**

10. **z-index property**

11. **HTML div tags**

12. **AP div tag**

13. **Liquid layout**

14. **CSS page layouts**

15. **JavaScript behaviors**

16. **CSS Layout box model**

17. **Nested AP elements**

18. **Dynamic content**

a. A div tag with a specified, fixed position on a page

b. Pages built using div tags and CSS

c. A view that displays padding and margins for AP elements

d. The location used to control the properties of AP elements

e. Page content that changes through interaction between the viewer and the screen content

f. A layout with column widths based on percent of the browser window

g. An AP element whose code is inside another AP element's (parent) code

h. The property that determines the stacking order of multiple AP elements

i. Action scripts that allow you to create dynamic page content

j. HTML tags that determine the appearance and position of containers of content

▼ SKILLS REVIEW

(If you did not create this Web site in Unit B and maintain it during the preceding units, you will need to create a root folder for this Web site and define the Web site using files your instructor will provide. See the "Read This Before You Begin" section for more detailed instructions.)

1. Create a page using CSS layouts.

   a. Start Dreamweaver and open the blooms & bulbs Web site.

   b. Open the index page.

   c. Create a new blank HTML page with the 1-column fixed, centered, header and footer style, and attach the blooms_styles.css file to the page.

   d. Add the page title **blooms & bulbs – Your complete garden center** in the Title text box.

2. Add content to CSS layout blocks.

   a. Switch to the index page and copy the block of text, horizontal rule, and contact information (but not the copyright or last updated information).

   b. Paste the text in the mainContent container of the new, unsaved page, replacing the placeholder text.

   c. Switch back to the index page and copy the copyright and last updated information.

   d. Paste the text in the footer container of the new, unsaved page, replacing the placeholder text.

   e. Switch back to the index page, then select and copy both the banner and the navigation bar.

   f. Paste the banner and navigation bar in the header section of the new, unsaved page and delete any extra return characters if necessary. (*Hint*: The images will be broken until you save the file.)

   g. Close the index page.

   h. Save the new, untitled page as **index.html**, overwriting the original index page.

   i. Place the insertion point in the header section, then use the Property inspector to remove the H1 tag by setting the format to None.

3. Edit content in CSS layout blocks.

   a. Select the contact information and apply the body_text style.

   b. Save your work.

4. Edit CSS layout properties.

   a. Select the oneColFixCtrHdr #header style in the CSS Styles panel and change the background color to **#FFF**.

   b. Repeat Step a to change the background color of the oneColFixCtrHdr #footer to **#FFF**.

   c. Edit the body style to change the body background to **#FFF**.

   d. Save your work.

5. Insert an AP div.

   a. Use the Draw AP Div button to draw a rectangle, about two inches tall by one inch wide on the bottom half of your page, using a guide for placement.

   b. Select and rename this AP div **organic**.

   c. Set the Vis property to visible.

   d. Set the Overflow property to visible.

6. **Position and size an AP element.**

   a. Select the organic AP div, then set the Left property to 445px.

   b. Set the Top property to 230px.

   c. Set the Width property to 175px.

   d. Set the Height property to 219px.

   e. Set the Z-Index property to 1 if necessary.

   f. Save your work.

7. **Add content to an AP element.**

   a. Select the organic AP div, if necessary, then insert the background image peaches_small.jpg from the Unit G Data Files assets folder.

   b. Place the insertion point in the organic AP div, then type Organic Gardening.

   c. Insert a line break, then type Class begins soon!.

   d. Save your work.

   e. Preview the page in your browser, compare your screen with Figure G-28, then close the browser.

   f. Exit Dreamweaver.

FIGURE G-28

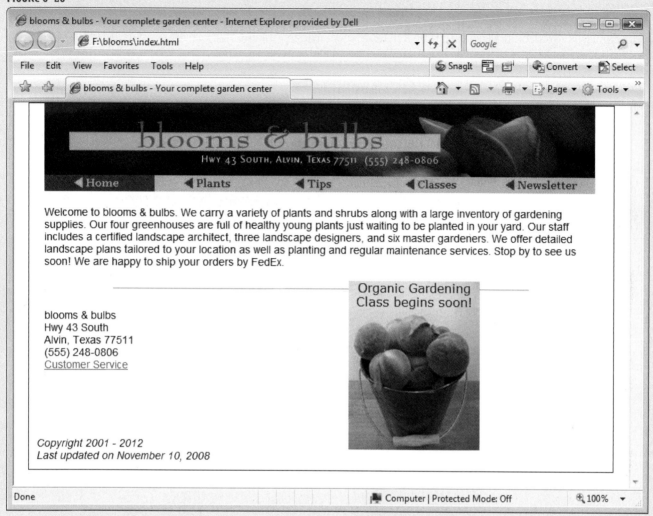

Important: *If you did not create the Web sites used in the following exercises in Unit B, you need to create a root folder for each Web site and define the Web sites using files your instructor provides. See the "Read This Before You Begin" section for more detailed instructions.*

▼ INDEPENDENT CHALLENGE 1

You continue your work on the Rapids Transit Web site. After studying Cascading Style Sheets, you have decided to experiment with CSS predefined layouts. You begin by redesigning the index page based on a CSS layout.

a. Open the Rapids Transit Web site, then open the index page.

b. Create a new HTML page based on the 1 column fixed, centered, header and footer style, attaching the rapids_transit.css file to the page.

c. Add the page title **Rapids Transit – Buffalo River Outfitters**.

d. Copy the banner and navigation bar from the index page to the new, untitled page, replacing the header placeholder text, then remove the Heading 1 format.

e. Copy the paragraph and contact information from the index page and paste it in the main content block, replacing the placeholder text.

f. Copy the copyright and last updated statement from the index page and use it to replace the placeholder text in the footer of the new, untitled page.

g. Close the index page and save the new, untitled page as **index.html**, replacing the original index page.

h. Select the footer text and apply the contact_info style.

i. Change the background colors of the layout blocks to white and the page background to **#003**.

j. Add an AP div about one inch tall and two inches wide, then name it **river_level**.

k. Set the following properties for the river_level AP element: the left position to **400px**, the top position to **275px**, the width to **245px**, and the height to **70px**.

l. Set the background color of the AP element to **#FF9**, then add an inset border that is dark blue. (The inset border option is in the Border category.)

m. In the AP div, add the text **Current River Conditions: Good floating today with a few Class II spots**, using line breaks after the words "Conditions:" and "today".

n. Edit the river_level text style to change the Font-family to Verdana, Geneva, sans-serif; the Font-size to medium; and the Color to dark blue.

o. Make any spacing adjustments necessary, save your work, then preview the page in the browser.

p. Compare your screen to Figure G-29, then close the browser.

q. Close the page, then exit Dreamweaver.

FIGURE G-29

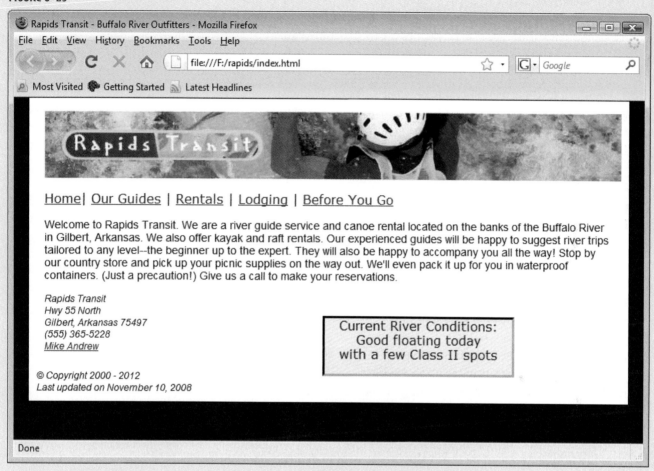

Rapids Transit - Buffalo River Outfitters - Mozilla Firefox

File Edit View History Bookmarks Tools Help

file:///F:/rapids/index.html   G· Google

Most Visited   Getting Started   Latest Headlines

Home| Our Guides | Rentals | Lodging | Before You Go

Welcome to Rapids Transit. We are a river guide service and canoe rental located on the banks of the Buffalo River in Gilbert, Arkansas. We also offer kayak and raft rentals. Our experienced guides will be happy to suggest river trips tailored to any level--the beginner up to the expert. They will also be happy to accompany you all the way! Stop by our country store and pick up your picnic supplies on the way out. We'll even pack it up for you in waterproof containers. (Just a precaution!) Give us a call to make your reservations.

Rapids Transit
Hwy 55 North
Gilbert, Arkansas 75497
(555) 365-5228
Mike Andrew

© Copyright 2000 - 2012
Last updated on November 10, 2008

Current River Conditions:
Good floating today
with a few Class II spots

Done

▼ INDEPENDENT CHALLENGE 2

You continue your work on the TripSmart Web site. The owner, Thomas Howard, wants you to create a section on the index page that advertises a special price on Packing Cubes, one of the catalog items.

a. Open the TripSmart Web site, then open the index page.

b. Create a new HTML page based on the one column fixed, centered CSS page layout, then attach the tripsmart_styles.css file.

c. Copy all content from the index page, then paste it into the new, unsaved page, replacing all placeholder text.

d. Close the index page.

e. Save the new page as the index page, overwriting the original index page.

f. Check the formatting for each text block to make sure each is formatted with a style from one of the style sheets, and apply a style to any unformatted text. Remove the heading format from the banner.

g. Draw an AP div that is approximately one inch tall and four inches wide in the middle of the page, then name it special.

h. Set the background color of the AP div to transparent by clicking the Strikethrough button on the color picker toolbar.

i. Click inside the AP div, then insert packing_cube.jpg from the Unit G Data Files assets folder into the AP div, adding appropriate alternate text. (This time you are not using the image for the background. You are inserting it on the AP div just like you have inserted images on a page.)

j. Set the Left property of the AP div to 300px and the Top property to 300px.

k. Set the Width property to 350px, the Height property to 80px, and the Z-Index property to 1 if necessary.

l. Add the following text to the right of the image: Packing cubes on sale this week!, with a line break before the word "this".

m. Select the packing cube image, then use the Align list arrow to set the Align option to Left.

n. Format the Packing cubes on sale this week! text using the heading style.

o. Enter a line break; type Large: $15.00; Medium: $10.00; then enter a line break; type Small: $5.00; then format this text with the body_text style.

p. Edit the #special style in the CSS Styles panel to add a double border around the AP div with the color #666.

q. Set the Overflow property of the AP div to visible.

r. Add the page title TripSmart – serving all your travel needs.

s. Save your work, preview the page in your browser, compare your screen to Figure G-30, close your browser, make any spacing adjustments necessary for the AP div size or position, then close the index page.

t. Exit Dreamweaver.

FIGURE G-30

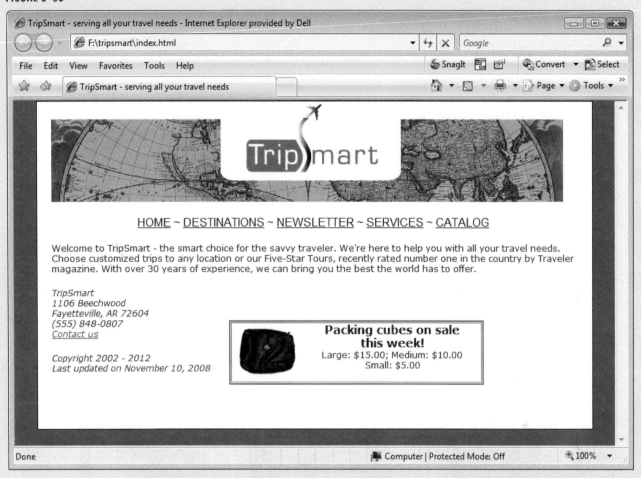

▼ INDEPENDENT CHALLENGE 3

Hernandez Santoro has recently been asked to redesign a Web site for a new restaurant. He has decided to use CSS for page layout. Because he has never developed a Web site based on CSS before, he decides to look at some other restaurant Web sites for ideas and inspiration.

a. Connect to the Internet, then go to www.jamesatthemill.com, as shown in Figure G-31.

b. View the source code for the index page and locate the HTML tags that control the CSS on the page.

c. How are CSS tags used in this site?

d. List at least five div tag IDs that you find on the index page.

e. Use the Reference panel in Dreamweaver to look up two sets of code used in this site for page layout that you don't understand.

FIGURE G-31

James at the Mill Web site used with permission from James at the Mill—www.jamesatthemill.com

Dreamweaver CS4

▼ REAL LIFE INDEPENDENT CHALLENGE

For this assignment, you will continue to work on the Web site that you have been developing since Unit A. You are building this Web site from unit to unit, so you must do each Real Life Independent Challenge to complete your Web site. There are no Data Files supplied. You will continue building your Web site by designing and completing a page that uses CSS for page layout.

a. Consult your storyboard to decide which page to create and develop for this unit. Draw a sketch of the page to show how you will use CSS to lay out the content.

b. Create the new page for the site using one of the predefined CSS layouts. Add or edit the div tags and AP elements on your page, making sure to name each one.

c. Add text, images, and background colors to each element.

d. Copy the navigation bar from an existing page to the new page.

e. Update the navigation bar if necessary to include a link to the new page.

f. Consider using the new page as an example to redesign the existing pages to also be based on CSS.

g. Save your work, preview each page in your browser, and make any necessary modifications to make the pages look attractive.

h. Close your browser, close all open pages, then exit Dreamweaver.

▼ VISUAL WORKSHOP

Use Figure G-32 as a guide to continue your work on the Carolyne's Creations Web site. Replace the index page with a new page based on the one column fixed, centered CSS page layout. Remember to attach the Web site style sheet to the page. Create an AP div on the page and insert the the cc_logo.jpg image from the Unit G Data Files assets folder. (*Hint*: Remember to add the page title. The background color shown in the figure is #963. The border was set to a black groove and the padding was set to 3px.)

FIGURE G-32

Positioning Objects with HTML Tables

You have learned how to place elements on a page, align them, and enhance them through various formatting options, such as div tags and CSS styles. Another way to position page elements is by using tables. **Tables** are placeholders made up of small boxes called **cells**, where you can insert text and graphics. Cells are arranged horizontally in rows and vertically in columns. Using tables on a Web page gives you total control over the placement of each object on the page. In actual practice, many designers use a combination of div tags, CSS styles, and tables, choosing the tool that is the best suited to the current design challenge. In this unit you learn how to create and format tables, work with table rows and columns, and format the contents of table cells. You also insert a Flash movie on the page. It is time to work on the cafe page. You have been given three images and a Flash animation to position attractively with the text on the page. You have decided to use a table to position some of the page elements within a div tag.

OBJECTIVES

- Understand table modes
- Create a table
- Resize tables, rows, and columns
- Merge and split cells
- Insert and align images in table cells
- Insert text
- Format and modify cell content
- Format cells
- Add media objects

UNIT

H

Dreamweaver CS4

Understanding Table Modes

There are two ways to create a table in Dreamweaver. You can use the Table button in the Common or Layout category on the Insert panel or use the Insert, Table command. There are two different modes for viewing a table. You use **Standard mode** to insert a table using the Table button. **Expanded Tables mode** is similar to Standard mode but has expanded table borders and temporary space between the cells to make it easier to work with individual cells. You can choose the mode that you want by clicking the Standard mode button, or the Expanded Tables mode button in the Layout category on the Insert panel. It is common to switch between modes as you work with tables in Dreamweaver. You can use the Standard mode most of the time, but you can switch to Expanded Tables mode when you are doing precise work with small cells that are difficult to select or move between. You can also use the Import Tabular Data command on the Insert, Table Objects menu to place an existing table with its data on a Web page. ▓▓▓▓ You review the two methods for creating tables using the Standard and Expanded Tables modes.

DETAILS

- ### Creating a table in Standard mode

  Standard mode is the mode you have used for page layout up to this point. To create a table in Standard mode, you click the Table button in the Common or Layout category on the Insert panel. The Table dialog box opens and allows you to enter values for the number of rows and columns, the table width, border size, cell padding, and cell spacing. The **border** is the outline or frame around the table and the individual cells. It is expressed in pixels. The **width** refers to the width of the table. The width is expressed either in pixels or as a percentage of page width. When expressed as a percentage, the table width adjusts to the width of the page in the browser window. When expressed in pixels, the table width does not change, regardless of the size of the browser window. **Cell padding** is the distance between the cell content and the **cell walls**, the lines inside the cell borders. **Cell spacing** is the distance between cells. Figure H-1 shows an example of a table created in Standard mode.

- ### Editing a table in Expanded Tables mode

  Expanded Tables mode lets you view a table with expanded table borders and temporary cell padding and cell spacing. This mode makes it easier to see how many rows and columns you have in your table. Often, especially after splitting empty cells, it is difficult to place the insertion point precisely in a table cell. The Expanded Tables mode lets you see each cell clearly. After you select a table item or place the insertion point, it's best to return to Standard mode to maintain the WYSIWYG environment. **WYSIWYG** is the acronym for What You See Is What You Get. This means that your Web page should look the same in the browser as it does in the Web editor. You can toggle between the Expanded Tables mode and Standard mode by pressing [Alt] [F6]. Figure H-2 shows an example of a table in Expanded Tables mode.

Using HTML table tags

When formatting a table, you should understand basic HTML table tags. The tags that represent a table are **<table></table>**. The tags that represent table rows are **<tr></tr>**. The tags that represent table data cells are **<td></td>**. Dreamweaver places the   code into each empty table cell at the time it is created. The ** ** code represents a **nonbreaking space**; this is a space that appears in a fixed location to keep a line break from separating text into two lines or, in the case of table cells, to keep an empty cell from collapsing. Some browsers collapse an empty cell, which can ruin the look of a table. The nonbreaking space appears in the cell until it is replaced with content.

FIGURE H-1: Table created in Standard mode

Layout category

Standard mode button

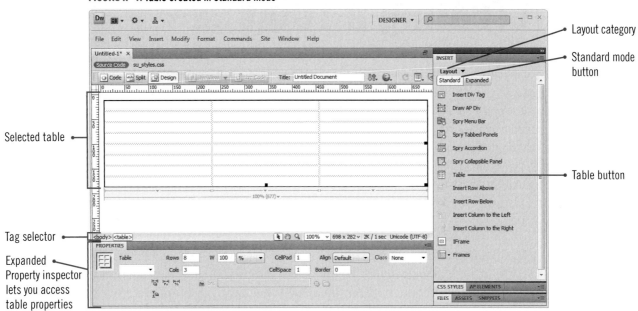

Selected table

Table button

Tag selector

Expanded Property inspector lets you access table properties

FIGURE H-2: Same table shown in Expanded Tables mode

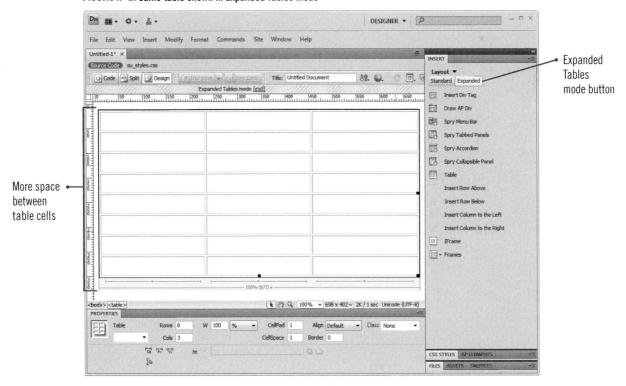

Expanded Tables mode button

More space between table cells

Creating a Table

Before you begin creating a table in any mode, it is imperative that you plan in advance how you want to place the table and how you want it to look. If you plan to insert images into a table, you should know exactly where you want them to appear on the page. Having an overall plan before you begin saves you a lot of development time. You should also consider whether you want the table borders and the cell walls to appear in the browser. You can make a table "invisible" by setting the border value to zero. Then the viewer will not be aware that you used a table to arrange the text or images on the page. You can also create a table inside a cell of another table to create a **nested table**. After consulting with the restaurant manager, you sketch your ideas for the new cafe page in The Striped Umbrella Web site, as shown in Figure H-3. You then insert a table using Standard mode.

STEPS

1. **Start Dreamweaver, open The Striped Umbrella Web site, open the file dwh_1.html from the drive and folder where your Data Files are stored, save it as cafe.html, overwriting your existing file, but not updating links, then close the dwh_1.html file**
   The cafe page needs a descriptive title.

2. **Type The Sand Crab Cafe in the Title text box on the Document toolbar, replacing Untitled Document, then press [Enter] (Win) or [return] (Mac)**

3. **Select the placeholder text Main content, delete it, click the Standard mode button** Standard **in the Layout category on the Insert panel if necessary, then click the Table button**
   The Table dialog box opens.

TROUBLE
There is a difference between leaving the Cell padding and Cell spacing text boxes blank and typing a zero in them. Typing a zero as their values will remove any space between table cells.

4. **Type 6 in the Rows text box, 3 in the Columns text box, and 735 in the Table width text box, click the Table Width list arrow, click pixels, type 0 in the Border thickness text box, (leave the Cell padding and Cell spacing options blank), click None in the Header section if necessary, type This table is used for page layout. in the Summary text box, as shown in Figure H-4, then click OK**
   A table with six rows and three columns appears on the page. Because the table is selected, the Property inspector displays the table settings that you entered in the Table dialog box. You can modify the table by changing its values in the Property inspector. Since the table, navigation bar, and the banner are the same width, the table lines up perfectly with the page banner and navigation bar.

5. **Compare your screen to Figure H-5, then save your work**
   As you place content into the table cells, the table will lengthen.

Selecting a table

There are several ways to select a table in Dreamweaver. First, you can click the insertion point in the table, click Modify on the Application bar (Win) or Menu bar (Mac), point to Table, then click Select Table. Second, you can select a table by moving the pointer slowly to the top or bottom edge of the table, then clicking the table border when the pointer changes to ⊞. Finally, if the insertion point is inside the table, you can click the table tag icon <table> on the tag selector on the status bar.

FIGURE H-3: Sketch for the table on the cafe page

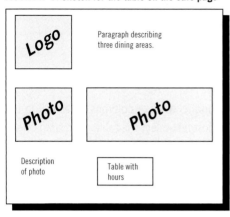

FIGURE H-4: Insert Table dialog box

Rows text box

Table width text box

Border thickness text box

No header option

Columns text box

Width list arrow

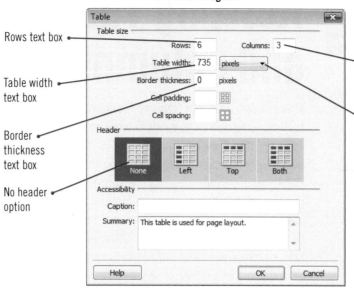

FIGURE H-5: Table inserted on the café page

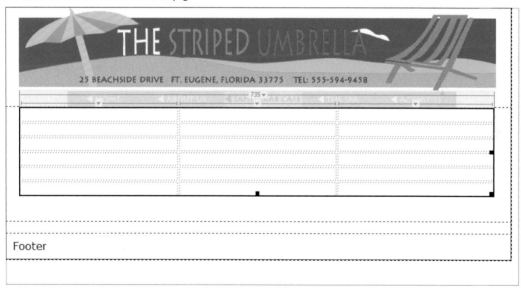

Footer

Design Matters

Setting table and cell widths for page layout

If you use a table to position text and graphics on an entire Web page, it is wise to set the width of the table in pixels. This way, the table does not resize itself proportionately if the browser window size is changed. If you set the width of a table using pixels, the table remains one size, regardless of the browser window size. Most designers today use a window size setting of 800×600 or 1024×768. By using a table width of slightly under 800, the table will cover the width of the window. Those viewers using higher resolutions can then view the table without having it spread out across the screen and altering your intended formatting, as would happen if the width were set using a percent. You can also set each cell width as either a percent of the table or as pixels. If you expect your users to print the page, consider making the table narrower so it will fit on a printed page.

Resizing Tables, Rows, and Columns

After creating a table in Standard mode, you can resize the table and its rows or columns by adjusting the borders. To resize a table, a row, or a column proportionately, you must first select the table, then drag one of three selection handles. To change all of the columns in a table so that they are the same size, drag the middle-right selection handle; dragging the middle-bottom selection handle resizes the height of all rows simultaneously, while dragging the right-corner selection handle resizes the entire table. To resize a row or column individually, you drag the interior cell borders up, down, left, or right. You can also resize column widths and row heights using the W and H text boxes in the Property inspector. You can resize cells using pixels or a percent as a measurement. Cells resized as a percent maintain that percent in relation to the width or height of the entire table, if the table is resized. It is a good idea to set the cell widths before you enter data; otherwise the widths tend to shift as you enter the data. ■■■■■ You want to make sure that the contents of the three cells in the last row will be distributed according to your plan. You set the width of each by entering width values using percentages. You also experiment with resizing a row height.

STEPS

QUICK TIP

You do not actually have to select the cell to see or edit cell properties; you can place the insertion point inside the cell instead.

1. **Click inside the bottom-left cell, then click the cell tag <td> on the tag selector, as shown in Figure H-6**

   The **tag selector**, located on the status bar, displays HTML tags for the various page components, including tables and cells. Clicking a table tag selects the table associated with that tag. Clicking a cell tag selects the corresponding table cell. The cell is now selected with a dark border surrounding it. The Property inspector displays properties of the selected cell.

QUICK TIP

Type the % sign next to a number you want expressed as a percent. Otherwise, it will be expressed in pixels.

2. **Expand the Property inspector if necessary, then type 30% in the W text box in the Property inspector, then press [Tab]**

   The cell width is set to 30% of the table width. Now, as you add content to the table, you can be sure that this column will remain 30% of the width of the table. Notice that the cell width, 30%, appears above the table, as shown in Figure H-6.

3. **Repeat Steps 1 and 2 for the next two cells in the last row, using 30% for the middle cell and 40% for the last cell**

   The combined widths of the three cells add up to 100%. If your widths do not add up to 100%, the table may not appear as you intended. Now you experiment with changing the height of the first row.

QUICK TIP

The height of a row also automatically increases to accommodate the height of its contents.

4. **Click inside one of the cells to deselect the last selected cell, place the pointer over the bottom row border of the first row until the pointer changes to a resizing pointer ‡, then click and drag downward as shown in Figure H-7, to increase the height of the row slightly**

   The color of the border becomes darker as you drag it.

5. **Click Window on the Application bar (Win) or Menu bar (Mac), click History to open the History panel if necessary, then drag the slider in the History panel up until Set Height is dimmed, to undo the Set Height command**

   The row returns to the original height.

6. **Save the file**

FIGURE H-6: Selecting a cell

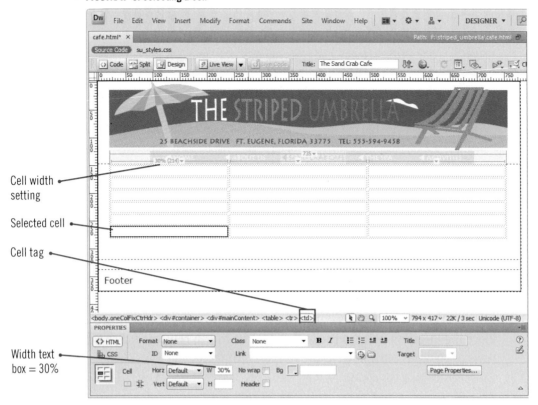

Cell width setting

Selected cell

Cell tag

Width text box = 30%

FIGURE H-7: Resizing the height of a row

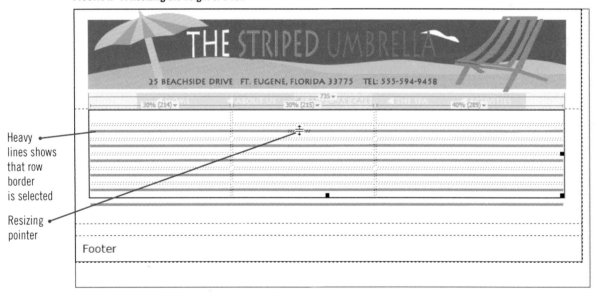

Heavy lines shows that row border is selected

Resizing pointer

Footer

Resetting table widths and heights

After resizing columns and rows in a table, you may want to return your table to the default column widths and row heights. To do this, select the table, click Modify on the Application bar (Win) or Menu bar (Mac), point to Table, then click Clear Cell Heights or Clear Cell Widths. You can also use these commands to tighten up any extra white space in a cell. Using the Clear Cell Heights command forces a cell border to align with the bottom of an inserted image.

Merging and Splitting Cells

In addition to resizing table columns and rows you may need to adjust the table cells by splitting or merging them. To **split** a cell means to divide it into multiple rows or columns. To **merge** cells means to combine multiple cells into one cell. Splitting and merging cells gives you more flexibility for inserting images or text into your table. When cells are merged, the HTML tag used to describe them changes from a width size tag to a column span or row span tag. You can split merged cells and merge split cells.  You merge some cells to make room for a wide image. You then split one cell that will be used to place an image with descriptive text under it.

STEPS

1. **Click to place the insertion point in the second cell in the fourth row, then drag the pointer across the next cell to the right**

   A black border surrounds the cells, indicating that they are selected.

QUICK TIP

You can only merge cells that, together, form a rectangle.

2. **Click the Merges selected cells using spans button ⬚ in the Property inspector**

   The two cells are merged into one cell, as shown in Figure H-8. This row will contain a photo of the cafe. You decide to experiment with splitting cells.

3. **Place the insertion point in the first cell in the fourth row, then click the Splits cell into rows or columns button ⬚ in the Property inspector**

   The Split Cell dialog box opens.

4. **Click the Split cell into Rows option to select it if necessary, type 2 in the Number of rows text box if necessary, as shown in Figure H-9, then click OK**

   The dialog box closes, and the cell is split into two rows.

5. **Click the Show Code view button ⬚ Code on the Document toolbar**

   The code for the split and merged cells appears. Table tags denote the column span and the nonbreaking spaces ( ) inserted in the empty cells. The tag <td colspan="2"> about half-way through the table code refers to the two cells that have been merged into one cell that spans two columns to provide room for the banner.

6. **Click the Show Design view button ⬚ Design, then save your work**

Adding and deleting rows and columns

As you add new content to your table, you may find that you have too many, or not enough rows or columns. You can add or delete one row or column at a time or add several at once, using commands on the Modify menu to add and delete table rows and columns. When you add a new column or row, you must first select an existing column or row to which the new column or row will be adjacent. The Insert Rows or Columns dialog box lets you choose how many rows or columns you want to insert and where you want them placed, relative to the selected row or column. To add a new row to the end of a table, simply press [Tab].

FIGURE H-8: Merging selected cells into one cell

Resulting merged cells

Merge selected cells using spans button

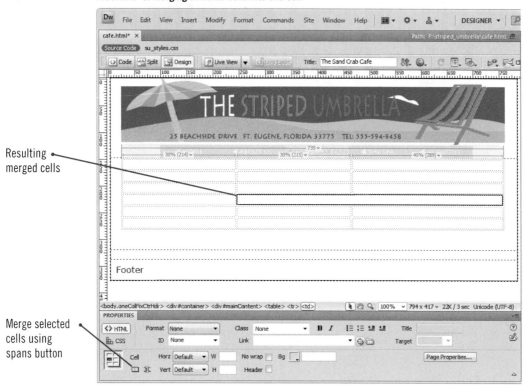

FIGURE H-9: Splitting a cell into two rows

Rows option button

Number of rows text box

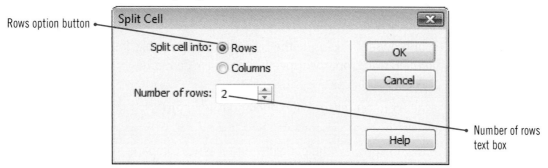

Inserting and Aligning Images in Table Cells

Designers use tables for page layout because by placing text and images in table cells, they can control the exact location of text and images on a page. You can type or paste text into table cells and you can insert images into cells just as you would place them on a page, using the Insert panel. As you add content to cells, the cells expand in height to make room for the content.  You insert three images into the table on the cafe page, then center each within its cell.

STEPS

TROUBLE

If you do not see an alternate text dialog box, type the text in the Alt text box in the Property inspector.

1. **Click to place the insertion point in the first cell in the second row, click to select the Image button in the Common category on the Insert panel, navigate to the drive and folder where your Unit H Data Files are stored, double-click or click the assets folder, double-click cafe_logo.gif, inserting the alternate text Sand Crab Cafe logo when prompted, click OK, then refresh the Files panel**

   The cafe logo appears in the cell and is saved in the assets folder of the Web site. The last button that was selected on the Insert panel becomes the default button for that group until you choose another one. Click the list arrow to select a different one.

2. **Click to place the insertion point in the first cell in the fourth row (the top row in the set of split cells), click the Image button in the Common category on the Insert panel, navigate to the drive and folder where your Unit H Data Files are stored, double-click the assets folder, double-click cheesecake.jpg, insert the alternate text Banana Chocolate Cheesecake when prompted, click OK, then refresh the Files panel**

   The image appears in the cell and is saved in the assets folder of the Web site.

QUICK TIP

You can press [Tab] to move your insertion point to the next cell in a row, and press [Shift] [Tab] to move your insertion point to the previous cell.

3. **Repeat Step 2 to insert the cafe_photo.jpg image in the merged cells to the right of the cheesecake image, using The Sand Crab Cafe as the alternate text**

   The image is placed on the page and saved in the assets folder.

4. **Save your work, click the Preview/Debug in browser button [icon], then click Preview in [your browser name]**

   The cafe page appears in the browser window. You need to improve the alignment of the images.

5. **Close your browser, click inside the cell with the cheesecake image, click the Horz list arrow in the HTML Property inspector, then click Center**

   The image is horizontally centered in its cell.

6. **Repeat Step 5 to center the cafe logo and cafe photo**

   Compare your screen to Figure H-10.

7. **Save your work, preview the page in your browser, compare your screen to Figure H-11, then close the browser**

   You cannot see the table or cell borders in the browser because the table borders are set to zero. If you click the links on the navigation bar, you will notice that the index page and the cafe page work well together now. The other pages seem to "jump" or change positions slightly when you click on one of those links. The index and cafe page are both based on the same CSS page layout. The others are not based on a CSS page layout. Ideally, once you have decided on a CSS page layout for one page, you would redesign all pages to use the same layout.

FIGURE H-10: Aligning images in cells

Centered images

FIGURE H-11: Viewing the table in a browser

Footer

Vertically aligning cell contents

In addition to aligning cell contents horizontally, you can also align them vertically, in the top, middle, bottom, or on the baseline of the cell. To vertically align an image, select the image, click the cell tag icon <td> on the tag selector; or place the insertion point in the cell, click the Vert list arrow in the HTML Property inspector, then choose an alignment type. See Figure H-12.

FIGURE H-12: Vertically aligning cell contents

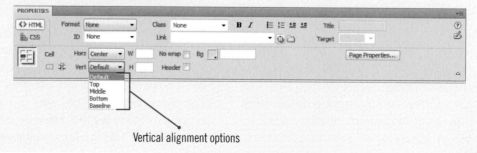

Vertical alignment options

Inserting Text

You can enter text in table cells by typing it in the cell, copying it from another source and pasting it into the cell, or importing it into the cell from another program. Then you can format the text for readability and appearance. If you import text from another program, you should use the Clean Up HTML or Clean Up Word HTML command to remove unnecessary code. ██████ You import a Microsoft Word file that describes the cafe, type two short text descriptions, then enter the three different dining area hours using a nested table.

STEPS

1. **Merge the second and third cells in the second row, click in the newly merged cell, then use the File, Import, Word Document command to import the Word document** cafe.doc **from the Unit H Data Files folder (Win) or copy and paste the text (Mac)**
   The text appears in the merged cell.

2. **Click in the cell under the cheesecake photo, type** Banana Chocolate, **press** [Shift] [Enter] **(Win) or** [Shift] [return] **(Mac), type** Cheesecake, **press** [Shift] [Enter] **(Win) or** [Shift] [return] **(Mac), then type** Our signature dessert

3. **Click in the next cell down and type** Reservations are recommended for The Dining Room during the peak summer season.
   You are ready to enter the cafe hours. You will use a nested table for this.

4. **Merge the two empty cells under the cafe photo, place the insertion point inside the newly merged cell, then click the** Table button **in the Common or Layout category on the Insert panel**

5. **Type** 4 **in the Rows text box, type** 2 **in the Columns text box, type** 300 **in the Table width text box, click the** Table width list arrow, **click** pixels **if necessary, type** 0 **in the Border thickness text box if necessary, then leave the Cell padding and Cell spacing blank**

6. **Click the** Top row header icon **in the Header section, type** This table contains the cafe hours. **in the Summary text box, compare your Table dialog box to Figure H-13, then click** OK
   The Top header option will automatically center and bold the text that is typed into the top cells of the table. The header will be read by screen readers, providing more accessibility for the table.

7. **Merge the top row of cells in the nested table, click in the newly merged cell, then type** The Sand Crab Cafe Hours

8. **Enter the cafe dining area names and their hours, as shown in Figure H-14, then save your work**

Using nested tables

Inserting another table inside a table is similar to adding a new row or column to a table, and creates what is called a **nested table**. To create a nested table, click to place the insertion point inside the cell where you want the nested table to appear, click Insert on the Application bar (Win) or Menu bar (Mac), then click Table, or click the Table button on the Insert panel. The nested table is a separate table that you can format differently from the table in which it is placed. Nested tables can be used effectively if you want part of your table data to have visible borders and part to have invisible borders. For example, you can nest a table with red borders inside a table with invisible borders. Careful planning is important when you work with nested tables. It is easy to get carried away and have too many, which can make them difficult to select and edit. You may be able to achieve the same results by adding rows and columns or splitting cells instead of inserting a nested table.

FIGURE H-13: Table dialog box settings for nested table

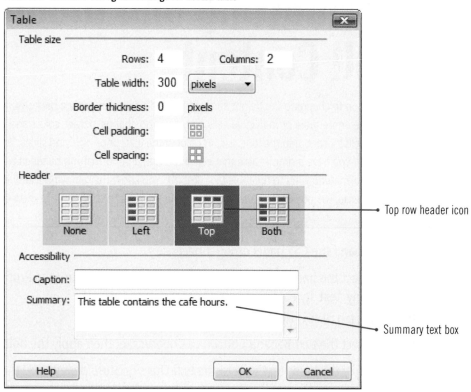

Top row header icon

Summary text box

FIGURE H-14: Adding a nested table

Importing and exporting tabular data

You can import and export tabular data into and out of Dreamweaver. **Tabular data** is data that is arranged in columns and rows and separated by a **delimiter**: a comma, tab, colon, semicolon, or similar character that tells Dreamweaver where to break the data into table cells. **Importing** means to bring data created in another software program into Dreamweaver, and **exporting** means to save data that was created in Dreamweaver in a special file format so that other programs can read it. Files containing tabular data that are imported into Dreamweaver must first be saved as delimited text files. Programs such as Microsoft

Word and Excel offer many file formats for saving files, including saving as delimited text. To import a delimited file, click File on the Application bar (Win) or Menu bar (Mac), point to Import, then click Tabular Data. The Import Tabular Data dialog box opens, offering you choices for the resulting table that will appear on the Web page. To export a table that you created in Dreamweaver, click File on the Application bar (Win) or Menu bar (Mac), point to Export, then click Table. The Export Table dialog box opens, letting you choose the type of delimiter and line breaks you want for the delimited file when you save it.

Formatting and Modifying Cell Content

In addition to changing the height and width of cells, you can apply a background color or a background image to fill the entire table or individual cells. You can also change border colors and border widths. You can format text in cells by changing the font, size, or color of the text, or by applying styles. You can also resize images placed in cells. If you have a simple table that can share the same formatting between all of the table elements, you can add all formatting rules to the table tag. ▚▚▚▚ You know that applying the styles from the Web site style sheet makes sense, so you use the styles from the style sheet file to format the text on the page.

STEPS

1. **Expand the CSS panel group if necessary**

2. **Select the paragraph under the navigation bar, then use the Property inspector to apply the body_text style**

   The text changes to reflect the settings in the body_text style.

3. **Select the text** Banana Chocolate Cheesecake**, then apply the bold_blue style**

4. **Apply the body_text style to the text** Our signature dessert **and the reservation information**

5. **Apply the body_text style to the nested table text, as shown in Figure H-15**

   All text on the page now has a style applied. The table heading remains bold because it is a table header.

QUICK TIP
You may need to make minor adjustments to the spacing on the page if you have extra space above or below the table.

6. **Save your work, preview the cafe page in your browser, then close your browser**

   Formatting the text in the table cells makes the cafe page look more professional.

Formatting cells and cell content

As you have learned, you can format cell content using the Property inspector, but formatting cells is not the same as formatting the content inside them. You can format a cell by simply clicking to place the insertion point inside the cell that you want to format, then choosing options in the Property inspector. For example, you can click a cell, then choose a fill color for the cell by clicking the Bg Color list arrow in the Property inspector and selecting a color. (You must expand the Property inspector to see this option.) However, to format the cell content, you must select the content, not the cell itself. For instance, you can set a cell alignment to center align, but format individual cell contents to different alignments by selecting each one individually and formatting it. Thus, you can have left-aligned text and a centered image in a cell that has been formatted as center aligned.

FIGURE H-15: Styles applied to text

body_text
style applied

bold_blue
style applied

body_text
style applied

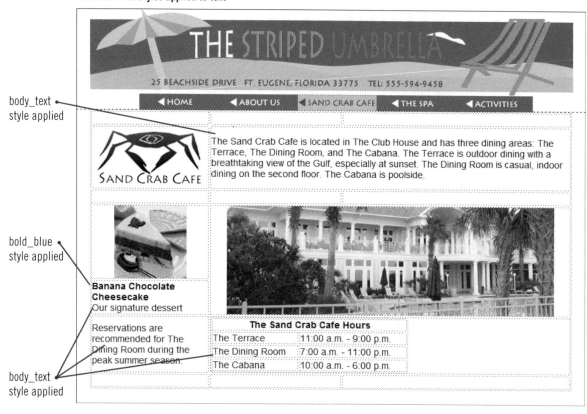

Design Matters

Setting Accessibility Preferences for Tables

You can make tables more accessible to visually-handicapped viewers by adding table captions or table summaries that can be read by screen readers. A table caption will appear on the screen, but a table summary will not. These features are especially useful for tables that are used for tabular data. **Table headers** are another way to provide accessibility. Table headers can be placed at the top or sides of a table. They are automatically centered and bold, and are used by screen readers to help viewers identify the table content. You create table captions, summaries, and headers using with settings found in the Table dialog box.

Formatting Cells

Formatting a cell can include setting properties that visually enhance the cell's appearance, such as setting a cell width, assigning a background color, or setting global alignment properties for the cell content. To format a cell, you need to either select the cell or place the insertion point inside the cell you want to format, then choose the cell formatting options you want to use in the Property inspector. Formatting cells is different from formatting cell contents. When you format cell contents, you must select the contents before you can format them.  You change the horizontal and vertical alignment settings for some of the table cells to improve the appearance of the cell contents on the page.

STEPS

QUICK TIP

You do not need to select the cell content because you are setting the alignment for all contents in the cell, even if there is only one object in the cell at the time.

1. Click to place the insertion point in the cell with the reservations text

2. Click the Vert list arrow in the Property inspector, then click Middle to force the cell contents to the middle of the cell

   Even if the cell is enlarged, the contents will stay aligned in the middle of the cell.

3. With the insertion point in the cell with the reservations text, click the Horz list arrow, then click Center to center the cell contents

   This alignment command centers everything in the cell.

4. Repeat Step 3 to horizontally center the cell contents for the cell with the cheesecake name and the cell with the nested table, then compare your screen to Figure H-16

5. Save your work, preview the cafe page in your browser, then close your browser

---

Design Matters

Using visual aids

Dreamweaver lets you hide or display page features such as table borders, image maps, and frame borders, known as **Visual Aids**, that appear in Design view but not in the browser. You can control the Visual Aids display using the View menu or the Visual Aids button on the Document toolbar. You can show or hide all visual aids or selectively show or hide individual items. Table borders and similar features are helpful as you edit and format a page, but hiding them lets you quickly see how the page will appear in the browser without having to open it in the browser window.

FIGURE H-16: Setting horizontal and vertical cell alignment

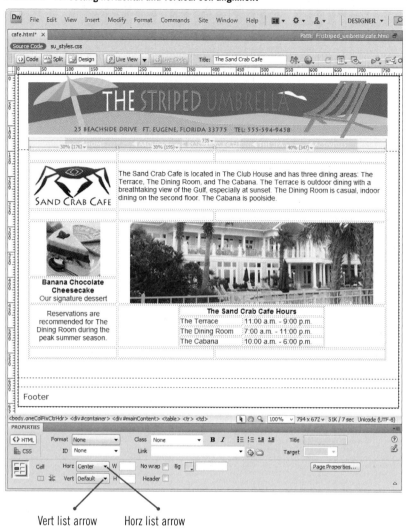

Vert list arrow   Horz list arrow

Using grids and guides for positioning page content

Dreamweaver offers View menu options to help you position your page content more precisely. **Grids** consist of horizontal and vertical lines resembling graph paper that fill the page. You can edit the colors of the lines, the distance between them, whether they are displayed using lines or dots, and whether or not objects "snap" (or automatically align to) to them. **Guides** are horizontal or vertical lines that you drag onto the page from the rulers. Grids and guides are used to position page elements using exact measurements on the ruler. You can edit both the color of the guides and the color of the **distance**, a

feature that shows you the distance between two guides when you hold down the control key and place the mouse pointer between the guides. You can lock the guides so you don't accidentally move them, and you can set them either to snap to page elements or have page elements snap to them. To display either feature, click View on the Application bar (Win) or Menu bar (Mac), point to Grid or Guides, then select an option from the menu. Grids and guides only appear in Dreamweaver, not in the browser.

Adding Media Objects

You can use Dreamweaver to insert a variety of rich media objects on your Web pages, including Flash video; Flash buttons, movies, and text; and a series of built-in JavaScript behaviors, such as sounds, rollover images, popup messages, and menus. **Adobe Flash** is a software program that allows you to create animations and interactive elements that can be placed on your Web pages. These animations use a series of vector-based graphics that load quickly and merge with other graphics and sounds to create short movies. In order to view Flash movies, you need the Adobe Flash Player, a software program that is embedded in the latest versions of most browsers, including Internet Explorer, Mozilla Firefox, and Opera. If you are using an older browser that does not support the version of Flash used to create your movie, you can download the latest Flash player from the Adobe Web site, located at www.adobe.com. You have been given a simple Flash animation that uses the cafe logo to incorporate animation and sound on the Web page. You place it in a cell near the top of the page.

STEPS

QUICK TIP
To play Flash movies in Dreamweaver and in your browser, you must have the Flash Player installed on your computer. If the Flash Player is not installed, you can download it at the Adobe Web site (www.adobe.com). To hear the sound, you must have your speakers turned on and the sound volume turned on in the computer sound settings.

1. Delete the crab image in the left cell in the second row

2. Click the Media list arrow in the Common category on the Insert panel, then click SWF

3. Navigate to the unit_h Data Files folder, click crab.swf, click OK (Win) or Choose (Mac), then click Yes to close the dialog box asking if you want to copy the file to the Web site

4. Save the movie in the root folder of the Web site, type Flash movie of crab logo in the Title text box of the Object Tag Accessibility Attributes dialog box, then click OK

   A Flash movie placeholder appears on the page, as shown in Figure H-17.

5. With the placeholder image selected, as shown in Figure H-17, click Play in the Property inspector to play the crab.swf movie, then click Stop

6. Save your work, click OK in the Copy Dependent Files dialog box, then preview the page in your browser

   A Scripts folder with two files that control the Flash content has been created in the root folder. The crab movie plays in the browser one time, then stops.

QUICK TIP
If you are using a different browser or a version of Internet Explorer that is earlier than 6.0, look for a similar setting.

7. If the movie did not play in Internet Explorer, click Tools on the menu bar, click Internet Options, click the Advanced tab, scroll down to the Security section, then click the Allow active content to run in files on My Computer check box, then click OK

8. Close your browser, position the pointer so that it points to the left side of the first row, then when the pointer becomes an arrow →, click once to select the row, click Modify on the Application bar (Win) or Menu bar (Mac), point to Table, then click Delete Row

   The extra space under the navigation bar is not necessary. Removing the empty row moved the rest of the page contents closer to the top of the page. Lastly, you edit the footer rule and finalize the footer text.

9. Edit the #footer rule as follows: Font-family: Arial, Helvetica, sans-serif; Font-size: small; Font-style: italic; Text-align: center

10. Replace the Footer placeholder text with The Striped Umbrella Copyright 2002 - 2012

QUICK TIP
The nested table text displays as centered in the browser unless you specify the cells to be left-aligned.

11. Save your work, preview the page in the browser again, compare your screen to Figure H-18, then close the browser

12. Close Dreamweaver

FIGURE H-17: Flash movie placeholder on the cafe page

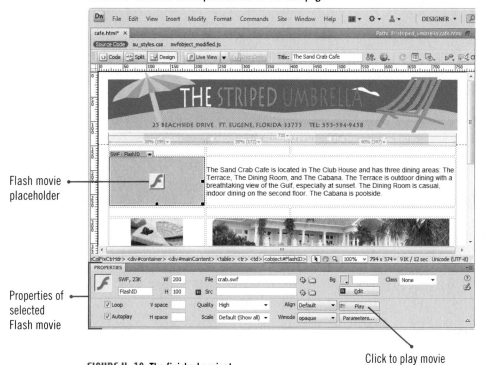

Flash movie placeholder

Properties of selected Flash movie

Click to play movie

FIGURE H-18: The finished project

Editing Flash movies from Dreamweaver

When you create a movie using Adobe Flash, you create two different files: a source file with an .fla file extension, and a player file with an .swf file extension. The player file is the file that is used on Web pages, but it cannot be edited. To make changes to the movie, such as adding or deleting frames, you must have the source file. If you have Adobe Flash installed on your computer and the source file in your Web site root folder, you can edit the source file from Dreamweaver. To do this, select the Flash movie placeholder on a page open in Dreamweaver, then click the Edit button in the Property inspector. The source file will open in the Flash program and be ready to edit. After completing the edits, save and close the file. Flash will update both the source and player files.

Practice

▼ **CONCEPTS REVIEW**

Label each element in the Dreamweaver window shown in Figure H-19.

FIGURE H-19

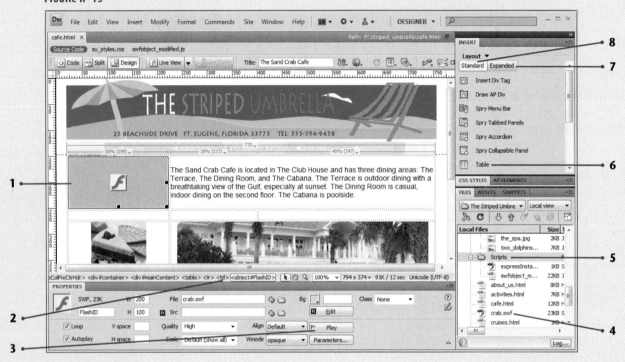

1. _____   5. _____

2. _____   6. _____

3. _____   7. _____

4. _____   8. _____

Match each of the following terms with the statement that best describes its function.

9. **Small boxes that make up columns and rows**

10. **Expanded Tables mode**

11. **Cell padding**

12. **Standard mode**

13. **Border**

14. **Import**

15. **Cell spacing**

16. **Export**

17. **Tag selector**

a. The mode that displays temporary cell padding and cell spacing

b. The space between cell content and cell walls

c. Displays HTML tags for the various page components, including tables and cells

d. Cells

e. The mode that you use to create a table with a specific number of rows and columns

f. Save data that was created in Dreamweaver in a special file format

g. The space between table cells

h. The outline of a table or an individual cell

i. To bring data into Dreamweaver from another program

Select the best answer from the following list of choices.

18. Which of the following is true about nested tables?

    a. Only one nested table can be inserted into a table.

    b. Nested tables are inserted using the Insert Nested Table button.

    c. Nested tables can have visible or invisible borders.

    d. Nested tables cannot be formatted like regular tables.

19. Which of the following is used to select a row in a table?

    a. <div>   **c.** <tr>

    b. <td>   **d.** <table>

20. Which pointer is used to select a row?

    a. ➡   **c.** ◤

    b. ✛   **d.** ▤

▼ SKILLS REVIEW

Important: *If you did not create this Web site in Unit B and maintain it during the preceding units, you will need to create a root folder for this Web site and define the Web site using files your instructor will provide. See the "Read This Before You Begin" section for more detailed instructions.*

1. Understand table modes.

    a. Open the blooms & bulbs Web site.

    b. Open the file dwh_2.html, then save it as **classes.html**, overwriting the existing file, but not updating links.

    c. Close dwh_2.html, then use the Insert panel to change to the Layout category, then change to Expanded Tables mode. Click OK to close the Getting Started in Expanded Tables Mode dialog box if necessary.

    d. Change back to Standard mode.

2. Create a table.

    a. Type **Master Gardener classes begin soon!** in the Title text box on the toolbar, replacing Untitled Document.

    b. Delete the main content placeholder text, then use the Insert panel to insert a table on the page with the following settings:

        Rows = 4   Width = 735 pixels   Cell padding = 5   Header: None

        Columns = 3   Border = 0   Cell spacing = 5

        Enter the text **This table is used for page layout.** in the Summary text box.

    c. Save the file.

3. Resize tables, rows and columns.

    a. Select the first cell in the first row and set the cell width to 25%.

    b. Select the second cell in the same row and set the cell width to 40%.

    c. Select the third cell in the same row and set the cell width to 35%.

    d. Save your work.

4. Merge and split cells.

    a. Merge the first two cells in the first row.

    b. Merge the third cell in the second row with the third cell in the third row.

    c. Split the first cell in the third row into two columns.

    d. Merge the three cells in the last row, then save your work.

5. Insert and align images in table cells.

    a. Use the Insert panel to insert **flower_bed.jpg** in the last row. You can find the flower_bed.jpg file in the unit_h assets folder where your Data Files are stored. Add the alternate text **Flower bed in downtown Alvin** to the flower_bed.jpg image when prompted, then place the insertion point next to the image in the cell and set the horizontal alignment to Center.

    b. Use the tag selector to select the cell containing the flower_bed.jpg image, then set the vertical alignment to **Top**.

    c. Save your work.

6. Insert text.

    a. Type **Master Gardener Classes Beginning Soon!** in the first cell in the first row.

    b. Type **Who are Master Gardeners?** in the second cell in the first row.

    c. Type **Schedule** in the first cell in the second row.

    d. Type **Registration** in the second cell in the second row.

    e. Type the dates and times for the classes from Figure H-20 in the first and second cells in the third row, using line breaks between each line. (Don't be concerned if your text does not neatly line up. You will align it when you format the cells and cell content.)

    f. Either copy and paste or use the Import Word Document command on the File menu to import the file **registration.doc** from the Unit H Data Files into the third cell in the third row.

    g. Repeat Step f to place the text from the gardeners.doc file into the next empty cell.

    h. Save your changes to the page. (*Hint*: Don't worry if your table content does not look like the figure. It will after you format the cells and cell content. If you select the <table> tag on the Tag selector, the cells will tighten up and make it easier to work with the table.)

FIGURE H-20

7. Format and modify cell content.

    a. Apply the body_text style from the blooms style sheet file to the dates, times, and two paragraphs of text.

    b. Create a new class style in the blooms_styles.css style sheet named **subheadings** with the following settings: Font-family: Arial, Helvetica, sans-serif; Font-size: 14; Font-weight: bold; Color: #036.

    c. Create another new class style in the blooms_styles.css style sheet named **reverse_text** with the following settings: Font-family: Arial, Helvetica, sans-serif; Font-size: 14; Font-style: normal; Font-weight: bold; Color: #FFF.

    d. Apply the reverse_text style to the word "Registration" and the subheadings style to the text "Who are Master Gardeners" and "Schedule." (The reverse text style will not be visible until you change the cell background in the next set of steps.)

    e. Apply the seasons style to the text "Master Gardener Classes Beginning Soon!"

    f. Save the file.

8. Format cells.

    a. Set the horizontal alignment for the cells with the dates, times, and the flower_bed image to Center.

    b. Set the horizontal alignment for the cells describing registration and Master Gardeners to Left.

    c. Select the cell with the word "Registration" in it, then change the cell background color to #000099.

    d. Select each cell that contains text (including headings) and set the vertical alignment to Top.

▼ SKILLS REVIEW (CONTINUED)

e. Select each of the four cells with headings and set the horizontal alignment to center. (Master Gardener Classes Beginning Soon!, Who are Master Gardeners?, Schedule, and Registration)

f. Save your work.

9. Add media objects.

a. Insert the **garden_quote.swf** Flash movie located in the unit_h Data Files folder two line breaks below the paragraph about registration, copy the file to the blooms root folder, then enter **Garden quote** in the Object Tag Accessibility Attributes dialog box. (*Hint*: Remember to refresh the Assets panel if necessary.)

b. Play the garden_quote.swf movie in Dreamweaver using the Play button in the Property inspector.

c. Replace the footer placeholder text with **blooms & bulbs Copyright 2001 – 2012**.

d. Make any spacing adjustments necessary to improve the page appearance.

e. Save your work, preview the page in your browser, then compare your screen to Figure H-20.

f. Close the browser, close the page, and exit Dreamweaver.

Important: *If you did not create these Web sites in Unit B and maintain them during the preceding units, you will need to create a root folder for each Web site and define the Web site using files your instructor will provide. See the "Read This Before You Begin" section for more detailed instructions.*

▼ INDEPENDENT CHALLENGE 1

You have been hired to create a Web site for a river expedition company named Rapids Transit, located on the Buffalo River in Arkansas. In addition to renting canoes, kayaks, and rafts, they provide overnight accommodations for those who want to spend more time on the river. River guides are available, if requested, to accompany clients on float trips. The clients range from high-school and college students to families to vacationing professionals. The owner's name is Mike Andrew. Mike has asked you to develop the page for the Web site that lists the equipment available for rental. Refer to Figure H-21 as you work on this page.

a. Start Dreamweaver and open the Rapids Transit Web site.

b. Open the file dwh_3.html from the location where your Data Files are stored, save it as **rentals.html**, overwriting the existing file, but not updating links, then close dwh_3.html.

c. Delete the main content placeholder text, then replace it with a table with two rows, two columns, 740 pixels wide, zero border, no header, and type **Table used for page layout.** in the Summary text box. Leave the cell padding and cell spacing settings blank.

d. Split the first cell in the first row into two rows.

e. Type **Equipment Rentals** in the first of the two split cells in the first row, then center the cell contents horizontally.

f. Format the Equipment Rentals text using the lodging style.

g. Insert the image kayak.jpg from the assets folder where your Unit H Data Files are stored into the second of the two split cells, adding **Kayaking is fun!** as the alternate text.

h. Set the horizontal alignment for the cell with the kayak image to center.

i. Use the tag selector to select the cell with the image and change the cell width to **30%**.

j. Import the text from the Unit H Data File rentals.doc into the cell that is to the right of the kayak image.

k. Format the paragraph with the body_text style, and set the vertical alignment for the cell to Top.

l. Merge the cells in the bottom row.

m. Insert a nested table in the bottom row with **4 rows**, **4 columns**, **100% width**, and a border of **1**; set the cell padding and cell spacing for the nested table to zero; select the Top header option; type **This table contains rental prices.** for the table summary.

n. Set each cell width to **25%**, then merge the cells in the top row to make room for the table header.

o. Enter the rental information from Figure H-21 into your table and format the heading, items, and prices with the body_text style.

p. Save your work and preview the page in your browser. (*Hint*: If your nested table header is not centered in the browser, set the cell alignment for the table header to Center.)

q. Modify the footer placeholder text to read **Rapids Transit Copyright 2000 – 2012**.

r. Close your browser, then exit Dreamweaver.

FIGURE H-21

▼ INDEPENDENT CHALLENGE 2

Your company is designing a new Web site for TripSmart, a travel outfitter. TripSmart specializes in travel products and services. In addition to selling travel products, such as luggage and accessories, they sponsor trips and offer travel advice. Their clients range from college students to families to vacationing professionals. You are now ready to work on the catalog page. The catalog page will feature three items from their catalog.

a. Start Dreamweaver and open the TripSmart Web site.

b. Open the file dwh_4.html, save it as **catalog.html**, and the title **TripSmart featured catalog items**, then close the dwh_4.html file.

c. Replace the main content text with a table with five rows, three columns, a width of 715 pixels, a border of zero, cell padding and spacing of zero, no header, and an appropriate table summary, then set the cell widths in the second row to **33%**, **33%**, and **34%**.

d. Merge the three cells in the first row and type **Our products are backed by a 100% guarantee.**, then set the horizontal cell alignment to Center.

e. In the three cells in the second row, type **Protection from harmful UV rays**; **Cool, light-weight, versatile**; and **Pockets for everything**, then set the horizontal alignment in each cell to Center.

f. In the three cells in the third row, place the files hat.jpg, pants.jpg, and vest.jpg from the unit_h Data Files assets folder, and add the following alternate text to the images: **Safari Hat**, **Kenya Convertible Pants**, and **Photographer's Vest**, then set the horizontal cell alignment for each cell to Center.

g. In the three cells in the fourth row, type **Safari Hat**, **Kenya Convertible Pants**, and **Photographer's Vest**, then center align each cell.

h. In the first cell in the fifth row, type **Item number 50501** and **$29.00** with a line break between them, then center align the cell.

i. Type **Item number 62495** and **$39.50** with a line break between them in the second cell in the fifth row, then center align the cell.

j. Type **Item number 52301** and **$54.95** with a line break between them in the third cell in the fifth row, then center align the cell.

k. Apply the body_text style to the three descriptions in the second row.

l. Create a new class style in the tripsmart_styles.css style sheet named reverse_text with the following settings: Font-family: Verdana, Geneva, sans-serif; Font-size: 14; Font-style: normal; Font-weight: bold; color: #FFF.

m. Apply the reverse_text style to the text in the first row, then change the cell background color to #666666.

n. Apply the reverse_text style to the three item names under the images, then change the three cell background colors to #999999.

o. Create a new class style called item_numbers with the following settings: Font-family: Verdana, Geneva, sans-serif; Font-size: x-small; Font-style: normal; Font-weight: bold.

p. Apply the item_numbers style to the three item numbers and prices.

q. Save your work, preview the page in the browser, and compare your page to Figure H-22.

r. Close your browser, then exit Dreamweaver.

FIGURE H-22

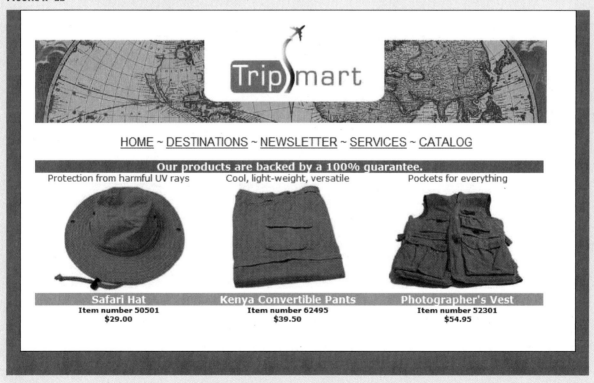

▼ INDEPENDENT CHALLENGE 3

Dell Patterson has opened a new shop called CollegeFandz, an online source for college students' clothing and collectibles. She is considering creating a Web site to promote her services and products and would like to gather some ideas before she hires a Web designer. She decides to visit Web sites to look for design ideas.

    a. Connect to the Internet and go to the Neiman Marcus Web site at www.neimanmarcus.com.

    b. Use the Source command on the View menu (Internet Explorer), or the Page Source command on the View menu (Firefox), to view the source code and determine if the page layout is based on the use of CSS layouts, tables, or a combination of both.

    c. Go to the Dakini Web site at www.dakini.com, as shown in Figure H-23.

    d. View the source code and determine if the page layout is based on the use of CSS layouts, tables, or a combination of both.

    e. Using your word processing software or paper, list five design ideas that you like from either of these pages and tell which page was the source of each idea.

    f. Exit the browser.

FIGURE H-23

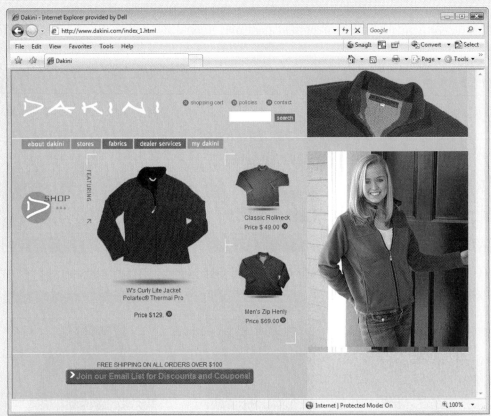

Dakini Web site used with permission from Dakini, Inc.—www.dakini.com.

▼ INDEPENDENT CHALLENGE 4

This assignment will continue to build on the personal Web site that you created in Unit B. In Unit C you created and developed your index page. In Unit D you added a page with either an ordered or an unordered list, a CSS Style Sheet with a minimum of two styles. In Unit E you added a page that included at least two graphics. In Unit F you added a page that included several links and an image map. In Unit G, you converted the index page to a page based on a CSS layout. In this lesson, you will be working with one of the other pages in your Web site.

   a. Consult your storyboard and decide which page you would like to develop in this lesson.

   b. Sketch a layout for your page using a table for placement of some of the page elements.

   c. Experiment with splitting and merging cells and adding and deleting rows.

   d. Create content for this page and format the text attractively on the page using settings for Font, Size, Text Color, Style, and Alignment.

   e. Save the file and preview the page in the browser.

   f. Consider adding a table to position selected page elements.

After you are satisfied with your work, verify the following:

   a. Each completed page has a page title.

   b. All links work correctly.

   c. The completed pages view well using a screen resolution of 800 × 600 and 1024 × 768.

   d. All images are properly set showing a path to the assets folder of the Web site.

   e. All images have alternate text and are legal for you to use.

   f. The link checker shows no broken links or orphaned files. If there are orphaned files, note your plan to link them.

   g. All main pages have a consistent navigation system.

▼ VISUAL WORKSHOP

Use Figure H-24 to continue your work on the Carolyne's Creations Web site. You are now ready to begin work on a page that will showcase the catering services using a table to list menu items. Open the file dwh_5.html, save it as catering.html. overwriting the existing file, and begin by replacing the main content placeholder text with the table shown in Figure H-24. Use the new image from the unit_h Data Files folder called muffins.jpg. The text for the menu items can be found in the file menu items.doc. (*Hint*: Open the file in Word, then copy and paste each section to the appropriate cell in the table.) Remember to add alternate text for each new image. Make any spacing adjustments necessary to improve the page appearance. The table in Figure H-24 is 750 pixels wide.

FIGURE H-24

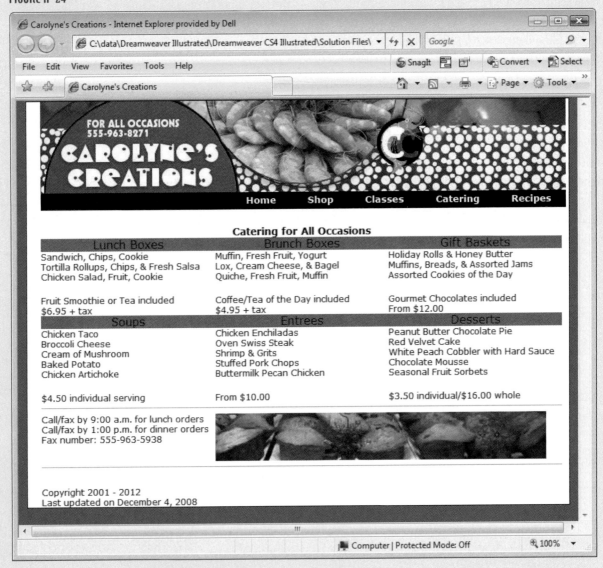

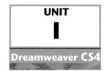
Collecting Data with Forms

Forms are a way to add interactivity to a Web page. Forms present users with a series of options for entering information. Dreamweaver lets you easily create forms containing form objects, such as check boxes and option buttons. The form then sends information that users enter to the host Web server to be collected and processed. Forms are useful for tasks, such as ordering merchandise, responding to requests for customer feedback, and requesting information. The Striped Umbrella Marketing Department has asked you to design a form for the bottom of the activities page; the form will provide another way for interested clients to request additional information about fishing and dolphin cruises.

OBJECTIVES

Understand forms and form objects

Insert a form on a page

Add a text form field

Add a radio group

Add a check box

Insert a Submit and a Reset button

Format and test a form

Update files

Understanding Forms and Form Objects

Forms are a convenient and efficient way to obtain information from Web site users. A form can either be a page by itself, collecting several pieces of information from a user with numerous form objects, or it can take up only a small part of a page. See Figures I-1 and I-2 for examples of long and short forms. **Form objects** are the individual form components that accept individual pieces of information. They include check boxes, radio buttons, text fields, and buttons. Many pages include a form with only one form object, such as a text box. You can insert tables in more complex forms to help organize the objects into rows and columns. It is possible for a page to have more than one form. However, you cannot place a form inside a form. In the HTML code, forms are surrounded by beginning and ending form tags. You decide to place the form at the bottom of the activities page. Before you begin work, you review the various form objects you might use.

DETAILS

As you create forms, you can choose from the following objects:

- **Form fields**

  A **field** is a form area into which users can insert a specific piece of data, such as their last name or address. Form fields include text fields, hidden fields, and file fields. **Text fields** can accept both numbers and letters, known as **alphanumeric** data. A text field can contain single or multiple lines of data. **Hidden fields** store information about the user and can be used by the company originating the form at a later time, such as the next time the user visits their Web site. **File fields** allow users to browse to a file on their computer and **upload**, or send, it to the form host Web server. In this unit, you will work with text fields.

- **Radio buttons**

  Radio buttons are small empty circles on a form that users click to select a choice. A selected radio button has a black fill. Radio buttons in a group are mutually exclusive, meaning that the user can select only one choice at a time.

- **Check boxes**

  Check boxes are small squares on a form. To select a choice, users click to place a check mark inside the box(es). In a series of check boxes, it is possible to select more than one check box.

- **List/menus**

  List/menus provide the user with a list or menu of choices to select. Lists display the choices in a scrolling format. Menus display the choices in a pop-up menu. List/menus provide a fast method of entering information that may be tedious for the user to type.

- **Buttons**

  Buttons (not to be confused with radio buttons) are usually small rectangular objects containing a text label. When a user clicks a button, a task is performed, such as submitting the form or clearing the form. To **submit** the form means to send the information on the form to the host Web server for processing. Clearing, or **resetting**, the form means to erase all form entries and set the values back to the default settings.

Design Matters

Planning form layout

Before you begin creating your form, you should take the time to write down the information you want to collect and the order that you want it to appear on the form. It's also a good idea to make a sketch of the form to make sure that all of the form objects are placed in a logical order that will make sense to the users. Since people using the Internet are notoriously in a hurry, put the most important information at the top of the form to make it more likely that users will include that information when they fill out the form. Putting the most important information at the top of the page, so that it can be seen without the user having to scroll, is similar to putting the most important news "above the fold," or at the top of, a newspaper page.

FIGURE I-1: Example of a long form

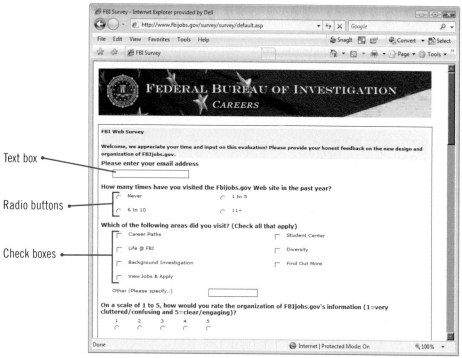

Text box

Radio buttons

Check boxes

Federal Bureau of Investigation Web site – www.fbijobs.gov

FIGURE I-2: Examples of small forms

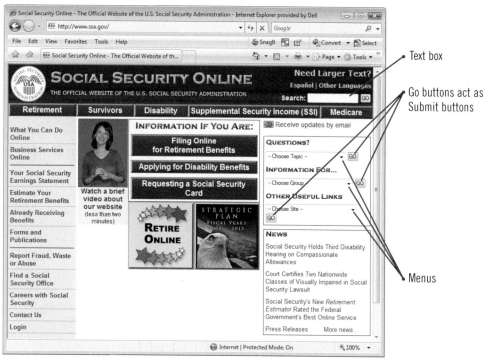

Text box

Go buttons act as Submit buttons

Menus

Social Security Administration Web site – www.ssa.gov

Accessible forms

To ensure that your forms are accessible, use the Accessibility preference for Form Objects. To select it, click Edit (Win) or Dreamweaver (Mac) on the Application bar (Win) or Menu bar (Mac), click Preferences, then click the Accessibility category and select the Form objects check box. With this option selected, each time you insert a new form, Dreamweaver will prompt you to enter a label tag that is then attached to the form. These labels are read by screen readers.

Inserting a Form on a Page

Before you can begin adding form objects to a page, you must create the form that will contain them. You can create a form by using the Form command on the Insert menu, or by using the Form button on the Insert panel. When you create a form, Dreamweaver adds beginning and ending form tags to the HTML code. You give the form a descriptive name that the program will use when it processes the data from the form.  You decide to create a form on the activities page that will include form objects for the client name and address information.

STEPS

1. **Start Dreamweaver, open** The Striped Umbrella Web site, **then open the** activities.html **page**
   The form will go at the bottom of this page.

2. **Place the insertion point after the last sentence on the page, then insert a paragraph break**

3. **Click the** Form button **in the Forms category on the Insert panel**
   A red dotted outline appears on the page. It doesn't contain any form objects yet. The Property inspector displays the form properties. If you try to insert a form object before you create the form, Dreamweaver will ask if you want to add form tags before inserting the form object.

> **TROUBLE**
>
> You might see a message box stating that you must be able to view invisible elements to see the form. If you do, click View on the Application bar (Win) or Menu bar (Mac), point to Visual Aids, then click Invisible Elements to see the form outline on the page.

4. **Select the form name in the Property inspector, type** feedback, **replacing the default form name, press [Tab] then compare your screen to Figure I-3**
   The rest of the form properties relate to how the information users enter will be processed. They can be filled out with information provided by your instructor, or left blank. (The programming involved in processing a form is beyond the scope of this book.) You can edit the form to add these properties at a later time. The form cannot be processed on a server without them.

5. **Click the** Show Code view button [Code]
   The form code appears, as shown in Figure I-4.

6. **Locate the tags for the form**
   You notice the tags for the form ID, form name, form method, and form action. The form method directs the way that the data will be sent to the server.

7. **Click the** Show Design view button [Design] **to return to Design view**

Design Matters

Creating user-friendly forms

When a form contains several required fields — fields that must be filled out before the form can be processed — it is a good idea to provide visual clues that label these fields as required fields. Often you see an asterisk next to a required field with a corresponding note at either the top or the bottom of the form explaining that all fields marked with asterisks are required. This encourages viewers to complete these fields initially, rather than submitting the form and then receiving an error message asking them to complete required fields that were left blank. Using a different font color for the asterisks and note is an easy way to call attention to them and make them more visible to users.

FIGURE I-3: Form on the activities page

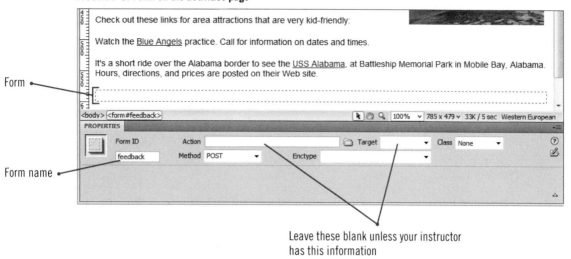

Form

Form name

Check out these links for area attractions that are very kid-friendly:

Watch the Blue Angels practice. Call for information on dates and times.

It's a short ride over the Alabama border to see the USS Alabama, at Battleship Memorial Park in Mobile Bay, Alabama. Hours, directions, and prices are posted on their Web site.

`<body> <form#feedback>`   100% ▾ 785 x 479 ▾ 33K / 5 sec Western European

PROPERTIES

Form ID feedback   Action   Target   Class None
Method POST   Enctype

Leave these blank unless your instructor
has this information

FIGURE I-4: HTML code for the form on the activities page

Form tags

```
      surf. Beware, though, of Ralph! Ralph is our resident blue heron. He knows what you fishermen have in
       your coolers and if you aren't careful, he'll take your catch off your hands and make a quick
      getaway.</span></p>
72    <p class="body_text"><img src="assets/two_dolphins.jpg" alt="Two dolphins surfing the wake" width=
      "225" height="159" hspace="5" vspace="5" align="right" />We can also arrange dolphin cruises. We have
       a unique approach -- two boats go out side by side about 50 yards apart. The dolphins love it
      because it generates a huge wake! You'll see them jumping right between the boats. </p>
73    <p class="body_text">You can arrange for tickets for <a href="fishing.html">fishing excursions</a> or
       <a href="cruises.html">dolphin cruises</a> at The Club House desk.</p>
74    <p class="body_text">Check out these links for area attractions that are very kid-friendly: </p>
75    <p class="body_text">Watch the <a href="http://www.blueangels.navy.mil">Blue Angels</a> practice.
      Call for information on dates and times. </p>
76    <p class="body_text">It's a short ride over the Alabama border to see the <a href=
      "http://www.ussalabama.com">USS Alabama</a>, at Battleship Memorial Park in Mobile Bay, Alabama.
      Hours, directions, and prices are posted on their Web site. </p>
77    <form id="feedback" name="feedback" method="post" action="">
78    </form>
79    <p class="body_text"> </p>
80    </body>
81    </html>
82
```

Processing forms

While it is very easy to create attractive, user-friendly forms, they are useless without a way to process and store the information. Although you can e-mail form information, this is not a great option because someone will have to open the e-mail, read the information, and enter it in a database if it is to be stored or processed. It is more practical to send the information directly to a server to read, store, and process the data. The data-collecting stage of form processing is called **front-end processing**; it is the beginning of the processing cycle. The processing stage is called **back-end processing** because it is the end of the processing cycle. Forms are processed according to the properties specified in the form action attribute. The **form action** attribute is the part of the form tag that specifies how the data in the form will be processed. If you do not need to save the data that a user enters on a form, it is better to use **client-side scripting**. This means that the form is processed on the user's computer. An example of this is a mortgage calculator that allows you to estimate mortgage payments. If you need to store and process the data, you must use **server-side scripting**. This means the form data is processed on the form's host Web server. An example of this is ordering books on a bookstore Web site. Client-side scripting is written with programs such as JavaScript or VBScript. Server-side scripting is written with a program such as Common Gateway Interface (CGI) script.

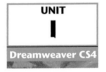
Adding a Text Form Field

One of the most common form fields is a text field. You can create a Single-line text field or a Multi-line text field. Each field should have a descriptive label so users have a visual clue as to what to enter in the field. Form field names should not include spaces, punctuation, or uppercase letters, to ensure that they can be read properly by the program that will process the form data. ██████ You begin creating your form by placing a table inside the form. The table will help you line up the form objects more precisely.

STEPS

1. **Place the insertion point inside the form if necessary**
   The table must be placed inside the form to work properly.

2. **Click the Table button in the Common category on the Insert panel**

3. **Set the table rows to 7, the table columns to 3, the table width to 700 pixels, the border to 0 if necessary, leave the cell padding text box blank, set the cell spacing to 3, a Top header option, type This table is used for form layout. for the Summary, then click OK**

> **QUICK TIP**
> Notice that the First Name label goes in the second row of the table; leave the top row blank for now.

4. **Using Figure I-5 as a guide, enter the labels for your text fields into the table, select and format the labels with the subheading style, then drag the column border closer to the edge of the text labels**
   You want the corresponding form fields to appear next to each label.

5. **Place the insertion point in the cell next to the First Name label, then click the Text Field button in the Forms category on the Insert panel**

> **QUICK TIP**
> The default Char width is 20 characters.

6. **Click the No Label tag style option in the Input Tag Accessibility Attributes dialog box, click OK, type first_name in the TextField text box in the Property inspector, replacing the default name, then type 30 in both the Char width and the Max chars text boxes**
   You have named the text field first_name. The character width and max characters settings set the size of the text field and the number of characters, respectively, that can be input in the field. If more characters are entered in the field than the character width setting allows, they will not all be visible. They will, however, be submitted with the form data. A user will not be able to enter more characters in the field than the max characters setting allows.

> **QUICK TIP**
> If you have to create many fields of the same size, you can copy the first field, paste it in the new locations, then change the name and properties for each one.

7. **Repeat Steps 5 and 6 to enter Single-line text fields for each text label, using the information in Table I-1**
   All text form fields now have labels, names, and settings for the character width on the screen, and the maximum characters the user can enter in each field.

8. **Drag the column border closer to the edge of the form fields, click the first_name field to select it, then save your work. (You are only selecting this field to be able to compare your field properties with the figure.)**
   Compare your screen to Figure I-6.

TABLE I-1: Form field attributes for the feedback form

label	form field name	char width	max chars
First Name	first_name	30	30
Last Name	last_name	30	30
Street	street	30	30
City	city	30	30
State	state	2	2
Zip Code	zip_code	10	10

FIGURE I-5: Adding and formatting form labels

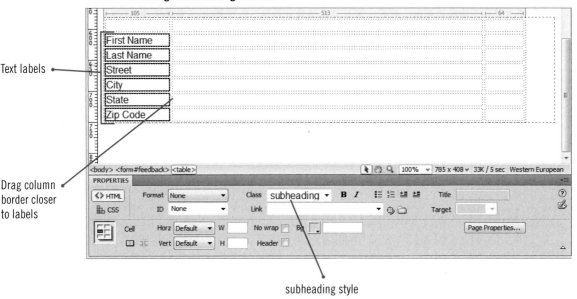

Text labels

Drag column
border closer
to labels

subheading style

FIGURE I-6: Text form fields added to the feedback form

Drag column
border closer
to form fields

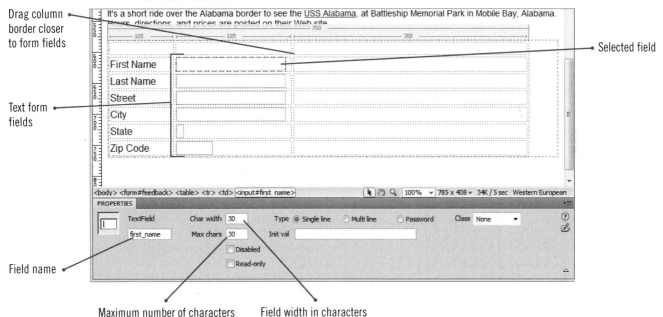

Selected field

Text form
fields

Field name

Maximum number of characters   Field width in characters

Understanding text fields

Dreamweaver has three types of text fields: Single-line text fields, Multi-line text fields, and Password fields. **Single-line text fields** are useful for small pieces of data, such as a name or telephone number. **Multi-line text fields**, also called Textarea fields, are useful for entering comments that may take several sentences to complete. **Password fields** are unique fields that display asterisks or bullets when the data is entered to prevent others from viewing the data as it is entered. There are three ways to create a Multi-line text field.

You can click the Text Field button in the Forms category on the Insert panel, select the field, then click the Multi line option on the Property inspector. Or you can create a Textarea field by clicking the Textarea button in the Forms category on the Insert panel. You can also use the Input Tag Accessibility Attributes dialog box if you have set your preferences to provide accessibility for form objects. To create a Password field, create a text field, select the field, then select the Password option in the Property inspector.

Adding a Radio Group

Radio buttons let users select options. Two or more radio buttons together are called a **radio group**. When used in a group, radio buttons are mutually exclusive; if a user tries to select two radio buttons in the same group, the first one becomes deselected when the second one is selected. Radio buttons are useful in situations where you want users to select only one choice from a group of possible choices. For example, on a shoe order form, radio buttons could represent the different shoe sizes. To order one pair of shoes, users would select only one size. You continue designing your form for the activities page by adding a group of two radio buttons for users to indicate whether they would like to receive newsletters in the mail.

STEPS

1. **Select the third cells in the second, third, and fourth rows, expand the Property inspector if necessary, then click the** Merges selected cells using spans button ▢ **in the Property inspector**

   The radio group will go in the space you created.

2. **Place the insertion point in the newly merged cell in the third column, then type** Would you like to receive our quarterly newsletters?

   It is important to include instructions so users will know how to fill in the form.

3. **Press** [Shift][Enter] **(Win) or** [shift][return] **(Mac), then click the** Radio Group button **in the Forms category on the Insert panel**

   The Radio Group dialog box opens, as shown in Figure I-7.

4. **Type** newsletters **in the Name text box**

   Newsletters is the name of the radio group. Next you configure the two buttons you will use for the group.

> **TROUBLE**
> If your table has extra space in the rows, click the <table> tag on the tag selector.

5. **Select** the first instance of Radio **in the Label column of the Radio Group dialog box to select it, then type** Yes

6. **Press** [Tab] **to select the** first instance of radio **in the Value column, then type** positive

   You specified that the first radio button will be named Yes and you set "positive" as the value that, after users select this option, will be sent to your script or program when the form is processed.

7. **Repeat Steps 5 and 6 to add another radio button named** No **with a value of** negative

> **TROUBLE**
> You may have to click the Table tag in the Tag selector to close up any empty space in the table.

8. **Verify that the** Lay out using: Line breaks (
 tags) **option is selected, compare your screen to Figure I-8, then click** OK

   The radio group appears on the form.

9. **Format the button labels with the** body_text style **and the sentence above them using the** subheading style, **save your work, then compare your screen to Figure I-9**

Design Matters

Creating good form field labels

When you create a form, you must include form field labels so that viewers know what information you want them to enter in each field of the form. Because labels are so important in identifying the information that the form collects, you must use labels that make sense to your viewers. For example, First Name and Last Name are good form field labels because viewers understand clearly what information they should enter. However, a label such as Top 6 Directory Names might confuse viewers and cause them to leave the field blank or enter incorrect information. When you create a form field

label, use a simple name that makes it obvious what information viewers should enter in the form field. If creating a simple and obvious label is not possible, then include a short paragraph that describes the information that should be entered into the form field. You can add labels to a form using one of three methods. You can simply type a label in the appropriate table cell of your form, or use the Label button in the Forms category on the Insert panel to link the label to the form object. Or you can use the Input Tag Accessibility Attributes dialog box if you have set your preferences to provide access for form objects.

FIGURE I-7: Radio Group dialog box

Enter Radio Group name

Add Radio button

Delete Radio button

Select to change label for Radio buttons

Click to change the button order

Select a layout to use

FIGURE I-8: Radio Group properties for newsletters radio group

Name of Radio Group

Labels for the two buttons

Button values

Lay out using Line breaks

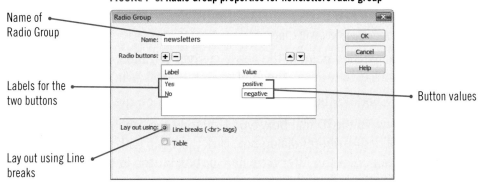

FIGURE I-9: Formatting the Radio Group

Sentence in subheading style

Radio group buttons and labels with body_text style

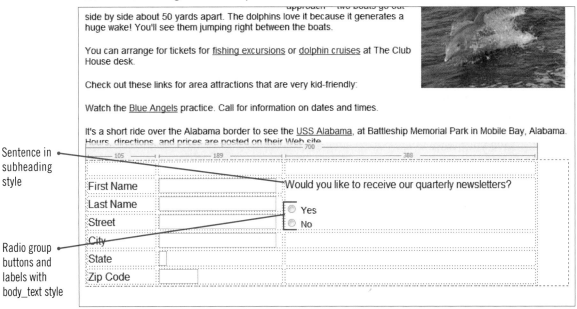

Design Matters

Using list/menus

Often a form will include a field where the user is asked to select only one item, but there are so many items from which to choose that radio buttons would take too much space on the form. In those cases, list/menus are the more appropriate choice for a form object.

This object can either take the form of a scrolling list or a shortcut menu. Lists differ from menus in that they allow form users to make multiple selections. Menus only allow one selection. Both make efficient use of space on a form.

Adding a Check Box

Check boxes are very much like radio buttons, in that a user can simply click one to select it. However, with check boxes, the user can select more than one choice when appropriate. For example, a form with options for checking your hobbies from a group would allow you to check more than one hobby since many people have more than one hobby. You insert check boxes in the form so users can request more information about the fishing trips and dolphin cruises.

STEPS

1. **Place the insertion point in the third row of the third column, drag to select that cell and the cell beneath it, then click the** Merges selected cells using spans button ⊞ **in the Property inspector**

   These newly merged cells will contain the check boxes.

2. **Place the insertion point in the newly merged cell and type** Please select the materials you would like to receive:, **then press [Shift][Enter] (Win) or [shift][return] (Mac)**

3. **Click the** Checkbox button **in the Forms category on the Insert panel**

> **TROUBLE**
>
> If you need to edit one of the check boxes, click the check box to select it and edit the properties in the Property inspector.

4. **Type** fishing **in the ID text box, type** Fishing **in the Label text box in the Input Tag Accessibilities Attributes dialog box, click the** Wrap with label tag option button **in the Style section, click the** After form item option button **in the Position section, as shown in Figure I-10, then click** OK

   A check box with the label "Fishing" appears in the cell.

5. **Select the check box, then type** fish **as the Checked value in the Property inspector**

   You have assigned the check box a name and a value, as shown in Figure I-11. You leave the initial state as unchecked, since you don't want the check box to be selected when the form is first opened.

6. **Click to place the insertion point after the word "Fishing" on the form, press [spacebar] once, then repeat Steps 3 through 5 to place one more check box on the form, using Figure I-12 as a guide for the check box properties and** Cruises **as the label on the page**

> **TROUBLE**
>
> You may need to resize your cell widths to match Figure I-13.

7. **Format the labels with the** body_text **style and the text line above it as the** subheading **style, then compare your screen to Figure I-13**

8. **Save your work**

Design Matters

Creating accessible HTML form objects

When users enter information in form fields, they use [Tab] to move the insertion point from field to field. By default, the insertion point moves through fields from left to right across the page and screen readers read from left to right. However, you can set your own tab order to override the default. For example, regardless of where the fields for First Name and Last Name are placed on the form, you can direct the insertion point to move directly from the First Name field to the Last Name field, even if there are other fields between them. To change an existing form object's tab order, right-click the form object (Win), or Ctrl + click the form object (Mac). Click Edit Tag <input>, click the Style Sheet/Accessibility category in the Tag Editor - input dialog box, then change the Tab index number. To make the field the second field to be selected after the user presses [Tab], place the number 2 in the Tab index box; enter 3 to make it the third field selected, and so forth. You can also assign Tab Index values in the Input Tag Accessibility Attributes dialog box when you create the tag. Tab orders will only work if each tab is assigned an index number.

FIGURE I-10: Input Tag Accessibility Attributes dialog box for Fishing label

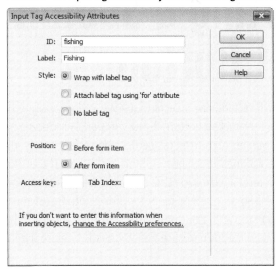

FIGURE I-11: Properties for first check box

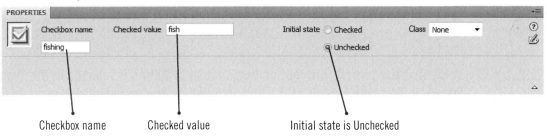

Checkbox name   Checked value   Initial state is Unchecked

FIGURE I-12: Properties for second check box

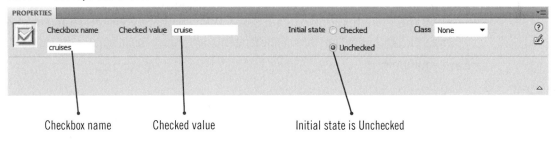

Checkbox name   Checked value   Initial state is Unchecked

FIGURE I-13: Formatting the check box text

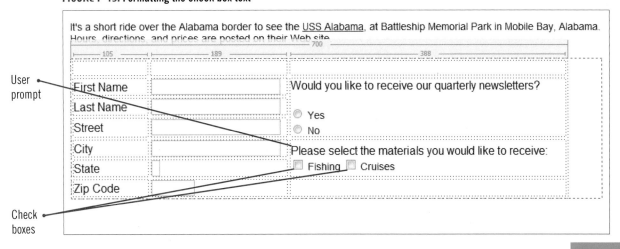

User prompt

Check boxes

Inserting a Submit and a Reset Button

Buttons are small rectangular objects that have actions assigned to them. **Actions** trigger events that take place after a user clicks a button. Button properties include a name, a label, and an action. As with all selected objects, you assign button properties using the Property inspector. There are two reserved button names that have assigned meanings: Submit and Reset. These should only be used for buttons that are used to submit or reset a form. No other buttons should use these names. **Submit** means to send the form data to the processing program or script for processing. **Reset** means to clear the form fields to the original values. You add a button to the bottom of the form that will submit the form for processing, and a button to clear the form in case the user needs to erase the information and start over.

STEPS

1. Place the insertion point in the third column of the last row

2. Click the Button button in the Forms category on the Insert panel, click the No label tag option in the Input Tag Accessibility Attributes dialog box, then click OK

   A Submit button appears on the form, without a label next to it, and the Property inspector displays its properties.

3. Verify that the Submit form option button next to Action is selected in the Property inspector, and type Submit as the button name, as shown in Figure I-14

   When a viewer clicks this Submit button, the information in the form will be sent to the processing script.

4. Click to place the insertion point to the right of the Submit button, click the Button button on the Insert panel, click the No label tag option in the Input Tag Accessibility Attributes dialog box if necessary, click OK, select the new button, click the Reset form option button next to Action in the Property inspector, verify that the Button name text box and the Value text box contain Reset, then compare your screen to Figure I-15

   When a viewer clicks this Reset button, the form will clear any information he or she has typed.

5. Save your work

Design Matters

Using the Adobe Exchange

To obtain form controls designed for creating specific types of forms, such as online tests and surveys, you can visit the Adobe Exchange. This is a central storage location on the Adobe Web site for program extensions, also known as add-ons. You can search the site by using keywords in the Search the Exchange text box, similar to the Dreamweaver Help Search text box. You can use the Advanced Search feature to search by categories such as Rich Media, Accessibility, or Navigation. You can also search by using the Category, License Type, Rating, Subcategory, Platform, and Publish Date search options. Go to www.adobe.com/cfusion/exchange/index.cfm.

FIGURE I-14: Inserting a Submit button

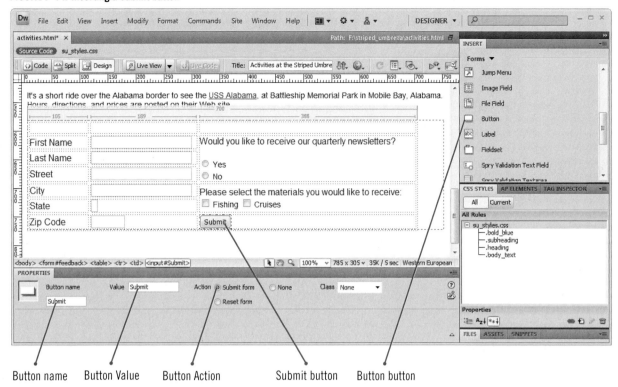

Button name   Button Value   Button Action   Submit button   Button button

FIGURE I-15: Inserting a Reset button

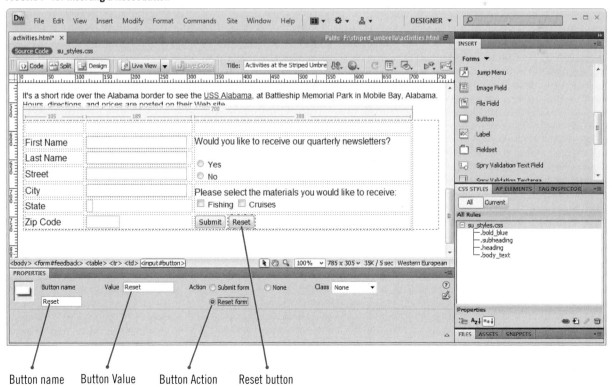

Button name   Button Value   Button Action   Reset button

Formatting and Testing a Form

In addition to adding descriptive labels to each form object, there are several ways you can format a form to make it easier to use. You can add brief instructions to the top of the form that will guide the user in filling it out. Simple formatting such as adding a horizontal rule above and below the form can set it off from the rest of the page content. Only the data the user enters using the form objects will be processed; any additional form text and formatting will not be processed. ▰▰▰▰ You add a short instructional sentence to serve as the form header at the top of the form, right-align some of the labels, then set off the form with a horizontal rule.

STEPS

1. **Merge the top three cells in the table, then in the merged cell type** To request further information please complete this form.

2. **Apply the** bold_blue **style to the sentence**
   The sentence is automatically centered across the table and appears bold because it is a table header.

3. **Select the labels in the first column and set the Horizontal alignment to right, as shown in Figure I-16**
   The labels are now closer to the text boxes.

4. **Place the insertion point in the last cell of the table, press [Tab] to create a new row, select all the cells in the new row, then merge them**
   The new row is merged. You will insert a horizontal line here to end the form.

5. **Place the insertion point in the newly merged cell, click** Insert **on the Application bar (Win) or Menu bar (Mac), point to** HTML, **click** Horizontal Rule, **then set the width to** 95% **and the alignment to** Center

QUICK TIP

Recall that you can click the table tag in the tag selector to select a table.

6. **Select the table, then center the table in the form**

7. **Save your work, click the** Preview/Debug in Browser button 🌐, **then select** Preview in [your browser name], **enter some dummy data in the form, then click the** Reset button
   The Reset button works correctly, but the Submit button will not work correctly because you have not set the form properties to send the data to a Web server. You need additional information from your instructor to do this.

TROUBLE

If the text in column 3 wraps to two lines, drag the right table border to widen the table.

8. **Compare your finished project to Figure I-17, close your browser window, then close the page**

FIGURE I-16: Formatting text field labels

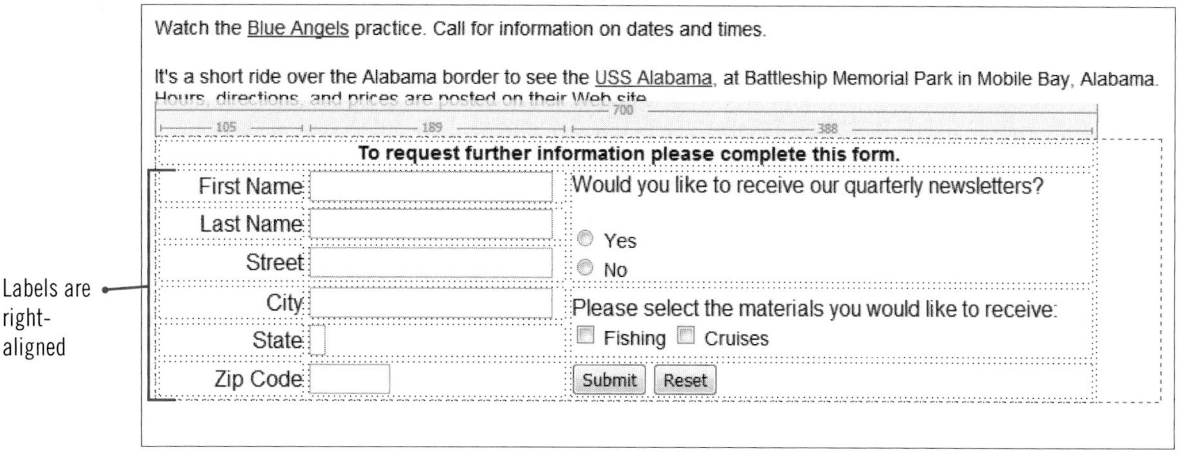

Watch the Blue Angels practice. Call for information on dates and times.

It's a short ride over the Alabama border to see the USS Alabama, at Battleship Memorial Park in Mobile Bay, Alabama. Hours, directions, and prices are posted on their Web site.

To request further information please complete this form.

First Name:

Last Name:

Street:

City:

State:

Zip Code:

Would you like to receive our quarterly newsletters?

Yes

No

Please select the materials you would like to receive:

Fishing Cruises

Submit Reset

Labels are right-aligned

FIGURE I-17: The finished project

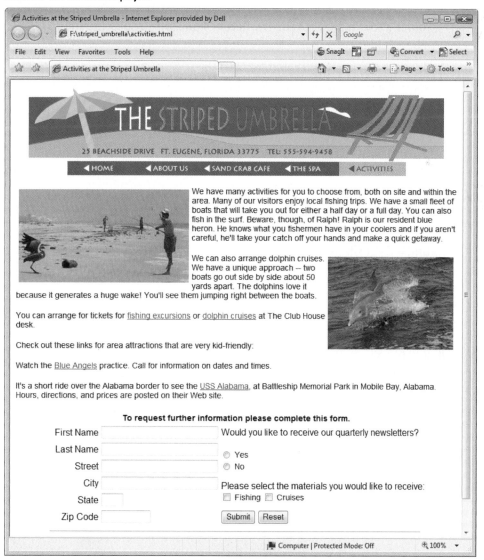

Updating Files

As your Web sites grow, it is easy to forget to take the time to keep your files in good order. Good "housekeeping" habits will save you lots of time later when you have many folders and files. In Unit F, you learned to run reports to identify broken links and orphaned files. When you are using incomplete pages as placeholder pages, they will not show up as orphaned files if they have links to them from other pages. Before publishing your site to a Web server, be sure to complete all pages; publishing incomplete pages is considered unprofessional. Deleting files that are no longer needed and keeping your other files updated are important to insure quality Web sites. ▰▰▰▰ You are ready to add content to the fishing and cruises pages so they will be ready for publication.

STEPS

1. Open the file dwi_1.html from the unit_i folder where your Data Files are stored, then save it as fishing.html in the striped_umbrella root folder, overwriting the existing fishing page, but not updating links

2. Click the broken link graphic placeholder, click the Browse for File icon 🗁 next to the Src text box in the Property inspector, then browse to the unit_i Data Files assets folder and double-click the file heron_small.jpg to copy the file to the striped_umbrella assets folder

3. Deselect the image placeholder, and the image appears as shown in Figure I-18
   Notice that the text is automatically updated with the body_text style. The code was already in place on the page linking the su_styles.css to the file.

4. Close the file dwi_1.html, then close the fishing page

5. Open the file dwi_2.html from the the unit_i folder where your Data Files are stored, then save it as cruises.html in the striped_umbrella root folder, overwriting the existing cruises page, but not updating links

6. Close the dwi_2.html page, click the broken link graphic placeholder, click the Browse for File icon 🗁 next to the Src text box in the Property inspector, then browse to the unit_i Data Files assets folder in your Data File location and double-click the file boats.jpg to copy the file to the striped_umbrella assets folder

7. Deselect the image placeholder, and the image will appear as shown in Figure I-19
   Notice that the text is automatically updated with the body_text style. The code was already in place on the page linking to the su_styles.css style sheet.

QUICK TIP
Recall that you can create reports using the Reports command on the site menu.

8. Run reports on the Entire Current Local Site to check for Missing Alt Text and Untitled Documents

9. Recreate the site cache, then run reports on broken links and orphaned files
   The cafe_logo.gif is listed as an orphaned file. You may use this later, so you decide to leave it temporarily in the assets folder.

10. Close the page, then exit Dreamweaver

FIGURE I-18: Fishing page updated

As you can see, Ralph scores occasionally. We certainly don't encourage you to feed Ralph. We feel it is important to intrude as little as possible with our wild friends and their diets. Just don't be surprised if you see him roaming the beach trying to blend in with the other fishermen.

FIGURE I-19: Cruises page updated

This is the Dolphin Racer at dock. We leave daily at 4:00 p.m.and 6:30 p.m. for 1 1/2 hour cruises. There are snacks and restrooms available on board. We welcome children of all ages. Our ship is a U.S. Coast Guard approved vessel and our captain is a former member of the Coast Guard. Call The Club desk for reservations.

Practice

▼ CONCEPTS REVIEW

Label each element in the Dreamweaver window shown in Figure I-20.

FIGURE I-20

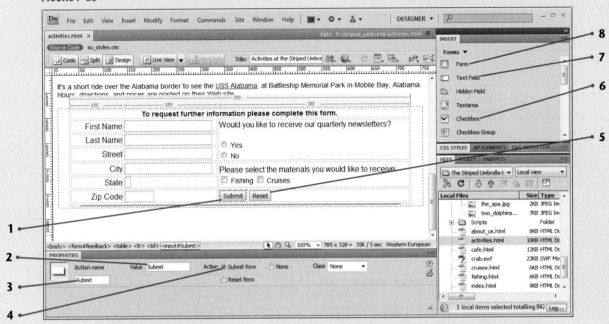

1. _____

2. _____

3. _____

4. _____

5. _____

6. _____

7. _____

8. _____

Match each of the following terms with the statement that best describes its function.

9. **Check boxes**	**a.** Set(s) the form object values to the default settings
10. **Radio buttons**	**b.** When in a group, are mutually exclusive; only one can be selected
11. **Submit button**	**c.** What happens after a button is clicked
12. **Reset button**	**d.** Display(s) data as asterisks or bullets
13. **Event**	**e.** Send(s) the data to be processed
14. **Password fields**	**f.** Contain(s) space for more than one line of data
15. **Multi-line text fields**	**g.** More than one can be selected

Select the best answer from the following list of choices.

16. Which of the following is not classified as a form field?

  a. text field

  b. hidden field

  c. default field

  d. file field

17. Button properties include:

  a. a name, a field, and an action.

  b. a name, a label, and an action.

  c. a name, a label, and a value.

  d. a name, a value, and an action.

18. Server-side scripting means that:

  a. the form is processed on the user's computer.

  b. the form is processed by a JavaScript program.

  c. the form is processed on the form's host server.

  d. b and c.

▼ SKILLS REVIEW

Important: If you did not create this Web site in Unit B and maintain it during the preceding units, you will need to create a root folder for this Web site and define the Web site using files your instructor will provide. See the "Read This Before You Begin" section for more detailed instructions.

1. Understand forms and form objects.

  a. Refer to Figure I-21 to locate a text field, a check box, a radio button, and a Submit button.

FIGURE I-21

2. Insert a form on a page.

   a. Start Dreamweaver and open the tips.html page in the blooms & bulbs Web site.

   b. Place the insertion point after the last sentence on the page and add two paragraph breaks to end the unordered list.

   c. Insert a form.

   d. Name the form **tips**.

   e. View the HTML code for the form.

   f. Return to Design view.

   g. Save your work.

3. Add a text form field.

   a. Place the insertion point inside the form and insert a table with 8 rows and 3 columns, a width of 750 pixels, a border of zero, the cell padding blank, cell spacing of 3, the Top header option, and a table summary **This table is used for form layout**.

   b. Center the table in the form.

   c. Using Figure I-21 as a guide, enter labels that will be used for Single line text fields in the first column, beginning in row 2.

   d. Format the labels with the body_text style.

   e. Drag the column border close to the text labels.

   f. Use the information in Table I-2 to add text fields with no label tags in the column next to the labels, beginning in row 2.

   g. Drag the column border close to the text fields.

   h. Save your work.

   i. Merge the second through fifth rows in the third column.

   j. Type **My favorite gardening tip:** in the resulting merged cell.

   k. Top-align the text.

   l. Create a line break after the text and insert a Multi-line text field (or a Textarea field) with no label tag.

   m. Name the new textarea field **my_tips** and set the Char width to 40 and the Num lines to 4.

   n. Click the table tag to remove any empty space displayed in the table, then save your work.

TABLE I-2: Form field attributes for the tips form

label	form field name	char width	max chars
First Name	first_name	40	40
Last Name	last_name	40	40
Street	street	40	40
City	city	40	40
State	state	2	2
Zip Code	zip_code	10	10
E-mail Address	e_mail	40	40

4. Add a radio group.

   a. In the third column in the last row, insert a radio group.

   b. Name the radio group **contact**.

   c. Enter the label **Please contact me with special offers** for the first radio button and a value of **yes**.

   d. Enter the label **Don't contact me** for the second radio button and a value of **no**.

   e. Use line breaks to lay out the radio group.

   f. Save your work.

5. Add a check box.

   a. In the cell below the text area, type **I would be interested in reading Gardening Tips:**.

   b. In the same cell, below the text, insert a check box with the label **On the Web** wrapped with the label tag after the form item. Name it **on_web** and assign it a Checked value of **web**.

   c. Enter a space after the check box text and insert a check box with the label **By e-mail** wrapped with the label tag after the form item, enter **e_mail2** as the name and **e_mail** as the Checked value.

   d. Enter a space after the check box text and insert a check box with the label **By mailouts** wrapped with the label tag after the form item, enter **mailout** as the name and **mail** as the Checked value.

   e. Save your work.

6. Insert a Submit and a Reset button.

   a. Add a new row to the table.

   b. Insert a Submit button with no label tag in the second column of the new row.

   c. Right-align the Submit button in the cell and change the button name to **Submit**.

   d. Insert a Reset button in the third column of the new row.

   e. Verify that **Reset** is the button name, **Reset** is the value, and the action is set to **Reset form**.

   f. Save your work.

7. Format a form.

   a. Merge the cells in the top row of the table, then type **Do you have a gardening tip you would like to share with us?** and format the text with the subheadings style.

   b. Right-align the labels in the first column of the form.

   c. Add a new row between the last two rows in the table and merge all cells in the row. (*Hint*: You can place the insertion point in the last row, then use the Insert, Table Objects, Insert Row Above command.)

   d. Place a horizontal rule in the new row and format it as 90%, centered.

   e. Format all text that is not formatted in the form with the body_text style.

   f. Select the table, then set the cell spacing to 5.

   g. Save your work, then preview the page in the browser, compare your screen to Figure I-21, test all fields, then test the Reset button. (*Hint*: Your text may wrap a bit differently.)

   h. Close the browser, then exit Dreamweaver.

8. Update files.

   a. Run reports to check for untitled documents and missing alternate text. Correct any omissions that you find.

   b. Check for broken links and orphaned files. Correct any errors that you find. (If you see any broken links, recreate your site cache and run the report again.)

Important: *If you did not create these Web sites in Unit B and maintain them during the preceding units, you will need to create a root folder for these Web sites and define the Web sites using files your instructor will provide. See the "Read This Before You Begin" section for more detailed instructions.*

▼ INDEPENDENT CHALLENGE 1

You have been hired to create a Web site for a river expedition company named Rapids Transit, located on the Buffalo River in Northwest Arkansas. Mike Andrew, the owner of Rapids Transit, has asked you to add a form to the page that describes the three categories of lodging available. The purpose of this form will be to allow users to request brochures for each lodging category.

   a. Open the Rapids Transit Web site.

   b. Open the page lodging.html.

   c. Place a paragraph break after the last sentence on the page and insert a form called **lodging**.

   d. Insert a table inside the form with 7 rows and 3 columns, 750 pixels wide, the border, cell spacing, and cell padding text boxes left blank, a Top header, an appropriate table summary, and left aligned.

   e. Enter text labels in the first column beginning with the second row, using Figure I-22 as a guide.

   f. Format the labels with the body_text style.

   g. Adjust the column border so it is adjacent to the text labels.

   h. Add Single line text fields in the column next to the text labels using 30 characters for the character width and maximum characters for all text fields, except use a width of 2 for the state and 10 for the zip code. Name the fields appropriately.

   i. Adjust the column border.

   j. In the third column of the second row type **Please check the brochures you would like to receive.**, then format the text with the body_text style.

   k. Place a check box in the third column of the third row named **option_1** with a checked value of **lodge** and a text label of **The Lodge**.

FIGURE I-22

l. Place a check box in the third column of the fourth row named **option_2** with a checked value of **jenny** and a text label of **Jenny's Cabins**.

m. Place a check box in the third column of the fifth row named **option_3** with a checked value of **john** and a text label of **John's Camp**.

n. Format the three labels next to the check boxes with the body_text style.

o. Insert a Submit button in the third column of the last row.

p. Insert a Reset button to the right of the Submit button in the same cell, and change the Action to **Reset form**, the button value to **Reset**, and the Button name to **Reset**.

q. Merge the cells in the top row, then type **If you would like to receive a brochure describing our lodging, please complete the form below.**.

r. Format the sentence with the **lodging** style.

s. Insert a new row at the end of the table and merge the cells in the new row.

t. Insert a horizontal rule with a 100% width, then copy the horizontal rule.

u. Add a new row between the first and second rows, merge the cells if necessary, and paste the horizontal rule in the merged cells.

v. Preview the page in the browser, compare it to Figure I-22, and test the text fields and the Reset button.

w. Make any adjustments to improve the page, then save your work.

x. Run reports for broken links, orphaned files, untitled documents, and missing alternate text, correcting any errors that you find.

y. Exit Dreamweaver.

▼ INDEPENDENT CHALLENGE 2

In this exercise you will continue your work on the TripSmart Web site. The owner, Thomas Howard, wants you to create a form to collect data from viewers who are interested in receiving more information on one or more of the featured trips.

a. Open the TripSmart Web site, then open the destinations page.

b. Insert a paragraph break after the last sentence on the page, then insert a form named **information**.

c. Insert a table in the form that contains 11 rows, 2 columns, a Table width of 700 pixels, a Border thickness of 0, Cell padding of 1, Cell spacing of 1, a Top header, and add an appropriate table summary. Left-align the table.

d. Merge the cells in the top row, type **Please complete this form for additional information on these tours.**, apply the reverse_text style, then change the cell background color to #666666.

e. Beginning in the second row, type the following labels in the cells in the first column: **First Name**, **Last Name**, **Street**, **City**, **State**, **Zip Code**, **Phone**, **E-mail**, and **I am interested in:**; adjust the column border to a position of your choice, then right-align the labels and apply the body_text style to each one.

f. Insert single-line text fields in the first eight cells in the second column and assign the following names: **first_name**, **last_name**, **street**, **city**, **state**, **zip**, **phone**, and **email**; setting the Char width to **30** and the Max Chars to **100** for each of these text fields. (*Hint*: To save time create the first_name field, then use copy and paste to create the other fields, changing the name of each pasted field in the Property inspector.)

g. In the second cell of the tenth row, insert a check box with the label **The Amazon**, the name **amazon**, and a Checked value of **yes**.

h. Add a space after the Amazon label, then repeat Step g to add another check box next to the Amazon check box with the label **Kenya**, the name **kenya**, and a Checked value of **yes**.

i. Apply the body_text style to The Amazon and Kenya.

j. Left-align the cells with the text boxes and check boxes, then set their vertical alignment to Top.

k. Insert a Submit button and a Reset button in the second cell of the eleventh row with appropriate names and actions.

l. Insert a new merged row at the bottom of the table, then insert a horizontal rule that is 100 percent wide.

m. Run reports for untitled documents, missing alternate text, broken links, and orphaned files.

n. Save your work, preview the page in your browser, test the form, compare your screen to Figure I-23, close your browser, then close the destinations page.

FIGURE I-23

businesspeople. Birding enthusiasts will enjoy adding to their bird lists with Kenya's over 300 species of birds. View the beginning of the annual migration of millions of wildebeest, a spectacular sight. The wildebeest are traveling from the Serengeti Plain to the Mara in search of water and grass. Optional excursions include ballooning over the Masai Mara, fishing on Lake Victoria, camel rides at Amboseli Serena Lodge, and golfing at the Aberdare Country Club. Lake Victoria is the largest freshwater lake in the world.

The price schedule is as follows: Land Tour and Supplemental Group Air, $4,500.00; International Air, $1,350.00; and Single Supplement, $1,000.00. Entrance fees, hotel taxes, and services are included in the Land Tour price. A deposit of $500.00 is required at the time the booking is made. Trip Insurance and Luggage Insurance are optional and are also offered at extra charge. A passport and visa will be required for entry into Kenya. Call us at *(555) 848-0807* for further information from 8:00 a.m. to 6:00 p.m. (Central Standard Time).

Please complete this form for additional information on these tours.

First Name	
Last Name	
Street	
City	
State	
Zip Code	
Phone	
E-mail	

I am interested in: ☐ The Amazon ☐ Kenya

[Submit] [Reset]

▼ INDEPENDENT CHALLENGE 3

Paul Patrick and his partner Donnie Honeycutt have a construction business in Southern California. They have recently published a Web site for their business and would like to add a search form to their Web site to help their customers quickly find the data they are looking for. They first do some research on the Internet to critique other Web site search pages.

a. Connect to the Internet and go to the Internal Revenue Service site at www.irs.gov.

b. Click the Advanced Search link to search the IRS site, as shown in Figure I-24.

c. How is the search form organized?

d. What form objects were used?

e. Click the Search Tips link. What information did you find to help viewers search the Web site?

f. Find one more example of a Web site that uses a search page and explain which of the two sites you prefer and why.

FIGURE I-24

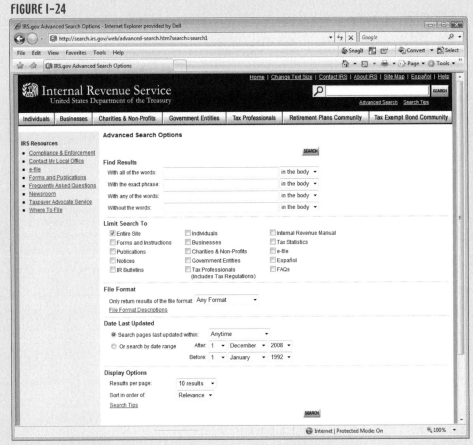

Internal Revenue Service Web site – www.irs.gov

▼ INDEPENDENT CHALLENGE 4

This assignment will continue to build on the personal Web site that you created in Unit B. In Unit C you created and developed your index page. In Unit D you added a page with either an ordered or an unordered list and a CSS Style Sheet with a minimum of two styles. In Unit E you added a page that included at least two graphics. In Unit F you added a page that included several links and an image map. In Unit G you redesigned at least one page based on a Cascading Style Sheet. In Unit H, you used a table to position page elements. In this lesson, you will add a form to one of the pages in your Web site.

   a. Consult your storyboard and decide which page you would like to develop in this lesson.

   b. Sketch a layout for your page to place the form objects you would like to use.

   c. Create the form using at least three different form objects. Include clear instructions that will help users fill out the form correctly.

   d. Add text labels to each form object.

   e. Add a Submit and Reset button and format them appropriately.

   f. Format the form attractively to help it stand out on the page.

   g. Save the file and preview the page in the browser, testing the Reset button to make sure it works correctly.

   h. Make any adjustments that are necessary to improve the appearance of your form.

After you are satisfied with your work, verify the following:

   a. Each completed page has a page title.

   b. All links work correctly.

   c. The completed pages look good using a screen resolution of 800 × 600 and 1024 × 768.

   d. All graphics are properly linked to the assets folder of the Web site.

   e. All images have alternate text and are legal to use.

   f. The link checker shows no broken links or orphaned files. If there are orphaned files, note your plan to link them.

   g. All main pages have a consistent navigation system.

   h. The form is attractive and easy to understand and use.

▼ VISUAL WORKSHOP

Use Figure I-25 as a guide to continue your work on the Carolyne's Creations Web site. You are adding a form to the catering page that will allow customers to fax a lunch order for pickup that day. Since the customers are faxing the order, there is no need for a Submit button. You can add a Reset button if you wish. Use form properties of your choice.

FIGURE I-25

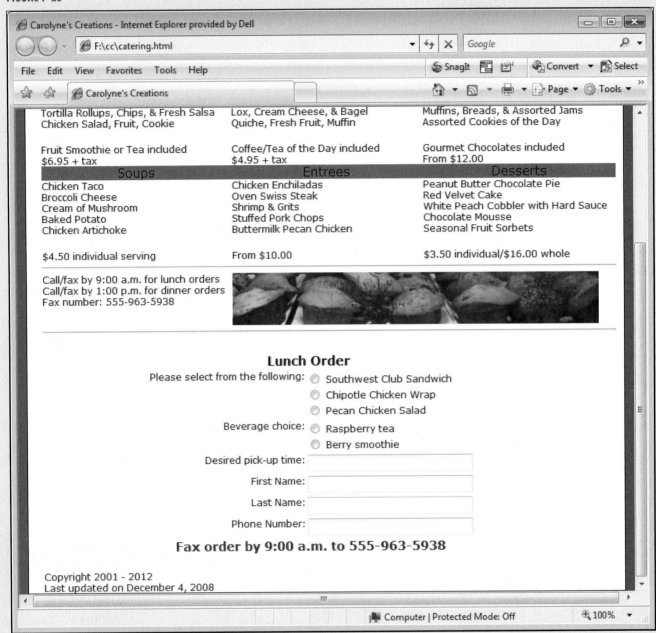

Maintaining and Publishing Your Web Site

As you prepare to publish your site, it is important to develop an effective site-maintenance routine that you will continue to follow after it is published. If you have used template-based pages, you can update information quickly and easily. Several relatively easy maintenance tasks can help you keep your Web site clean and vibrant. These include checking, testing, and organizing site components. You should tackle these tasks at regular intervals to prevent Web site errors. As you manage your site, you can also use a program called Adobe Bridge to manage your site assets. After you have run your initial maintenance checks and you are assured that your Web site works correctly, the Web site is ready to publish. Before you can publish your site, you must select the settings to transfer the files to the Web server. You begin by looking at the advantages that templates offer for creating and updating Web sites.

OBJECTIVES   Use templates

Manage your site with Adobe
    Contribute

Maintain your site

Manage your assets with Adobe
    Bridge

Test your Web pages

Set up remote access

Publish your site

Using Templates

When you create a Web site, it's important to make sure that each page has a unified look so that viewers know they are in your site no matter what page they are viewing. Common elements, such as the navigation bar and company banner, should appear in the same place on every page, and every page should have the same background color. If you are the only site developer, you can easily copy elements from one page to another. As your organization grows and your Web site becomes more complex, one way to update your site and maintain a consistent appearance on every page is through the use of templates. **Templates** are Web pages that contain the basic layout for related pages in a Web site. ████ Your organization is growing. You consider the advantages of incorporating templates in your increasingly complex Web site.

DETAILS

- **Templates save development time, especially when different people will be creating pages for your site.** The ideal process for using templates is for one person (the template author) to create a page and save it as a template. Other team members then use the template to create pages for the site. The template author creates **locked regions**, areas of the page that other designers cannot modify, and **editable regions**, in which they can add or change content. Locked regions contain design elements common to every page in the site. Figure AP-1 shows a template with an editable region.

- **Templates ensure both continuity and flexibility throughout a Web site.** Each page that a team creates from a template is connected to the original template file, so if the template author changes the template, all pages to which the template is attached can be automatically updated. **Nested templates** are templates that are based on other templates. Templates also allow for design flexibility; an **optional region** is an area in the template that other contributors can choose to show or hide.

- **Templates simplify the updating process.** A Web site needs to change with the times: When changes occur in your company, you will need to change your Web site. If your Web site pages are based on a template or a group of nested templates, you will be able to make those changes quickly and easily.

  Once the author develops the template (by either creating one or modifying one of the template page options shown in Figure AP-2) and distributes it to other team members, they, in turn, can apply the template to their site pages, adding appropriate content to the editable regions of each page.

STEPS

To create a new template:

1. **Click File on the Application bar (Win) or Menu bar (Mac), click New, click Blank Template, click HTML template, chose a layout from the Layout column, then click Create**
   As the Web page author, you would usually select the HTML template option.

2. **Place the insertion point where you want the object to appear, click Insert on the Application bar (Win) or Menu bar (Mac), point to Template objects, click the region type you want to add, name the region, then add content for the region if necessary**
   See Table AP-1 for a description of the available regions. By default, all template content is locked except for editable regions, which allows content contributors to add their own content.

3. **Click File on the Application bar (Win) or Menu bar (Mac), click Save As, type a template name, noting that the Templates folder is the save location, and .dwt is the file extension for the template page, then click Save**

To create a page based on a template:

1. **Click File on the Application bar (Win) or Menu bar (Mac), click New, then click Page from Template**

2. **Verify that the site name is selected, then double-click the template name**
   A new Dreamweaver document opens, based on the template.

3. **Add text to the template regions, then save the page**

FIGURE AP-1: Template with editable regions

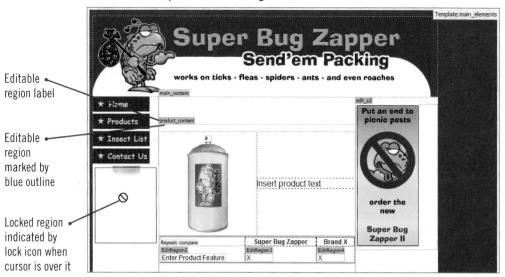

Editable region label

Editable region marked by blue outline

Locked region indicated by lock icon when cursor is over it

FIGURE AP-2: Template Type and Layout options

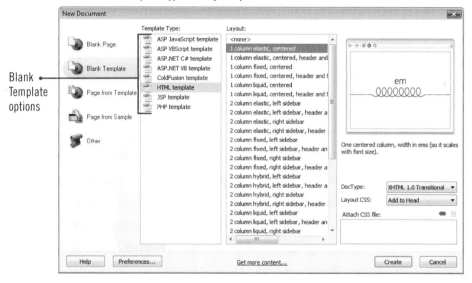

Blank Template options

TABLE AP-1 Template regions

region type	meaning to users
Editable	A region that allows users to edit the content
Optional	A region that allows users to choose to either show or hide content
Repeating	A region that contains content that is used multiple times
Editable Optional	A region that allows users to both edit the content and choose to show or hide the content
Repeating Table	A table that has a predefined structure and allows users to add content

Managing Your Site with Adobe Contribute

Adobe Contribute is a Web development tool that can be invaluable to both professional Web developers and non-technical Web content contributors. With Contribute, Web developers can design pages similar to templates that others can then use to insert content specific to their area. For example, a university might decide that all faculty members should have a Web page on the school Web site with their photo, a brief biography, and a list of the classes that they teach. This would be a difficult task for faculty members without a technology background. With Contribute, the school's webmaster can design a page to be used by all faculty members. The faculty members would then open the page in Contribute and simply insert their own photo, bio, and classes. They would not need a copy of Dreamweaver on their computer. There are several levels of permissions that can be attached to the pages that will allow contributors to add their own content without changing the basic layout. Figure AP-3 shows the Contribute Start page. You explore the advantages of using Contribute in your organization to develop Web content.

DETAILS

The advantages for Web professionals include the following:

- **Consistency across the Web site**

  By designing pages that can be used as the template for many similar pages, developers can create a Web site with a consistent, professional look without the webmaster's direct involvement in developing each page.

- **Time savings**

  Contribute is a huge timesaver for the Web professional. The ability to create templates for others to use gives the developer control over the pages, but frees up the time that would have been spent working on each page individually.

- **Support for basic features**

  Contribute supports basic features, such as Cascading Style Sheets and Dreamweaver templates, that promote continuity across a Web site. Contribute also includes Flash paper. **Flash paper** converts existing documents into Flash (.swf) files so they may be distributed as printable documents over the Internet.

The advantages for content contributors include the following:

- **Ease of use**

  Content contributors can open, edit, and publish a Web page with only basic computer skills. For example, they can easily drag and drop content from applications with which they may be more familiar, such as Microsoft Word or Microsoft Excel. In Contribute, they can correct errors using a feature that allows them to revert back to a previously-saved version of each page. The Contribute interface is simple and includes a tutorial that incorporates a practice Web site, as shown in Figure AP-4.

- **More freedom for advanced users**

  With the different levels of permissions possible, a person with more Web experience can be given more freedom than one who is not comfortable with Web editing. Less experienced users can be required to have their pages reviewed before publishing, while more experienced users can publish their pages without review.

FIGURE AP-3: Contribute Start page

Help files

Quick tour

Interactive
tutorial

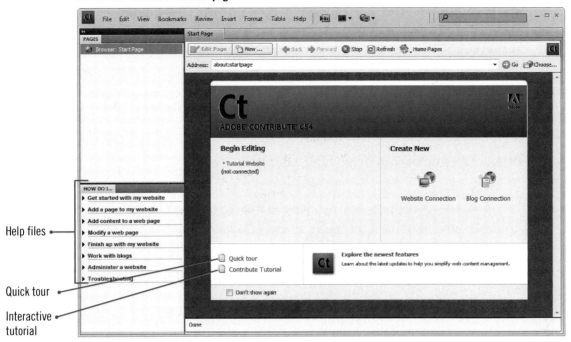

FIGURE AP-4: Editing a Web page using the tutorial

Publish button
connects to
Web server

Send for Review
sends the page to
be reviewed
before publishing

Interactive
tutorial uses a
practice Web
site that is
included in the
Contribute
installation

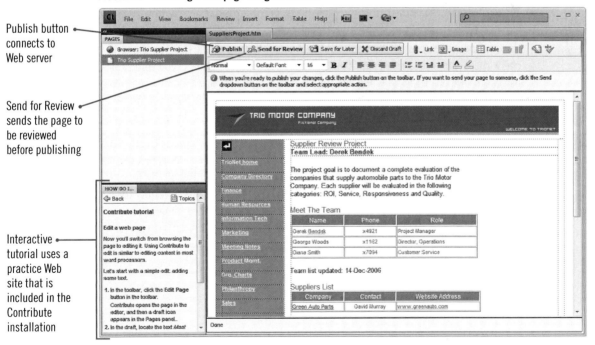

Maintaining Your Site

At fairly frequent intervals, you should perform routine Web site maintenance tasks. As you have probably learned from working on the projects for this book, Web sites can quickly become complex and difficult to manage. Checking links and organizing the Assets panel will help you keep a Web site "clean." You review the routine maintenance tasks to make sure your Web sites are always in great shape.

DETAILS

Follow these guidelines to maintain your Web site:

- **Check links**

  Use the Link Checker to check all links in the Web site, both external and internal. The Link Checker, in the Results panel, alerts you to any broken internal links and helps you repair them. It also lists the external links but does not verify their validity. In addition, the Link Checker alerts you to orphaned files. **Orphaned files** are files that are not linked to any other pages in the Web site. Often, orphaned files are simply files that you have not completed so are not yet ready to be linked to the Web site. If you find orphaned files, evaluate each file, then either delete it or develop it further. Even if you are not ready to link these files, routinely running a list of orphaned files will remind you of the work you must complete in preparation for linking them to the Web site. Figure AP-5 shows the options for using the Link Checker. You can either check the links on a single page, the entire Web site, or selected files or folders. You can open the Link Checker as a panel, or access it by right-clicking a file in the Files panel, then clicking Check Links, clicking Window in the Application bar, pointing to Results, and then clicking the tab Link Checker (Win), or by clicking Site in the Menu bar and clicking Check Links Sitewide (Mac). Once you have located broken links or orphaned files, you must fix them. You can fix a broken link in the Link Checker panel, or by using the Property inspector. To correct a broken link, use the Browse for File icon to browse to the file that is the correct destination.

- **Organize the Assets panel**

  Use the Assets panel to check the list of images and colors used in your Web site. If there are images listed that are not in use, consider moving them to a storage folder outside the Web site until you need them. Also, check the Colors list to make sure that all colors listed are Websafe. If you find non-Websafe colors in the list, locate the elements to which the non-Websafe colors are applied and apply Websafe colors to them. Figure AP-6 shows a list of colors in a Web site. One of the colors shown is non-Websafe, and should be replaced with a Websafe color.

  QUICK TIP
  Note that you can only designate assets as favorites, not .html files.

  If your list of images or media files has grown to the point that much scrolling is required to find one, consider creating subfolders in the Assets panel to organize them. You can categorize some files as favorites. **Favorites** are files you designate as those that you expect to use frequently in your Web site. They then appear in a separate window in the Assets panel to provide fast access. Scrolling through long lists of assets to find them is not necessary. Figure AP-7 shows files that have been designated as favorites. Favorites still appear in the list of Site files. To designate a file as a favorite, right-click (Win) or [ctrl]-click (Mac) the file in the Assets panel, then click Add to Favorites (Win) or Add to Image Favorites (Mac). Then when you select the Favorites option at the top of the Files panel, only your Favorites appear.

FIGURE AP-5: Link Checker options

Click list arrow to access options

Show Options

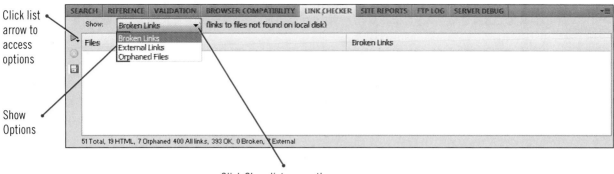

Click Show list arrow, then choose the type of report to run

FIGURE AP-6: Locating Non-Websafe colors

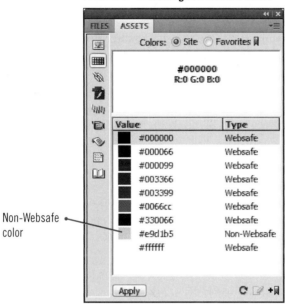

Non-Websafe color

FIGURE AP-7: Favorites category on Assets panel

Image files listed in the Favorites list, in addition to the Site list

Favorites option selected

Managing Your Assets with Adobe Bridge

Another useful tool you can use with Dreamweaver is a file management program called Adobe Bridge. Bridge provides many organizational tools to help you search, sort, and identify your project files. It also provides an easy way to view your files before you bring them into your site. Bridge is an integrated application, letting you access commands from Photoshop and Illustrator. You realize that the number of images and media files in the Web site is growing and could become difficult to manage. You familiarize yourself with the management capabilities of Adobe Bridge.

DETAILS

The advantages of using Adobe Bridge are as follows:

- **Manage Web site assets**

  Because it works with other Adobe programs, Bridge provides a common tool for managing graphic files. You can also use Bridge to add meta tags and to search your files to help you quickly find your files when you need them. As you learned in Unit C, meta tags are HTML codes that include information about a file. Just as you add meta tags to Web pages to help viewers find your pages with search engines, you can add meta tags to your images to help you find them as you search through your folders. For instance, you could add the keyword "beach" to all of the photos you took during your last beach vacation. Metadata in Bridge includes the file name, file size, date the file was created, dimensions, and resolution, to name a few. See Figure AP-8.

- **Organize photos**

  Adobe Bridge is a useful tool for managing digital photos. In Bridge you can not only open, view, and sort photos, but also download the files from your digital camera. Bridge will work with **camera raw** files, a file type used by many photographers that contains unprocessed data from a digital camera's sensor.

STEPS

To start Bridge from Dreamweaver:

1. Click File, then click Browse in Bridge

or

1. Click the Browse in Bridge button on the Standard toolbar, as shown in Figure AP-8

   Bridge opens.

2. Navigate to the folder where your images are stored

   To perform tasks in Adobe Bridge, use the commands listed in Table AP-2.

To insert a file from Bridge into an open page in Dreamweaver:

1. In Dreamweaver, place the insertion point in the target location in Design view

2. Go to Bridge, select the file you want to place, click File, point to Place, click In Dreamweaver, enter alternate text if necessary, then click OK

or

1. Arrange the Dreamweaver and Bridge windows next to each other, then drag the image from Bridge onto the open page in Dreamweaver, entering alternate text if necessary, as shown in Figure AP-8

FIGURE AP-8: Opening Adobe Bridge

Browse in
Bridge button

Selected
image

Drag a selected
image from Bridge
to an open page in
Dreamweaver

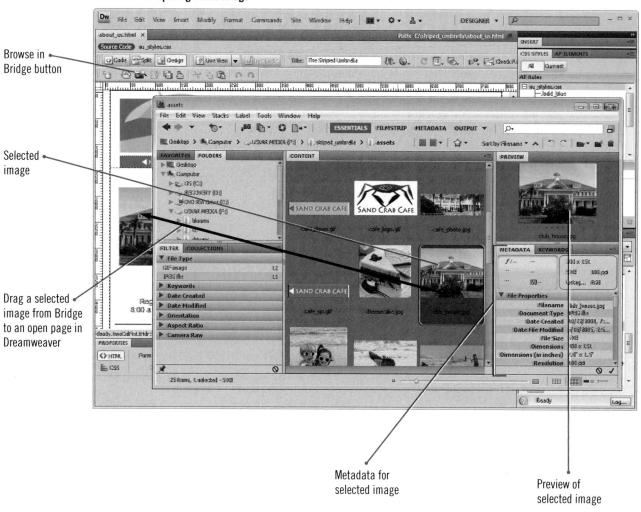

Metadata for
selected image

Preview of
selected image

TABLE AP-2: Performing other tasks in Bridge

task	to	menu commands
Rotate assets	Rotate 90 or 180 degrees	Edit, [Rotate command]
View slide show of selected assets	Examine any asset group	Select assets, click View, Slideshow
Sort assets	Change asset order	View, Sort, [sort by option]
View asset details	See dates created and modified; file size, document type and resolution	View, As Details
Stack assets	Group files under one thumbnail image	Select images, Stacks, Group as Stack
Label assets	Rate or classify assets	Label, [select rating]
View assets in different layouts	Customize your asset view	Window/Workspace, Essentials, Filmstrip, Metadata, Output, Keywords, Preview, Light Table, Folders
Perform tasks in Photoshop or Illustrator	Perform Photoshop or Illustrator tasks after Bridge automatically opens the programs for you	Tools, Photoshop or Tools, Illustrator

Testing Your Web Pages

Dreamweaver has several helpful reports you can run that identify problems in your Web site. You should run these reports on a regular schedule. The more frequently you run them, the easier it will be to correct any errors. If you allow errors to build up, it will be more difficult to find and correct them. Besides taking advantage of the Dreamweaver report features, nothing takes the place of actually viewing your pages in a browser so you can see what editing and formatting changes are necessary. ▰▰▰▰ You review the site report features available in Dreamweaver and consider how you can use them in your Web sites.

DETAILS

- ### Site reports

  The Reports command on the Site menu provides a checklist of reports that you can generate for your Web site. Figure AP-9 shows the Reports dialog box. You can create reports for the current document, the entire local site, selected files in the site, or a selected folder by clicking the Report On list arrow and choosing an option. You can create a Workflow report to see files that other designers are using or create a report to view Design Notes, which are notes you can add to a file for other designers who are working on different parts of your site. You can also create a Workflow report that will list all files that have been modified recently. There are six HTML reports that you can generate: Combinable Nested Font Tags, Accessibility, Missing Alt Text, Redundant Nested Tags, Removable Empty Tags, and Untitled Documents. The Missing Alt Text and the Untitled Documents are especially important for Web site accessibility. After you run a report, you can save it as an XML file. You can then import it into a database, spreadsheet, or template to view.

- ### Test pages

  Test each page again for design layout, using several types and versions of browsers. Test each page using many different screen resolutions, and test your site on different platforms. Test all external links to make sure they connect to valid, active Web sites. Notice how long it takes each page to download, and consider trimming pages that download slowly. Considering the volatility of the Web, testing external links should be done at regular intervals, such as once a week. Few things are more frustrating to a user than to click on a link that no longer works.

- ### Enjoy positive feedback and respond to negative feedback

  Everyone enjoys hearing positive feedback. When you receive positive feedback, record the comments so that you can refer to them in the future as you edit the site. Note the negative feedback and use it to your advantage to improve the Web site.

FIGURE AP-9: Reports dialog box

Report on options

Workflow reports

HTML reports

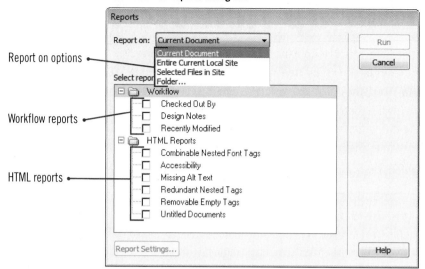

Setting Up Remote Access

Once your files are ready to publish, you must tell Dreamweaver where to place your files. Most Dreamweaver users begin first by creating a local root folder to house all of their Web site files. This is called the **local site**. Next, they gain access to a remote site. A **remote site** is a folder on a Web server that is connected to the Internet, hosts Web sites, and is not directly connected to the computer housing the local site. Often the **ISP**, or Internet Service Provider, will furnish users with space for publishing Web pages. This space then becomes the remote site. ▰▰▰▰ You review the processes available in Dreamweaver for setting up a remote site.

DETAILS

- **Using the Site Definition Remote Info dialog box**

  When your pages are ready to publish, the files must be transferred from the local site to the remote site. In Dreamweaver, you use the Site Definition Remote Info dialog box to enter the information about the remote site, such as the FTP host, host directory, the login, and the password. **FTP (File Transfer Protocol)** is the process of uploading and downloading files to and from a remote site. After the remote site information is entered, the files are transferred using the Put button in the Files panel. Figure AP-10 shows the Site Definition dialog box. You open this window by using the Site, New Site or Site, Manage Sites command, clicking Edit to open the Site Definition dialog box, clicking the Advanced tab, then clicking the Remote Info category. The choices for remote access appear when you click the Access list arrow.

- **Setting up FTP**

  The method most people use to transfer files is FTP. If you choose the FTP option, you then see several text boxes you need to complete, as shown in Figure AP-11. This information will come from your ISP. The FTP Host is the address on the Internet where you will send your files. The Host Directory is your folder on the remote server where you will place your files. The Login and Password will be provided by your ISP. There are also some security options that you can check when transferring your files.

STEPS

To set up remote access on an FTP site:

1. Click Site on the Application bar (Win) or Menu bar (Mac), then click Manage Sites

2. Click the Web site name in the Manage Sites dialog box, then click Edit

3. Click the Advanced tab, click Remote Info in the Category list, click the Access list arrow, then click FTP

4. Enter the FTP host, Host directory, Login, and Password information in the dialog box

5. Click Test to test the connection to the remote site

6. If the connection is successful, click Done to close the Dialog box

7. Click OK, then click Done to close the Manage Sites dialog box

To view a Web site on a remote server:

1. Click the View list arrow in the Files panel, then click Remote view

2. Click the Expand to show local and remote sites button to view both the Remote Site and the Local files panes

3. Click the Collapse to show only local or remote site button to return to Design view

FIGURE AP-10: Site Definition dialog box

Advanced tab

Remote Info category

Access options

Mac users will not see this option

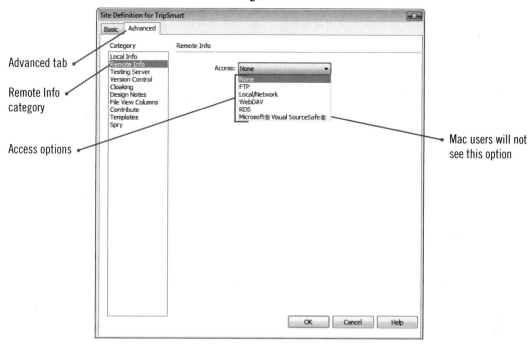

FIGURE AP-11: Site Definition dialog box

FTP Access

FTP host

Host directory

Login

Password

Security options

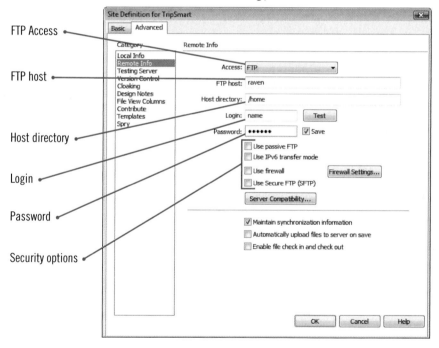

Choosing remote access options

Remote access choices include FTP, Local/Network, WebDAV, RDS, and Microsoft® Visual SourceSafe®. Local/Network refers to publishing a Web site on either the local drive (that is, your own hard drive) or a local network drive. WebDAV stands for Web-based Distributed Authoring and Versioning. WebDAV is used with servers such as the Microsoft Internet Information Server (IIS) and Apache Web server. RDS stands for Remote Development Services and is used with a remote folder running ColdFusion. Microsoft Visual SourceSafe is available under the Windows platform using Microsoft Visual SourceSafe Client.

Publishing Your Site

After setting up remote access and completing your Web site, you transfer your files to the remote server through the Files panel. The transfer is easily accomplished by using the Put button on the Files panel. This is similar to the process used by FTP client programs. Transferring your files from your computer to a remote computer is called **uploading**. Transferring files from a remote computer to your computer is called **downloading**. You review the processes available in Dreamweaver for publishing a Web site.

DETAILS

- **Using Put**

  Click the Put File(s) button in the Files panel (Win), shown on Figure AP-12, to transfer the files from the Local site to the Remote site. Click the Get File(s) button to transfer the files from the Remote site to the Local site. (There is also a Connects to remote host button that connects to the remote host, but the Put File(s) button also connects automatically.) After selecting the files you want to transfer, click the Put File(s) button. Answer Yes when asked if you want to transfer dependent files; this transfers associated files, such as image files, in the Web site.

- **Synchronizing files**

  You can choose to **synchronize** your site. The Synchronize command allows you to transfer only the latest versions of files, rather than all the Web site files. To synchronize your site, click Site on the Application bar (Win) or Menu bar (Mac), then click Synchronize Sitewide. The Synchronize Files dialog box will open, as shown in Figure AP-13. If no files have changed since the last transfer, Dreamweaver notifies you that you do not need to synchronize.

STEPS

To upload files to publish a Web site:

1. Click the file, folder, or site you want to publish, then click the Put Files(s) button in the Files panel

2. Click Yes to include the dependent files if necessary

To synchronize files:

1. Click Site on the Application bar (Win) or Menu bar (Mac), click Synchronize Sitewide

2. Click the Synchronize list arrow, then click Entire (Site name)

3. Click the Direction list arrow, then click Put newer files to remote

4. Click Preview, then click OK

FIGURE AP-12: Files panel

Get File(s) button

Connects to remote host

Put File(s) button

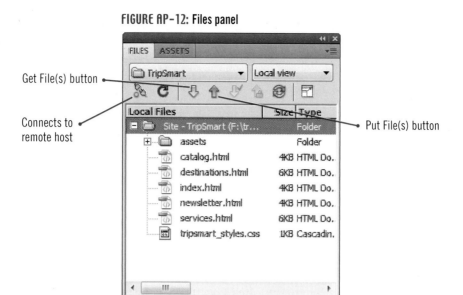

FIGURE AP-13: The Synchronize Files dialog box

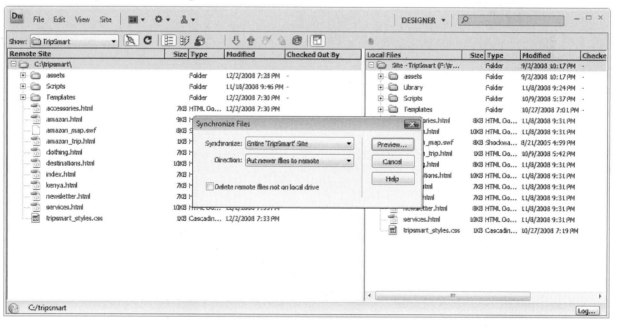

Practice

Match each of the following terms with the statement that best describes its function.

1. Put File(s) button
2. Get File(s) button
3. Orphaned files
4. Favorites file list
5. Missing Alt Text
6. Link Checker
7. Checked Out By
8. Template

a. Files that are not linked to any other pages in a Web site
b. An HTML report
c. Transfers the files from the remote site to the local site
d. Checks for broken links
e. Files that have been designated to use frequently in your Web site
f. Transfers the files from the local site to the remote site
g. Pages that can be used as a basis for creating other pages
h. A Workflow report

Select the best answer from the following list of choices.

9. **FTP is the acronym for:**
   a. File Transfer Protocol.
   b. File Transfer Process.
   c. File Transfer Pending.
   d. File Transferring Process.

10. **The most commonly used process to transfer files is:**
    a. Local/Network.
    b. RDS.
    c. FTP.
    d. SourceSafe Database.

11. **Adobe Bridge can be opened from Dreamweaver using the:**
    a. Document toolbar.
    b. Standard toolbar.
    c. Insert panel.
    d. Property inspector.

12. **The Link Checker can check for broken links on:**
    a. one Web page.
    b. the entire Web site.
    c. selected files and folders.
    d. all of the above.

13. **An area in a template where users can add or change content is called:**
    a. a locked region.
    b. an editable region.
    c. an optional region.
    d. a hidden region.

Data Files List

To complete the lessons and practice exercises in this book, students need to use Data Files that are supplied by Course Technology. Once they obtain the files, students select where to store the Web site files they create using the Data Files, such as to the hard disk drive, network server, or USB storage device.

Below is a list of the Data Files that are supplied and the unit or practice exercise to which the files correspond. For information on how to obtain Data Files, please refer to page xvi in the front part of this book. The following list includes only Data Files that are supplied; it does not include the Web site files students create from scratch or the files students create by revising supplied files.

Unit	File supplied	Location file is used in unit
Unit A	**Unit A folder** about_us.swf accommodations.swf activities.swf cafe.swf dwa_1.html index.swf shop.swf spa.swf **Unit A Assets folder:** pool.jpg striped_u_background.jpg striped_umbrella_banner.gif **Unit A Scripts folder:** AC_RunActiveContent.js	**Lessons** (The Striped Umbrella site)
	Unit A folder: dwa_2.html **Unit A Assets folder:** blooms_banner.jpg blooms_logo.jpg	**Skills Review** (blooms & bulbs site)
	Unit A folder: dwa_3.html **Unit A Assets folder:** tripsmart_banner.jpg	**Independent Challenge 1** (TripSmart site)
Unit B	**Unit B folder:** dwb_1.html **Unit B Assets folder:** striped_umbrella_banner.gif	**Lessons** (The Striped Umbrella site)
	Unit B folder: dwb_2.html **Unit B Assets folder:** blooms_banner.jpg	**Skills Review** (blooms & bulbs site)
	Unit B folder: dwb_3.html **Unit B Assets folder:** rapids_banner.jpg	**Independent Challenge 1** (Rapids Transit site)

Unit	File supplied	Location file is used in unit
	Unit B folder: dwb_4.html **Unit B Assets folder:** tripsmart_banner.jpg	**Independent Challenge 2** (TripSmart site)
	Unit B folder: dwb_5.html **Unit B Assets folder:** cc_banner.jpg	**Visual Workshop** (Caroline's Creations site)
Unit C	**No Data Files supplied**	
Unit D	**Unit D folder:** dwd_1.html spa.doc **Unit D Assets folder:** striped_umbrella_banner.gif the_spa.jpg	**Lessons** (The Striped Umbrella site)
	Unit D folder: dwd_2.html gardening_tips.doc **Unit D Assets folder:** blooms_banner.jpg garden_tips.jpg	**Skills Review** (blooms & bulbs site)
	Unit D folder: dwd_3.html **Unit D Assets folder:** rapids_banner.jpg	**Independent Challenge 1** (Rapids Transit site)
	Unit D folder: dwd_4.html **Unit D Assets folder:** tripsmart_banner.jpg	**Independent Challenge 2** (TripSmart site)
	Unit D folder: dwd_5.html **Unit D Assets folder:** cc_banner.jpg cranberry_ice.jpg	**Visual Workshop** (Caroline's Creations site)
Unit E	**Unit E folder:** dwe_1.html **Unit E Assets folder:** boardwalk.jpg club_house.jpg pool.jpg sago_palm.jpg sports_club.jpg striped_umbrella_banner.gif stripes_back.gif umbrella_back.gif	**Lessons** (The Striped Umbrella site)

Unit	File supplied	Location file is used in unit
	Unit E folder: dwe_2.html	**Skills Review** (blooms & bulbs site)
	Unit E Assets folder: blooms_banner.jpg daisies.jpg lantana.jpg petunias.jpg verbena.jpg	
	Unit E folder: dwe_3.html	**Independent Challenge 1** (Rapids Transit site)
	Unit E Assets folder: buster_tricks.jpg rapids_banner.jpg	
	Unit E folder: dwe_4.html	**Independent Challenge 2** (TripSmart site)
	Unit E Assets folder: lion.jpg tripsmart_banner.jpg zebra_mothers.jpg	
	Unit E folder: dwe_5.html	**Visual Workshop** (Caroline's Creations site)
	Unit E Assets folder: cc_banner.jpg pot_knives.jpg	
Unit F	**Unit F folder:** dwf_1.html	**Lessons** (The Striped Umbrella site)
	Unit F Assets folder: about_us_down.gif about_us_up.gif activities_down.gif activities_up.gif cafe_down.gif cafe_up.gif heron_waiting.jpg home_down.gif home_up.gif spa_down.gif spa_up.gif striped_umbrella_banner.gif two_dolphins.jpg	
	Unit F folder: dwf_2.html	**Skills Review** (blooms & bulbs site)

Unit	File supplied	Location file is used in unit
	Unit F Assets folder: b_classes_down.jpg b_classes_up.jpg b_home_down.jpg b_home_up.jpg b_newsletter_down.jpg b_newsletter_up.jpg b_plants_down.jpg b_plants_up.jpg b_tips_down.jpg b_tips_up.jpg blooms_banner.jpg	
	Unit F folder: dwf_3.html	**Independent Challenge 1** (Rapids Transit site)
	Unit F Assets folder: buffalo_fall.gif rapids_banner.jpg	
	Unit F folder: dwf_4.html	**Independent Challenge 2** (TripSmart site)
	Unit F Assets folder: tripsmart_banner.jpg	
	Unit F folder: dwf_5.html dwf_6.html dwf_7.html	**Visual Workshop** (Caroline's Creations site)
	Unit F Assets folder: cc_banner.jpg cc_banner_with_text.jpg children_cooking.jpg cookies_oven.jpg dumplings1.jpg dumplings2.jpg dumplings3.jpg fish.jpg	
Unit G	**Unit G Assets folder:** contestants_bak.jpg	**Lessons** (The Striped Umbrella site)
	Unit G Assets folder: peaches_small.jpg	**Skills Review** (blooms & bulbs site)
	Unit G Assets folder: packing_cube.jpg	**Independent Challenge 2** (TripSmart site)
	Unit G Assets folder: cc_logo.jpg	**Visual Workshop** (Caroline's Creations site)

Unit	File supplied	Location file is used in unit
Unit H	**Unit H folder:** cafe.doc crab.swf dwh_1.html **Unit H Assets folder:** about_us_down.gif about_us_up.gif activities_down.gif activities_up.gif cafe_down.gif cafe_logo.gif cafe_photo.jpg cafe_up.gif cheesecake.jpg home_down.gif home_up.gif spa_down.gif spa_up.gif striped_umbrella_banner.gif su_logo.jpg	**Lessons** (The Striped Umbrella site)
	Unit H folder: dwh_2.html garden_quote.swf gardeners.doc registration.doc **Unit H Assets folder:** b_classes_down.jpg b_classes_up.jpg b_home_down.jpg b_home_up.jpg b_newsletter_down.jpg b_newsletter_up.jpg b_plants_down.jpg b_plants_up.jpg b_tips_down.jpg b_tips_up.jpg blooms_banner.jpg flower_bed.jpg	**Skills Review** (blooms & bulbs site)
	Unit H folder: dwh_3.html rentals.doc **Unit H Assets folder:** kayak.jpg rapids_banner.jpg	**Independent Challenge 1** (Rapids Transit site)
	Unit H folder: dwh_4.html **Unit H Assets folder:** hat.jpg pants.jpg tripsmart_banner.jpg vest.jpg	**Independent Challenge 2** (TripSmart site)

Unit	File supplied	Location file is used in unit
	Unit H folder: dwh_5.html menu_items.doc **Unit H Assets folder:** cc_banner.jpg cc_banner_with_text.jpg cell_back.jpg muffins.jpg	**Visual Workshop** (Caroline's Creations site)
Unit I	**Unit I folder:** dwi_1.html dwi_2.html **Unit I Assets folder:** about_us_down.gif about_us_up.gif activities_down.gif activities_up.gif boats.jpg cafe_down.gif cafe_up.gif heron_small.jpg home_down.gif home_up.gif spa_down.gif spa_up.gif striped_umbrella_banner.gif	**Lessons** (The Striped Umbrella site)

Glossary

Absolute path A path containing an external link that references a link on a Web page outside the current Web site, and includes the protocol "http" and the URL, or address, of the Web page.

Absolute positioning Positioning an AP element so it will hold its position in the browser window when the window size changes.

Action A response to an event trigger that causes a change after a button is clicked, such as text changing color or a form being processed.

Adobe Breeze An Adobe program that produces multimedia presentations for Web communications.

Adobe Bridge An integrated file management tool that allows you to organize, search, and add meta tags to media files.

Adobe Community Help A collection of materials that includes tutorials, published articles, or blogs, in addition to the regular Help content. All content is monitored and approved by the Adobe Community Expert program.

Adobe Flash A software program used for creating vector-based graphics and animations. *See also* Vector-based graphics.

Adobe Flash Player A free program included with most browsers that allows you to view content created with Adobe Flash.

Advanced style A style used to format combinations of page elements. Also known as a Compound style.

Alias (Macintosh) An icon that represents a program, folder, or file stored on your computer.

Align an image Position an image on a Web page in relation to other elements on the page.

Alphanumeric A type of form field that will accept both numbers and letters or a combination of the two.

Alternate text Descriptive text that can be set to display in place of an image, while the image is downloading or when users place a mouse pointer over an image.

AP div tag A div tag that is assigned a fixed position on a page (absolute position).

AP element A container that is created from an AP div tag.

AP Elements panel The panel used to control the properties of all AP elements on a Web page.

Application bar (Win) A bar across the top of the Dreamweaver window that lists the names of the menus that contain Dreamweaver commands.

Asset In Dreamweaver, a file that is not a Web page, such as an image, audio file, or video clip.

Assets folder A subfolder in which most of the files that are not Web pages, such as images, audio files, and video clips are stored.

Assets panel A panel that contains nine categories of assets, such as images, used in a Web site. Clicking a category button will display a list of those assets.

Back-end processing The end of the form processing cycle when the data is processed.

Background color A color that fills the entire Web page, a table, or a cell.

Background image An image used in place of a background color.

Banner An image that generally appears across the top of the screen and can incorporate a company's logo, contact information, and navigation bars.

Baseline The bottom of a line of text, not including letter descenders such as in "y" or "g."

BCC *See* Browser Compatibility Check.

Behavior A preset piece of JavaScript code that can be attached to page elements.

Body The part of a Web page that includes text, images, and links, that is visible when the page is viewed in a browser window.

Border An outline that surrounds an image, cell, or table.

Bread crumbs trail A list of links that provides a path from the initial page you opened in a Web site to the page that you are currently viewing.

Broken link A link that cannot find the intended destination file.

Browse box A Dreamweaver Help area that lets you view other Adobe products' Help topics.

Browser *See* Web browser.

Browser Compatibility Check (BCC) A feature on the Adobe Web site that is used to check for problematic CSS issues.

Bullet A small image used to call attention to items in an unordered list.

Bulleted list A list of items that does not need to be placed in a specific order; also called an unordered list.

Button On a form, a small rectangular object with a text label that usually has an action attached to it.

Cache Space on the hard drive used for temporary memory.

Camera Raw file A file type used by many photographers that contains unprocessed data from a digital camera's sensor.

Cascading Style Sheet (CSS) A file used to assign sets of common formatting characteristics to page elements such as text, objects, and tables.

Cell A small box within a table that is used to hold text or images. Cells are arranged horizontally in rows and vertically in columns.

Cell padding In a table, the distance between the cell content and the cell walls.

Cell spacing In a table, the distance between cells.

Cell wall In a table, the edge surrounding a cell.

Check box A classification of a form object that appears as a box that, when clicked by the user, has a check mark placed in it to indicate that it is selected.

Class style A style that can be used to format any page element.

Client-side scripting A script that is processed on the user's computer.

Clip art collection A group of image files collected on CDs and sold with an index, or directory, of the files.

Code and Design view The view that is a combination of Code view and Design view.

Code Navigator A pop-up window that displays the name of the CSS rule, the style sheet name, and the properties of a selected page element.

Code view The view that shows a full screen with the HTML code for the page. Use this view to read or directly edit the code.

Coder layout A layout in the Dreamweaver workspace in which the panels are docked on the left side of the screen and Code view is the default view.

Coding toolbar A toolbar used when you are working with the code and that can only be accessed in Code view.

Column A group of table cells arranged vertically.

Comment Helpful text describing portions of the HTML code, such as a JavaScript function.

Compound style *See* Advanced style.

Computer server *See* Server.

Cropping Removing part of an image, both visually (on the page) and physically (the file size).

CSS Advisor A part of the Adobe Web site that offers solutions for problems with CSS.

CSS Layout Box Model A way to view layout blocks in Design view with the padding and margins of a selected layout visible.

Data file A file created using a software program; for example: a letter, report, or Web page, that you save on a drive so you can open and use it again later.

Debug To correct errors in HTML code.

Declaration Part of a Cascading Style Sheet; contains a property and a value.

Default alignment For images, the automatic alignment with the text baseline.

Default base font Size 3 text without any formatting applied to it.

Default font color The color the browser uses to display text, links, and visited links if no other colors are assigned.

Default link color The color the browser uses to display links if no other color is assigned. The default link color is blue.

Define a Web site Specify the site's local root folder location to help Dreamweaver keep track of the links among Web pages and supporting files and set other Web site preferences.

Definition list A list composed of terms with indented descriptions or definitions.

Delimiter A comma, tab, colon, semicolon, or similar character that separates tabular data in a text file.

Deprecated Features that are being phased out and will soon be invalid or obsolete, such as Directory or menu lists, which are deprecated in HTML 4.

Description A short summary of Web site content that resides in the Head section.

Design view The view that shows a full-screen layout and is primarily used when designing and creating a Web page.

Designer layout A layout in the Dreamweaver workspace, in which panels are docked on the right side of the screen and Design view is the default view.

Distance A feature that shows you the distance between two guides when you hold down the control key and place the mouse pointer between the guides.

Div tag An HTML tag that is used to format and position Web page elements.

Document toolbar A toolbar that contains buttons for changing the current Web page view, previewing and debugging Web pages, and managing files.

Document window The large area to the left of the Dreamweaver panels; displays open documents, each one represented by a tab.

Document-relative path A path referenced in relation to the Web page that is currently displayed.

Domain name An IP address expressed in letters instead of numbers, usually reflecting the name of the business represented by the Web site, such as tripsmart.com.

Down Image state The state of a page element when the element has been clicked with the mouse pointer.

Download To transfer files from a remote computer to a different computer.

Download time The time it takes to transfer a file to another computer.

Drive A computer storage device designated by a drive letter (such as C:) and a drive name (such as Local Disk).

Drive letter *See* Drive.

Drive name *See* Drive.

DSL Digital Subscriber Line; a type of Internet connection.

Dual Screen layout A layout that utilizes two monitors: one for the document window and Property inspector and one for the panels.

Dynamic content Content that the user can change by interacting with content on the screen.

Dynamic image A Web page image that changes frequently. *See also* Recordset.

Edit To insert, delete, or change page content, such as inserting a new image, adding a link, or correcting spelling errors.

Editable region In a template, an area the template author creates that allows other design team members to inset text or images.

Elastic layout A CSS layout that uses columns expressed in "ems."

Element In the Insert Navigation Bar dialog box, an image link.

Embedded style A style whose code is part of a Web page, rather than in a separate external file. *See also* Internal style.

Enable Cache A setting to direct the computer system to use space on the hard drive as temporary memory, or cache, while you are working in Dreamweaver.

Event A reaction to an action that causes a behavior to start.

Expanded tables mode An environment for creating tables that features expanded borders and expanded white space between cells.

Export data To save data that was created in Dreamweaver in a special file format to bring into another software program.

External cascading style sheet A file that contains formatting code and can be attached to multiple Web pages to quickly apply formatting to their content. *See also* Internal style and Inline style.

External link A link that connects to a Web page in another Web site.

Favorite An asset that you expect to use repeatedly while you work on a site and that is categorized separately in the Assets panel; also, the Dreamweaver Help feature that allows you to add topics to the Favorites window that you might want to view later without having to search again.

Field A form area into which users can insert a specific piece of data, such as their last name or address.

File field In a form, a field that lets users browse to and send files.

File hierarchy A tree-like structure that connects all the drives, folders, and files on your computer.

File management Organizing, saving, and finding files and folders on a computer.

File server *See* Server.

File Transfer Protocol *See* FTP.

Files panel A Dreamweaver panel similar to Windows Explorer or Finder, which contains a listing of all the folders and files in your Web site.

Fixed layout A CSS layout that uses columns expressed in pixels that will not change sizes when viewed in different window sizes.

Flash movie An animation created with the Adobe Flash program that is viewed using the Adobe Flash Player and has a .swf file extension.

Flash Paper An Adobe product that converts existing documents into Flash (.swf) files so they may be distributed as printable documents over the Internet.

Flash Player *See* Adobe Flash Player.

Flash video Flash files that include both video and audio and have a .flv file extension.

Fold line The line on a newspaper where the newspaper is folded. The most important information goes above the fold line.

Folder A named location on a disk that helps you group related files together, similar to the way you might group papers in file folders in a file cabinet.

Font combination A group of similar fonts such as Arial, Helvetica, sans-serif.

Form A collection of input fields that allows one to obtain information from Web site users.

Form action Part of a form tag that specifies how the form will be processed.

Form field A classification of form objects that includes text fields, hidden fields, and file fields.

Form object An individual component of a form that accepts an individual piece of information.

Format To adjust the appearance of page elements, such as resizing an image or changing the color of text.

Frameset A document that contains the instructions that tell a browser how to lay out a set of frames showing multiple individual documents on a page.

Front-end processing The beginning of the processing cycle when the data is collected.

FTP Stands for File Transfer Protocol, the process of uploading and downloading files to and from a remote site.

GIF file A Graphics Interchange Format file; a type of file format used for images placed on Web pages.

Graphic A picture or design element that adds visual interest to a page.

Graphic file A graphic in digital format.

Grid A set of horizontal and vertical lines that provide a graph-paper-like view of a page.

Guide A horizontal or vertical line that you drag onto a page from a ruler. Used to position objects, guides are not visible in the browser.

Hard drive The main storage disk on a computer.

Head content Items such as the page title, keywords, and description that are contained in the Head section. *See also* Head section.

Head section A part of a Web page that is not visible in the browser window. It includes meta tags, which are HTML codes that include information about the page, such as keywords and descriptions.

Heading One of six different text styles that can be applied to paragraphs: Heading 1 (the largest size) through Heading 6 (the smallest size).

Height property (H) The width of an AP element expressed either in pixels or as a percentage of the page.

Hexadecimal value A value that represents the amount of red, green, and blue in a color.

Hidden field On a form, an invisible field that stores user information.

History panel A Dreamweaver panel that lists the steps that have been performed while editing and formatting a document.

Home page The first Web page that appears when users go to a Web site.

Horizontal and vertical space Blank space above, below, and on the sides of an image that separates the image from the text or other elements on the page.

Hotspot A clickable area on an image that, when clicked, links to a different location on the page or to another Web page.

HTML The acronym for Hypertext Markup Language, the language Web developers use to create Web pages.

HTML div tag *See* Div tag.

HTML form A Web page or a portion of a Web page that includes one or more form objects that allow a user to enter information and send it to a host Web server.

HTML style A style used to redefine an HTML tag.

http Hypertext transfer protocol; the hypertext protocol that precedes absolute paths to external links.

Hybrid layout A CSS layout where the main column is expressed as liquid and the side columns as elastic.

Hyperlink *See* Link.

Hypertext Markup Language *See* HTML.

Image A picture or photograph.

Image map An image that has clickable areas defined on it that, when clicked, serve as links that take the viewer to other locations.

Import data To bring data created in another software program into Dreamweaver.

Index The Dreamweaver Help feature that displays topics in alphabetical order; also, a directory of files on a CD containing image files.

Inline style A style that uses code stored in the body content of a Web page. *See also* Embedded style and Internal style.

Insert panel A panel containing buttons organized by categories that allow you to insert objects, such as images, tables, and horizontal rules.

Inspector A panel that displays the properties of the currently selected object; allows you to make formatting changes quickly and easily, without having to open menus.

Interlaced graphic A characteristic of JPEG files that allows an image to appear on a Web page before the browser has fully downloaded it, giving the viewer something to look at while they are waiting for the image to finish downloading.

Internal link A link to a Web page within the same Web site.

Internal style A style that uses code stored in the head content of a Web page. *See also* Embedded style sheet and Inline style.

Internal style sheet A style sheet that is contained in the code for an individual Web page.

Internet Protocol *See* IP address.

Internet Service Provider *See* ISP.

Intranet An internal Web site without public access; companies often have intranets that only their employees can access.

IP address Also called an Internet Protocol address, an assigned series of numbers, separated by periods, that designates an address on the Internet.

ISP Stands for Internet Service Provider, a company that supplies accounts that allow Internet access.

JavaScript Code that adds dynamic content, such as rollovers or interactive forms, to a Web page.

JavaScript behavior An action script that allows you to add dynamic content to your Web pages.

JPEG file A file format that stands for Joint Photographic Experts Group file; used for images that appear on Web pages. Many photographs are saved in the JPEG file format.

Keyword A word that relates to the content of the Web site and resides in the Head section. Keywords are used by many search engines to match viewer queries with Web pages.

Left property (L) The distance between the left edge of an AP element and the left edge of the page or parent AP element that contains it.

Line break Code that places text on a separate line without creating a new paragraph. You create a line break by pressing [Shift] [Enter] (Win) or [Shift] [return] (Mac).

Link An image or text element on a Web page that users click to display another location on the page, another Web page on the same Web site, or a Web page on a different Web site. Links are also known as hyperlinks.

Liquid layout A CSS layout that uses columns expressed as percents based on the browser window width, so they will change sizes according to the window size.

List/Menu A classification of a form object that provides the user with a list or menu of choices to select. Lists display the choices in a scrolling menu. Menus display the choices in a shortcut menu.

Local disk *See* Drive.

Local root folder A folder on your hard drive, Zip disk, or USB device that will hold all the files and folders for a Web site.

Local site The folder location that contains all the files for a Web site.

Locked region An area on a page that is controlled by the template author. Other design team members cannot change it.

Mapped drive An icon representing a network drive, identified by a letter such as "J" or "K" and a name.

mailto: link An e-mail address on a Web page that is formatted as a link that will open the default mail program with a blank, addressed message.

Menu A list of commands that you can display by clicking a menu name on the menu bar, just under the title bar.

Menu bar (Mac) A bar across the top of the Dreamweaver window that lists the names of the menus that contain Dreamweaver commands.

Merge cells To combine multiple cells into one cell.

Meta tag An HTML code that includes information about the page, such as a keyword and description, and resides in the head section.

Multi-line text field In forms, a data entry area that is useful for entering text that may take several sentences to complete. Also called a Textarea field.

Multiple Document Interface (MDI) All the document windows and panels are positioned within one large application window.

Named anchor A specific location on a Web page that is used to link to that portion of the Web page.

Navigation bar A set of text or image links that viewers can use to navigate among the pages of a Web site.

Nested AP element An AP element whose HTML code resides inside another AP div tag.

Nested table A table that is placed inside the cell of another table.

Nested template A template that is based on another template.

Network drive A remote drive connected to another computer, but not directly connected to your computer, as is a local drive.

Nonbreaking space A space that appears in a fixed location to keep a line break from separating text into two lines or, in the case of table cells, to keep an empty cell from collapsing.

Non-Websafe color A color that may not appear uniformly across platforms.

Object Web page content such as a table, image, form, and layer.

Optional region In a template, an area that a development team member can choose to show or hide.

Ordered list A list of items that needs to be placed in a specific order and is preceded by numbers or letters.

Orphaned file A file that is not linked to any page in the Web site.

Over Image state The state of a page element when the mouse pointer is over the element.

Over While Down Image state The state of a page element when the mouse pointer is being held down over the element.

Panel An individual window that displays information on a particular program area, such as Files or History.

Panel group A collection of panels such as Design, Code, Application, and Files, that is displayed through the Window menu. Sets of related panels are grouped together. Also called a Tab group.

Panel group title bar The bar at the top of each panel group; contains the expander arrow that opens the panel group, and the Panel options list arrow, which you click to select commands that affect that panel group.

Password field In a form, a field that displays asterisks or bullets when a user types in a password.

Path A series of folder and file names separated by backslashes (\) that describes the exact location of a file on a computer, starting with the highest level in the file hierarchy; Microsoft Windows uses paths to store and locate files on a computer.

PNG file A file format that stands for Portable Network Graphics file; used for Web page images and is capable of showing millions of colors, but is small in file size.

Point Refers to, such as an image that points to its source file by displaying its path on the Property inspector.

Point of contact A place on a Web page that provides viewers a means of contacting a company, usually an e-mail link. *See also* mailto: link.

Program file Software such as Microsoft Word or Adobe Dreamweaver that allows you to perform specific tasks, such as writing letters or creating Web pages.

Property inspector A Dreamweaver panel that displays the characteristics of the currently selected object on the page.

Public domain Images or text that are free to use without restrictions.

Publish a Web site To make a Web site available for viewing on the Internet or on an intranet.

Quick Tag Editor A Dreamweaver panel that is used to insert or edit HTML code.

Radio button A classification of a form object that appears as a hollow circle on a form that, when clicked by the user, is then filled in to indicate that it is selected.

Radio group Two or more radio buttons grouped together on a form.

Recordset A database stored on a server that can contain image files for a dynamic image. *See also* Dynamic image.

Reference panel A panel that is used to find answers to coding questions, covering topics such as HTML, JavaScript, and Accessibility.

Refresh Local File List Automatically option A setting that directs Dreamweaver to automatically reflect changes made in your file listings.

Related Files toolbar The toolbar under the file tab (Win) or file title bar (Mac) that displays the names of files related to the open page file.

Relative path A path used with an internal link to reference a Web page or an image file within the Web site.

Relative positioning The placing of div tags in relation to other Web page elements.

Remote drive *See* Network drive.

Remote site The folder location on a Web server that contains all the files for a Web site.

Reset a form To erase the entries that have been previously entered in a form and set the values back to the default settings.

Rollover A screen element that changes in appearance as the user places the mouse over it.

Root-relative path A path referenced from a Web site's root folder.

Roundtrip HTML The Dreamweaver feature that allows HTML files created in other programs, such as Microsoft Expression Web, to be opened in Dreamweaver without adding additional coding, such as meta tags or spaces.

Row A group of table cells arranged horizontally.

Royalty-free graphic An image that you can purchase and use in your published Web pages without having to pay a royalty fee to the company that created it.

Rule A set of formatting attributes that defines styles in a Cascading Style Sheet.

Sans-serif font A block style character used frequently for headings, sub-headings, and Web pages. In this Glossary, all the blue terms are in a sans-serif font; they do not contain small strokes at the tops and bottoms of letters. The definitions are in a serif font.

Screen reader A device used by the visually impaired to convert written text on a computer monitor to spoken words.

Seamless image A tiled image that is blurred at the edges so that it appears to be all one image.

Search The Dreamweaver Help feature that allows you to enter a keyword to begin a search for a topic.

Selector In Cascading Style Sheets, the name or the tag to which the style declarations have been assigned.

Serif font A font with small extra strokes at the top and bottom of the characters; used frequently for paragraph text in printed materials. All the definitions in the Glossary are set in a serif font. The blue terms are in a sans-serif font.

Server A computer that is connected to other computers to provide file storage and processing services.

Server-side scripting A script that processes a form on the form's host Web server.

Shortcut (Win) An icon that represents a software program, folder, or file stored elsewhere on your computer system.

Single-line text field In a form, a data entry area that is useful for small pieces of data such as a name or telephone number.

Snippets panel A panel that lets you create, insert, and store pieces of code, called snippets, for reuse.

Split cells To divide cells into multiple rows or columns.

Standard mode A Dreamweaver mode that is used when you insert a table using the Insert Table icon.

Standard toolbar A toolbar that contains buttons for some frequently used commands on the File and Edit menus.

State On a graphical navigation bar, the appearance of an image, such as Up, Down, Over, and Over While Down.

Status bar A bar that appears at the bottom of the Dreamweaver window; the left end displays the tag selector, which shows the HTML tags being used at the insertion point location, and the right end displays the window size and estimated download time for the page displayed.

Storyboard A small sketch that represents each page in a Web site; like a flowchart, shows the relationship of each page to the other pages in the site.

Streaming video A video that uses buffers as it downloads to ensure a smoother playback.

Style A named group of formatting characteristics.

Style Rendering Toolbar A toolbar that contains buttons that can be used to render different media types.

Subfolder A folder inside another folder on a computer; you can have many subfolder levels on your computer.

Submit a form To send the information on a form to a host Web server for processing.

Synchronize To transfer the latest version of Web files to a server.

Tab group *See* Panel group.

Table A grid of rows and columns that can either be used to hold tabular data on a Web page or as a basic design tool for page layout.

Table header Text placed at the top or sides of a table on a Web page and read by screen readers.

Tabular data Data arranged in columns and rows and separated by a delimiter.

Tag An individual piece of HTML code.

Tag Chooser A Dreamweaver feature that lets you insert tags from the Dreamweaver tag libraries such as ColdFusion or ASP.NET tags.

Tag selector A location on the status bar that displays HTML tags for the various page elements, including tables and cells.

Target The location on a Web page that the browser will display in full view when the user clicks an internal link.

Template A Web page that contains the basic layout for similar pages in a Web site.

Text field On a form, a box in which a user can enter text. *See also* Single-line text field and Multi-line text field.

Tiled image A small graphic that repeats across and down a Web page, appearing as individual squares or rectangles.

Timeline A JavaScript feature that will cause an AP element to appear to move along a path, or change size, visibility, or position.

Title bar A bar across the top of the Dreamweaver window that displays the name of the program, the name of the file, and the title of the open page enclosed in parentheses; also includes buttons for minimizing, resizing, and closing the window in the upper-left or upper-right corner, depending on which type of computer you are using.

Top property (T) The distance between the top edge of an AP element and the top edge of the page or AP element that contains it.

Transparent background A background composed of transparent pixels, rather than pixels of a color, resulting in images that blend easily on a Web page background.

Unordered list A list of items that do not need to be placed in a specific order and are usually preceded by bullets.

Up Image state The state of a page element when the user's mouse pointer is not on the element.

Upload To send a form or files to a host Web server.

URL The acronym for Uniform Resource Locator. A URL is the "address" for a Web page that can be typed in the address box in a browser to open a Web page.

Vector-based graphic A graphic based on mathematical formulas rather than pixels.

Vertical space *See* Horizontal and vertical space.

Visited link A link that the user has previously clicked, or visited; the default color for a visited link is purple.

Visual Aid A page feature that appears in Design view but not in the browser, such as a table border.

Web browser Software used to display pages in a Web site. The two most common Web browsers are Internet Explorer and Mozilla Firefox. Also called a browser.

Web design program A program for creating interactive Web pages containing text, images, hyperlinks, animation, sounds, and video.

Web page A collection of text and images in HTML format.

Web server A computer that is connected to the Internet with a static IP (Internet Protocol) address.

Web site A set of related Web pages stored on a server that users can display using a Web browser.

Websafe color A color that will display consistently in all browsers, and on Macintosh, Windows, and Unix computers.

Websafe color palette A set of colors that appears consistently in all browsers and on Macintosh, Windows, and UNIX platforms.

White space An area on a Web page that is not filled with text or graphics; not necessarily white.

Width property (W) The width of an AP element either in pixels or as a percentage of the page.

Workspace The Dreamweaver interface made up of the document window, the menu bar, toolbars, inspectors, and panels.

Workspace switcher A drop-down menu on the Application bar (Win) or Menu bar (Mac) that allows you to change the workspace layout.

WYSIWYG An acronym for What You See Is What You Get, which means that as you design a Web page in Dreamweaver, you are seeing the page exactly as it will appear in a browser window.

XHTML The acronym for eXtensible HyperText Markup Language; the most recent standard for developing Web pages.

XML site map A listing of Web site links that can be made available to search engines such as Google, MSN, or Yahoo.

Z-index property The property used to specify the vertical stacking order of multiple AP elements on a page.

Index

su_styles.css file, 82

tags, 76

unordered lists, 78

viewing, 8, 60

Web pages, 10

HTML div tags, 156

HTML document, 4

.html file extension, 2, 8, 60–61

HTML files, 2, 8

HTML form objects and accessibility, 222

HTML (HyperText Markup Language), 2, 61

HTML Property inspector, 81, 164

Browse for File icon, 56, 130

Center option, 194

Class list arrow, 84, 88

Class list box, 81, 86

Format list arrow, 54, 86, 160

Horz list arrow, 194

Italic button, 54

Link text box, 128, 129

name of named anchor, 134

Paragraph option, 86

Point to File icon, 134

Relative to box, 130

text formatting attributes, 76

Unordered List button, 78

Vert list arrow, 195

HTML Reference panel, 60

HTML styles, 80

formatting text, 54

HTML table tags, 186

HTML tags

displaying, 190

redefining, 80

http (hypertext transfer protocol), 126

hybrid layout, 159

hyperlinks, 12

See also links

▶ I

image editors, 106

image files, 110

additional storage space, 114

deleting from Web site, 114

managing, 114, 117

image maps, 125, 138, 142

Image Tag Accessibility Attributes dialog box, 109

images, 2, 12, 101, 110

aligning, 104

aligning in cells, 194

alternate text, 108

borders, 106

centering, 156

copying to Web site, 36

creation, 116

cropping, 106

dynamic, 104

enhancing, 106

file formats, 116

finding, 116

versus graphics, 110

horizontal space, 106

horizontally centered, 194

inserting, 102

inserting in cells, 194

navigation bar, 136

original, 116

path, 36

public domain, 116

purchasing, 116

refreshing list, 114

resizing, 106, 107

reverting to original size, 106

from scratch, 116

smallest acceptable size, 107

vertical space, 106

vertically aligning, 195

Import Tabular Data command, 186

Import Tabular Data dialog box, 197

importing

cafe.doc file, 196

tabular data, 197

text, 74

index.html file, 34, 50, 88, 116, 160

linking hotspot to, 142

individuals with disabilities and Web sites, 48, 49

See also alternate text and accessibility

information, formatting, 160

inline styles, 80

Input Tag Accessibility Attributes dialog box, 218–220, 222, 224

Insert, Form command, 216

Insert, HTML, Horizontal Rule command, 226

Insert, Image Objects command, 136

Insert, Table command, 186, 196

Insert, Table Objects command, 186

Insert Navigation Bar dialog box, 136

Insert panel, 2, 186, 194

Button button, 224

buttons, 3, 6

categories, 3